Christian Moral Judgment

Other books by J. Philip Wogaman

A Christian Method of Moral Judgment

The Great Economic Debate: An Ethical Analysis

Christian Moral Judgment

J. Philip Wogaman

Westminster/John Knox Press
Louisville, Kentucky

G

Book design by Gene Harris

Published by Westminster/John Knox Press
Louisville, Kentucky

PRINTED IN THE UNITED STATES OF AMERICA

9 8 7 6 5 4 3 2 1

To JEANIE, PAUL, DONALD, and STEPHEN

Library of Congress Cataloging-in-Publication Data

Wogaman, J. Philip.
  Christian moral judgment.

  Rev. ed. of: A Christian method of moral
judgment. c1976.
  Bibliography: p.
  Includes index.
  1. Christian ethics. I. Wogaman, J. Philip.
Christian method of moral judgment. II. Title.
BJ1251.W58 1989   241   88-27711
ISBN 0-664-25004-1 (pbk.)

Contents

Preface

Thoughtful people often experience great difficulty in arriving at moral judgments. Even those who are most deeply committed to universal good can be frustrated by moral dilemmas and uncertainties encountered in the real world. For most of us, the problem is compounded by our own mixed motives. But still we struggle to be as honest, faithful, and intelligent as possible in forming judgments to express our central moral commitments. Part of the problem is that absolute certainty remains illusive. We need to find ways of coping with the inevitable uncertainties.

This book is offered as a resource for thoughtful, morally serious people who feel the need for help in thinking about the moral judgments they are called upon to make. In the main, it is presented as a Christian moral perspective. One of the issues vigorously debated today among ethical thinkers is whether there is anything uniquely *Christian* about Christian ethics—or, phrased differently, whether Christianity adds anything to ethics. I believe it does, as the first chapter will show. Nevertheless, the whole human family occupies common ground in the moral life. The approaches to moral judgment suggested in this book may be useful both to Christians and to non-Christians. Indeed, one of the tests of a method of moral judgment is the degree to which it helps clarify dialogue among persons of diverse backgrounds. Is it necessary to add that no book can provide a ready-made solution to all of our problems of moral judgment? The point is to explore fruitful ways of thinking about the moral decisions we face— not ways of avoiding the struggle.

This volume is a carefully revised edition of my earlier *A Christian Method of Moral Judgment,* published in 1976. In the dozen years since that book was published I have been able to learn much from the responses of readers and critics, some of them colleagues here and abroad, some of them students for whom this book was an introduction to Christian ethics, some of them pastors and lay professionals of various kinds. A strong positive response from Roman Catholics was especially gratifying, as evidence that the ecumenical movement has put down very deep roots in Christian ethics.

But however gratifying the response to the book, it remains true that "time makes ancient good uncouth." That may be particularly so in Christian ethics, where issues and problems change, new literature needs to be taken into account, and concrete illustrations become dated. I do not think the changing agenda of problems and issues has diminished the principal arguments of the 1976 book, but the presentation was in need of substantial revision.

Readers of the earlier work will note that I have deleted the final chapter on social strategy while adding new chapters on the theological basis of Christian ethics and on character and virtue. In the earlier work I called attention to the fact that the book presupposed the existence of persons of moral commitment. But in order to make the volume more generally useful in the field of Christian ethics I have decided to include a more explicit discussion of Christian character and moral virtues (chapter 2). I have also included a specific discussion of the use of the Bible in Christian ethics (in chapter 8), although any reader of the earlier work will note that I have always taken the Bible very seriously. While not wishing to change parts of the book that readers have found useful, I have examined the entire volume carefully and refined it at many points. In some cases this meant clarifying passages that readers found unclear; in others, the responses of critics or general readers led me to develop my own thinking further.

The principal thesis remains the same. I continue to believe that we best organize problems of moral judgment by seeking to clarify our moral presumptions and requiring exceptions or deviations to bear the burden of proof. I hope this volume will be helpful in clarifying that approach to Christian moral judgment.

It is dangerous to single out particular people whose responses to *A Christian Method of Moral Judgment* were most helpful in the development of the present work, since I am bound to overlook some. Nevertheless, I will risk a special word of thanks to John C. Bennett, Charles Curran, John Ferguson, James Gaffney, Garth Hallett, Richard Holloway, David Little, Edward LeRoy Long, Jr., James William McClendon, Jr., Marjorie Reilley Maguire, Haskell Miller, Charles S. Milligan, Ronald Preston, Larry Rasmussen, Max Stackhouse, Charles C. West, John Howard Yoder, and for the help of the late L. Harold DeWolf. In some respects, the generations of students who have used the book and argued with me vigorously about it have been the most helpful of all. I haven't been persuaded by every critic, of course, but even unresolved disagreements can contribute to clarification.

I am also grateful to Westminster/John Knox Press for making this new edition possible, and to editors Keith Crim and Cynthia L. Thompson for their support and suggestions. My wife, Carolyn, who has patiently endured the side effects of much writing, remains my most helpful critic and source of support.

We live at what continues to be an awkward but exciting juncture of human history. None of us should claim too much for our own wisdom. All of us should confront our responsibilities humbly and diligently, hoping that by our faithfulness the next generation will have more to work with and a better society to live in. It is in that spirit that I again dedicate this book to my children—now a bit older than the last time around—and to the members of their generation.

Wesley Theological Seminary   J.P.W.
Washington, D.C.

1

The Theological Basis
of Christian Ethics

A few years ago, one of the better-known scholars of Christian ethics wrote a book addressed to the question, *Can Ethics Be Christian?*[1] Other observers, taking note of the highly publicized moral failings of a number of prominent Christians, were more inclined to reverse the question by asking, "Can Christians be ethical?" The first question is theoretical, the second practical. Either way we are reminded that there is some relationship between the faith of Christians and ethics.

Even a casual student of church history quickly becomes aware that there has never been a time in the two thousand years since Christ that Christians have not perceived their faith as having serious moral implications.[2] Christians have often disagreed as to what those implications should be. But even hypocrisy, as the "tribute that vice pays to virtue" (Voltaire), implies that being a Christian ought to affect the way we live. It ought to lay some kind of moral claim on us. Writers of Christian ethics generally assume that being a Christian should affect how we *think* about ethics as well.

Does Theology Add Anything to Ethics?

But not everybody agrees with that. Some of the most respected recent philosophers, such as William Frankena and R. M. Hare, have argued that our thinking on ethical issues should not be based on religious beliefs. Frankena points out that tying ethics to religion would make it more difficult to come to agreement on moral principles "by peaceful or rational means."[3] Dealing with ethical principles can only be complicated by subjecting them to religious disputes. Moreover, if we tie religion to ethics, people who find religious views unacceptable may be skeptical about ethics as well. Of course, there are practical problems. If there really *is* a logical connection between religion and ethics, we cannot avoid these difficulties just by pretending they do not exist. Nor can we expect to avoid hard controversy by shutting out religious questions. Indeed, is there not just as much controversy over ethical views as there is over religion? Frankena may be mistaken in thinking we can arrive at agreement on ethics more easily than on religion.

But is there really a logical connection between religion and ethics? On that point we cannot be so sure. We can argue that a given moral viewpoint represents the "will of God," but how do we know? When we give reasons why we think some moral teaching is the will of God, the reasons may turn out to be secular and not religious ones. The point was made bluntly by R. M. Hare, who declared that the existence or nonexistence of God "cannot possibly make any difference, either to what we ought to do, or to what is going to be the case."[4] In his view, theology is quite *irrelevant* to ethics— except, perhaps, as it adds a certain emotional flavor. In our own time, most moral philosophers seem to agree with Hare, for they manage to deal with ethical questions without invoking Christian or other religious ethics at all. At best, Christian ethics would seem to be harmless baggage. One recalls Voltaire's remark that it is possible to kill a flock of sheep by means of witchcraft if one feeds the sheep enough arsenic at the same time.[5] Is it true that, whenever Christian ethics arrives at a moral viewpoint, a nontheological analysis provides the "arsenic" and the theological part is only incantation?

The problem can be stated in this way: Since morality pertains to our concrete actions and attitudes—always within the sphere of human culture and society—our *real* reasons for doing something will also arise within human culture and society. Any reasons other than these are not real reasons. They are only harmless baggage. At best, they only supply motivation for doing the things we know, on other grounds, we ought to do. Thus good Christians oppose war because it kills people and causes suffering and destroys property. These are good reasons for opposing war, Christian or not. Similarly, good Christians are opposed to racial discrimination because it undermines the unity of the human community and has harmful psychological results, among both the victims and the perpetrators of discrimination. These are good reasons for opposing racial discrimination, Christian or not. Likewise, Christians consider it to be a moral obligation to feed the hungry, because if the hungry are not fed they starve to death or suffer from malnutrition. These are good reasons for feeding the hungry, Christian or not. What, in each of these cases, has the "Christian" component added to the substantive ethical reasoning? To say that God wills it does not seem to add anything, because it is possible to describe the reasons why "God wills it" without changing in the slightest the reasons why any nonbeliever might also will it.[6]

Nevertheless, we should look at those "real reasons" more closely. Why should I act so as to oppose war, racial discrimination, and hunger? The reasons just given have to do with the actual *results* of such problems—the objective conditions we confront as a result of war, discrimination, and hunger. But what is wrong or bad about such conditions? Why should we be concerned about such things? Isn't the world full of people who are not concerned about these problems? For that matter, why should they even be described as "problems"? One way or another, every rigorous discussion of ethics has to deal with these questions. What is a problem to one person may not be to another. And if we are serious about ethics, we have to say why something like war or hunger should be treated as a moral problem. The question is, where do we *ultimately* get our values?

The nineteenth-century Utilitarians—echoing the ancient hedonists— argued that our values are fundamentally based on pleasure. They observed that all of us value pleasure and seek to avoid pain. The point seems self-evident, psychologically, except among people who have neurotic reasons for "enjoying" pain. The Utilitarians built a more sophisticated social ethic on the pleasure principle, emphasizing the greatest good for the largest number of people. But good, ultimately, still represented pleasure.

Even in its more sophisticated forms, the utilitarian doctrine proved vulnerable to what G. E. Moore called the "naturalistic fallacy."[7] Moore's point was that we cannot say something is "good" just because it exists factually. Most of us do find pleasure attractive, but this does not prove that pleasure is ultimately *good*. Something else has to be added to the fact that we like pleasure for us to be able to say that pleasure is therefore good. Moore thought we grasp the moral quality of goodness intuitively. Moral intuition is a part of human nature, just as our physical senses and rational minds are innately human. Moral quality cannot finally be explained on the basis of anything else (such as pleasure). It is like the color yellow; either we know what yellow means or we do not. It cannot be explained on the basis of something else.

Moore's point about the "naturalistic fallacy" is very important. It reminds us that nothing should automatically be treated as good, just because it exists.

But there is a problem with Moore's way of finding the good. If "good" cannot be explained reasonably, does it truly mean anything? A more recent British philosopher, A. J. Ayer, argued that nothing means anything to us unless we can verify it or state it in logical, mathematical terms. We can verify that most people really *do* like pleasure and dislike pain. But that is only a psychological statement; it is meaningful only in psychological terms. To go on to say that pleasure is "good" is to take it out of the psychological realm and make a value judgment. There is no way of validating the value judgment. But neither can we speak of an intuitive quality of moral goodness. That kind of language, to Ayer, is simple nonsense. Some people may claim to experience it, but if they do, that too is only a psychological fact. Ayer, on the basis of this kind of analysis, believed that neither ethics nor religion finally means anything at all except as subjective, emotive expressions.[8] For neither ethics nor religion can be verified except as psychological, emotional expressions. It is not that they are false but that they are meaningless.

So we are left with the important question of how we are to leap out of the descriptive level to any ethical statements at all. The question, as posed by Ayer, applies not only to Christian ethics but to moral philosophy as well. This is a very difficult problem: How are we to avoid the "naturalistic fallacy" of identifying the "good" with some quality or feeling just because it exists? How are we to establish clearly and firmly the basis of any statement about what is "good" or about what people "ought" to do or to be? The hard side of ethical reasoning—the arsenic, so to speak—can be surprisingly soft until it comes up with an acceptable *ultimate* rationale for its conception of the good. That applies to philosophical ethics quite as much as to religious ethics.

Purely formal ethics may try to avoid this problem by speaking of integrity as being intrinsically good. As Immanuel Kant argued, the only ultimately good thing is the good will itself. It is good to be good. It is good to be devoted to the good, to seek to do the good in every possible way. But what does *that* mean if we do not know what good we should seek? Is not "good" an empty term until we have a basis for saying that anything is or is not good? One could say that it is self-evidently good to be a person of integrity, to be an integrated self. But is that so merely because many people experience this as good? We have already seen that it is not enough to appeal to a psychological state of mind, for this is a form of the "naturalistic fallacy" of identifying something as good just because it exists. Are there not, in any event, numerous people who experience selfhood as evil and not good? It does not appear possible, in the final analysis, to speak of selfhood as a good apart from some ultimate frame of reference in which the self exists.

The various forms of existentialism present us with the same difficulties in ethics. There is a certain quality of absoluteness in the existentialist "courage to be." Philosophers like Jean-Paul Sartre argue that we claim our authentic humanness by act of will. It almost does not seem to matter what it is we decide, as long as we take responsibility for our own being—even if the decision is for suicide. But what is the importance of any decision apart from the ultimate context in which it is made? Perched atop some ledge, so to speak, what does one ask oneself in those last moments of decision unless it pertains to the ultimate worth of the venture of life? Doesn't the yes or no hinge upon some ultimate assessment of reality? Does it include, in Paul Tillich's perceptive phrase, "the acceptance of being accepted"?[9] It is possible to conceive of an existentialist faith commitment or decision based on utter individualism. But few moral philosophers would be interested in its ethical implications, and such a faith commitment would, in any case, be a form of religion.

This kind of analysis could be pursued at greater length, of course. But in the end we should have to agree that we do not have a basis for making ethical judgments until we can ground our conception of the good and of moral obligation on an ultimate framework of valuation. It is the judgment that the framework is ultimate that makes it possible to break out of the "naturalistic fallacy" to which we have referred. Nothing is good just because it exists; it all depends on how it relates to ultimate reality.

For example, if I am a nationalist, I can claim that everything that helps to enhance my country is good. It may be possible, within limits, to verify what does and what does not contribute to the survival, power, and prosperity of my native land. If I argue simply that such things are good because they do maintain and enhance the nation, I can be accused of commiting the "naturalistic fallacy." But if I go further and say that the nation is morally ultimate—not because it exists and I like it but because I really believe it to be the ultimate embodiment of value—then I may have escaped the "naturalistic fallacy" of saying something is good just because it exists.

But does this avoid Ayer's charge that ethical statements are meaningless because they are not verifiable? How would you go about verifying that something is or is not "ultimate"?

Our problem, when seeking to establish an ultimate frame of reference for values, is that we have to make judgments concerning the *whole* of reality. There is no doubt (at least in my mind) that the whole of reality exists. In principle, to answer Ayer, the character of the whole of reality could be verified if we had the means and the minds to do it. So a question about the nature of the whole of reality is a meaningful question.

It is true that the ultimate character of the whole of reality is permanently beyond actual human knowing. But that makes it no less real, and it is no less important for the ethical enterprise for us to come to terms with it. Even the very limited ethical value system represented by nationalism implicitly represents a view of reality as a whole: namely, that everything other than the nation-state is void of significance except insofar as it contributes to or detracts from the nation-state. That is also true of ethical humanism, which regards the human as the apex of existence and considers all other aspects of being (including other life forms) as possessing a lower order of reality. A Bertrand Russell or an Albert Camus can even view the universe as a profoundly hostile or absurd or meaningless environment but at the same time consider humanity to be an important enough reality to serve as center of moral value. My point is that such conceptions involve, in principle, more than the nation or humanity; they also involve the rest of reality—which means that such conceptions always extend far beyond actual knowledge.

Whether this is lamentable or not, it seems to be true of everybody. Nobody knows everything. Most of us, in fact, know very little—a point I shall emphasize in a different way later in the book. Yet if we are to come to terms with the good in any *ultimate* sense, we must have some conception of how our particular values or moral rules or principles are grounded in relation to reality as a whole. Therefore, it now seems clear, the ideas of the good on which we base our being and thinking entail a kind of faith about reality as a whole. The intellectual status of that faith cannot be one of certainty. We must in some sense base our conception of reality as a whole on supposition. And since the foundation of our understanding of the good cannot be based on demonstrable fact or absolute, undeniable truth, a "hard" science of ethics does not exist. But reality exists, and we exist as people who live by and for values. So ethics exists as our attempt to understand our values critically in their ultimate context.

My complaint about a good deal of philosophical ethics—and even some Christian ethics as well—is that it slides by the ultimate questions. But it is not enough to ground our thinking in psychological feeling or social custom, in national interests or abstract conceptions of justice. We must also struggle to understand such things in their ultimate context.

How are we to do that if we cannot, for certain, *know* the character of that context? If we take both truth and goodness seriously, we will seek to relate to ultimate reality on the basis of what we *can* know. Thus, what we believe about reality as a whole is an expression of some aspects of reality that we take to convey the truth about everything else. We interpret the unknown on the basis of the known. This is as true in ethics as it is in science. Some things are more decisive than others in conveying truth, and there is obvious disagreement among people about what it is that *really* points us toward the truth. We shall take up this point shortly, for it is at the heart of theological knowledge.

First, however, we must return to the problem with which we began. If a religious faith of some kind must be invoked as ultimate grounding for ethics, is that faith in itself the source of the *particular* moral values? Isn't it still true that what really counts is the more immediate perception that war, racism, hunger, etc., are to be combated because we can all see they are evils? Why do we have to retreat into the conjectural question of the nature of "reality as a whole" in order to deal with the ordinary evils of our common experience?

I believe it is not possible for a truly rigorous presentation of ethics to dispense either with the immediate experiences of good and evil in ordinary human life or with the question of how these experiences are related to our ultimate view of things. From the first is drawn the substance of ethics; from the second its ultimate grounding. That is why there is an inescapable element of subjectivity alongside the objectivity of ethics. That is why ethics is, as the theologians say, "circular." We encounter, in that world, what we and others take to be good. We relate the good to our understanding of the whole of reality; thence it measures and in turn is tested by other moral claims and realities as experienced by ourselves and others.

If ethics is ultimately circular, this is not to say that it is detached from reality, for all its claims are drawn in one way or another from actual experience. And even the religious contexts—about which there is so much disagreement and even bloodshed—constantly must face the test of their adequacy as a summary of our experience as a whole.[10]

Theological Sources

What, then, are the sources of the theological truths on the basis of which we can ground our ethics?

I have argued that our views of "reality as a whole" are based on our experience of those aspects of reality we take to be decisive. In that sense we must relate to the whole of reality through metaphor. Our choice of metaphors is obviously very important. It is decisive in determining the character of our view of reality and, in the long run, of our ethics.

I use the word "metaphor" here to refer to any aspects of experience that have ever functioned or will ever function as the basis for interpreting the whole of reality. For example, many people think of one or more of the natural sciences as the real clue. The Newtonians understood the whole universe in the mechanistic terms of the physics of their day, with even the deistic God conforming, more or less, to that conception. The Darwinian revolution in biology had a similar effect. Suddenly everybody was thinking of the universe in evolutionary terms, and progress was the watchword in ethics and theology. Twentieth-century psychological behaviorism has a tendency to treat everything in objective terms, even including human consciousness—as in B. F. Skinner's tendency to reduce ethics to a manipulative organization of human life in terms thought to be natural and reasonable.[11] When reality is seen only as a working of natural processes, some may consider a purely hedonistic ethic to be the logical outcome.

Other kinds of metaphor have had great influence in human history. The Nietzschean superman had great influence in the ethics and politics of certain societies during the first half of the twentieth century. Dialectical materialism combined with humanism, perhaps illogically, to produce the Marxist view of reality and to set a distinctive ethic in place. The exploration of the various metaphors by which humankind has interpreted ultimate reality and its moral responsibilities is obviously a very complex undertaking. But it is inevitable that we should be influenced, at the heart of our ethics, by those metaphors which speak to us most persuasively about the character of reality as a whole.

In this sense, it is useful to think of ethics as finally being based on "revelation," although this can be a very troublesome word. It is troublesome, I think, because people immediately see images of miraculous interventions from the divine into the human sphere. Sometimes "revelation" has been seen in conflict with "reason," and reasonable people have not wanted any part in it.

But revelation as I prefer to use the term is indispensable to reason, not in conflict with it. Revelation is what makes everything come into focus or fall into place. For instance, we may find a chance remark or a particular action to be "revealing" as we try to understand somebody. It is not because the remark or action is out of character—a total departure, so to speak, from previously observed behavior patterns. Rather, it is because the remark or action brings everything else we know about that person into better focus. Or, to use another illustration, a scientist may work for years on a complex puzzle when suddenly a clue appears that helps make sense out of all the other isolated pieces of data. That clue can also serve as a revelation. A religious revelation is of this sort: It is something that suddenly makes it possible for us to make sense out of everything else. In the case of religion one must emphasize *everything* else, for a religious faith is the basis of one's relationship to reality as a whole.

That surely includes one's relation to the natural world, whether based on sophisticated science or relatively common encounters with nature. It includes one's own feelings—the hopes and fears, the loves and hates, the joys and sorrows with which our interior life is populated. A religious revelation functions to bring all those things into perspective.

But religious revelation is also what finally makes the moral life meaningful, thereby making serious ethics a possibility. It is not, I repeat, that moral experience is only a product of religious revelation. We all experience value as a dimension of human existence, and specific values can arise in very ordinary life without reference to much else. But religious revelation, as we have been using the term, brings moral life into an ultimate focus. Such a revelation offers a compelling sense of what really matters and of how things hold together. It may highlight the importance of certain values and require us to abandon others.

This may appear to make religious revelation an entirely intellectual thing; if so, it is not what I intend. Some of the deepest religious spirits—those whose lives have expressed a profound integrity of mind, spirit, and will—have not really been intellectuals. But neither have they been *anti*-intellectual, for to be anti-intellectual is to be at war with an important part of our humanity. Profound religious revelation can bring unity to the mind without our having to become philosophers, but not if it requires us to set aside things we know to be true in order to keep faith with the revelation. And so we all live, more or less, on the strength of the metaphors we find most revealing of life's ultimate meaning.

Christian metaphors, to which we will soon attend more directly, are drawn from that complex stream of Hebrew and Christian history summarized in the Bible and Christian tradition: metaphors born out of both personal and communal experience—if it is ever finally possible to separate the personal from the communal. Persons who have been born into or drawn into that history have been influenced substantially by its metaphors, while often making their own contributions to the unfolding tradition. The Bible has a certain inescapable primacy among the resources for Christian moral thought, yet it defies simplistic use among people who hope to find there detailed answers to questions about what we should strive to do or to be. The problem is not that there are not detailed answers to many questions but that the answers may not accord with wisdom derived from subsequent Christian experience or even with deeper levels of truth suggested by scripture itself. So the Bible, while central to any Christian ethic, must still be interpreted and even corrected in light of human experience, tradition, and reason.[12] We shall have more to say about the Bible. But those who seek to use it simplistically as a guide to Christian ethics are likely to become frustrated in the long run. It is better to search out central truths and compelling metaphors that bring moral life into focus. And in doing so, the deeper Christian spirits of every age have found the Bible indispensable.

Three Key Theological Metaphors

Christian scripture and tradition present a vast treasure of suggestive theological metaphors. But of these, three fundamental ones draw us in ascending order, toward the heart of the Christian conception of reality. Each is crucial to the development of a Christian ethic.

The first is the personal metaphor, which understands ultimate reality to be founded in God as *personal being.* While some of the details of the emergence of this conception in Hebrew history remain murky, it represented a departure of great importance from other religious systems, which personified particular natural objects or processes—mountains or storms or rivers that were invested with individual spirits. The departure was to see all of creation as the work of a personal God, thus suggesting the unity of creation in the purposes of God but also despiritualizing and demystifying inanimate objects and processes. In its origins, the personal metaphor for reality as a whole may not have had much competition from an impersonal materialistic conception of ultimate reality, although the Greek nature philosophies supplied that contrast even in the ancient world. Where taken seriously, the personal metaphor compelled one in some sense to see moral reality as it reflects or contradicts the character imputed to God. It made it possible to think seriously of the moral life as having a grounding in the creative and sustaining source of the universe.

Is it, however, finally necessary to believe in God in order to be moral? Is that metaphor really so important, even to Christians? Efforts to reconstruct a Christian faith apart from God, such as those of Ludwig Feuerbach and the "death of God" theologies of the 1960s, generally emphasize the self-sufficiency of justification by faith and the primacy of love.[13] But apart from God, human relationship with reality remains curiously both subjective (because values can only be one's own creation) and impersonal (because there is no personal response from an absolutely impersonal universe). Part of the difficulty some people have with speaking of God in relation to ethics is the belief that a personal conception of ultimate reality limits the creative moral freedom of anyone who believes in it. On a purely human plane, it is indeed clear that interpersonal relationships limit our creativity or our freedom insofar as one party exercises some kind of tyranny over the other. But when human beings fully affirm each other and experience life together, the effect is not one of limiting but rather of expanding the boundlessness of human creative freedom. Paul's claim, to which we will return later, is that God—far from limiting our freedom—is, when understood in a Christian context, the *source* of it. It is in any event a serious question whether creative moral freedom is a real possibility in a universe in which moral freedom does not pertain to the essence of being. In such a universe, it is difficult to see human life as more than happenstance and tragedy. This may indeed be the human predicament, to be sure. Paul Kurtz and many others believe so. There is no way to *prove* the contrary. But the metaphorical presentation of ultimate reality as personal does seem to make better sense out of human moral existence than a contrasting conception of reality as "blind to human purposes and indifferent to human ideals," as Kurtz has put it.[14]

It is, of course, possible to personify ultimate reality with a notion of God while, at the same time, finding it difficult to believe in any kind of personal relationship between God and humankind. The physicist Albert Einstein and the moral theologian James Gustafson share that difficulty. Einstein was almost awestruck by the depth of the intelligence he took to be responsible for the intricacy of the universe, and he thought it a great trivialization to think of a God "whose purposes are modeled after our own—a God, in short, who is but a reflection of human frailty."[15] Gustafson comments that "one can be grateful for the divine governance, for all it sustains and makes possible, without conceptually personalizing the Governor."[16] Both find the ultimate character of the universe relevant to moral life, but without conceiving of a conscious relationship between God and human beings.

The second great biblical metaphor takes that important step with the notion of *covenant*. Initially the Hebrew conception, presented in much of the Old Testament, was of God's particular relationship to the people of Israel—though already in the Old Testament that is arguably developed into a more universal conception. The covenant is not simply between individuals and God but between all people and God. God, in fact, brings real community into being, for it is our relation to God that is understood to constitute the deeper ground of our relationship to one another. The Hebrew prophets, among others, sought to interpret the character of that divine-human and human-communal relationship. The personal conception of God combined with the covenantal conception of God's relationship to humanity thus invited morally sensitive people, such as the great eighth-century Hebrew prophets, to underscore new insights into moral reality as new insights into the character of the person of God and of the divine-human covenant.

Again, while one could hardly expect to "prove" the reality of this covenant, its moral consequences are considerable. To believe that the God who is the center and source of all being has purposes for human existence is at least an invitation to center the moral life in the discovery and embodiment of those purposes.

The third metaphor, the uniquely Christian one, presents the historical figure of Jesus Christ—the "Christ event"—as the deepest *revelation* about the nature of God and of the covenant God has with humanity. The New Testament letter to the Colossians puts the claim powerfully:

> He is the image of the invisible God, the first-born of all creation; for in him all things were created, in heaven and on earth, visible and invisible, whether thrones or dominions or principalities or authorities—all things were created through him and for him. He is before all things, and in him all things hold together. . . . For in him all the fulness of God was pleased to dwell, and through him to reconcile to himself all things, whether on earth or in heaven, making peace by the blood of his cross.
>
> Colossians 1:15–17, 19–20

Exactly *how* reality is revealed in Jesus Christ is, of course, subject to endless elaboration and to no little controversy among contending schools of theology. But the Colossians passage and much of the rest of the New Testament underscore that the significance of Christ for Christian ethics is by no means limited to the specific ethical teachings of Jesus. That is an important point, partly because biblical scholarship cannot have full confidence in its attribution of specific statements to Jesus and partly because it is the *character* of Jesus that matters most as revelation of the *character* of God. Words are important in the revelation of character, to be sure, but so are actions and patterns of relationship. Taken as a whole, the teaching and healing ministry of Jesus, the quality of his life, and the depth of his love revealed in the acceptance of the cross have been regarded by Christians as the decisive revelation of what goodness ultimately means. It means at least that God, the center and source of all being, truly cares about each human being—even, as the gospel of Matthew puts it poignantly, about each little creature, such as the sparrow. That this loving quality of Jesus is also attributed to God is underscored by the resurrection faith, although it may be important to add that the resurrection faith is not an arbitrary miracle story designed to impress us with suspension of normal processes of the phenomenal world. Rather, it is the deepest possible affirmation that the moral quality reflected in Jesus Christ is also a reflection of the governing power at the center of all being.

We must remind ourselves again that these central biblical metaphors for the nature of ultimate reality are not shared by everybody. Not everybody finds in them the kind of revelatory power that brings experience into meaningful focus. But for those who do, the moral consequences are clearly great.

Theological Entry Points Into Ethics

Theology has much more to add to moral discourse than the three basic metaphors we have just outlined, all too briefly. The Bible alone is a vast treasure-house of resources for Christian ethical reflection, and when one adds to the scriptures the insights accumulated by many centuries of gathering tradition and the work of innumerable theologians, the resources are incalculably large. How does one bring all this theological background to bear upon the work of Christian ethics?

After years of pondering the question, I think I begin to see why Christian ethics is so often annoying to many moral philosophers who seek great systemic precision in the presentation of ethical truth. There is so often an irritating imprecision in Christian ethics for people who prefer their ethics, like their mathematics, in exact categories. And such people are right, of course, insofar as Christian ethicists proceed eclectically, applying inconsistent values and principles to suit desired outcomes on particular questions. Christian ethics cannot be unsystematic in the sense of containing fundamental inconsistencies without risking rejection by orderly minds.

But the theological points we have already made in this chapter suggest that the ultimate sources for all ethics are transcendent. Human beings are not mechanical objects; a serious presentation of the moral life is finally open and creative, not subject to criteria to be applied mechanically to the human person. A theological ethics, pointing as it does to the transcendent but caring God, has even more openness to it. It is not that nothing can be known about God; it is that what is believed about God points toward depths of being and caring that no human being can fully comprehend, let alone exhaustively express in creaturely existence. There is always something more to be grasped, always more possibilities for growth in the moral life. The theological tradition itself, expressing as it does the profound spiritual and moral experience of vast numbers of people, presents us with intricate nuances of meaning into which we may gain greater insight the longer we live with them and struggle with them. So, to employ a distinctly modern metaphor, we must not expect to be able to create a computer program for the Christian moral life upon which we can then rely for all the answers!

Still, it is the office of Christian ethics to *think* about these things, to present relevant aspects of the tradition in manageable form to people eager to live and act and decide on the basis of their faith and not in conflict with their faith.

A part of the answer to the problem of Christian ethics is to recognize that the treasure-house of scripture and theological tradition present us with variable "entry points"[17] into different kinds of ethical problems. A great theological tradition such as this one is a vast repository of suggestive avenues into moral reality. Some particular theological symbols or doctrines may be more relevant to specific problems of being and doing than others are. This is not at all to say that the different symbols or doctrines are inconsistent with one another, or that we can invoke different entry points in an arbitrary or subjective manner to rationalize what we want to do for quite different reasons. Reality, ultimately, is one; the moral life cannot ultimately be self-contradictory. All entry points, if authentic presentations of theological truth, are expressions of the same deep realities. But some ways of bringing the deep realities to bear upon particular problems may be more authentic and fruitful than others. The test of whether this is really so is partly the question of whether those who do this work are fundamentally consistent and whether their work, as a whole, is internally coherent. The response of theology to one kind of problem should not undercut the answer given to a different kind of problem—it being understood that none of us can be perfectly consistent, that moral and intellectual growth mean change, and that change implies some inconsistency between present perceptions and behaviors and those reflecting a less mature point in our development and thinking.

Mining the theological entry points for the work of Christian ethics is thus partly a work of art, if one understands art more as the effort to represent ultimate reality than to emit subjective feelings for their own sake or to present superficial impressions photographically. Truly significant work in ethics is thus more frequently a matter of exploring resources and possibilities than of erecting airtight moral systems. But again, the integrity of Christian ethics depends on its faithfulness to the central metaphors of faith.

Theology and the World

Those metaphors are surprisingly worldly at many points, but special attention still must be given to a crucial problem in all theological ethics: How are we to make the leap from the purely spiritual or relational aspects of Christian life to the objective world? Many of the crucial terms in the Christian tradition, including "God," "covenant," "life in the Spirit," "salvation," "justification," "sanctification," and "love," can be expressed, so to speak, above the world. It can even be said that since it is our covenantal relationship with God that finally matters, the concrete realities of our existence in the world are of little consequence. Cannot even love for other people be reduced to "spiritual love" and warm sympathy for the suffering that some must endure in this vale of tears?

The point is that much of the language of Christian faith can occur on this plane because whatever else we may say about the painful realities of an earthbound existence, those realities are not the source of the *meaning* of human life. Every pastor of a Christian congregation who has chanced to preach upon themes injurious to the material interests of part of the congregation has doubtless been reminded that Christianity is, after all, a "spiritual" faith and that pastors are well advised to restrict their preaching to that sphere! In one sense this is right. Interpersonal relationships transcend the material sphere. Compounding this problem of relating the material world to spiritual reality is the problem of relating this present age to the anticipated consummation of God's purposes for human history. This problem can also be posed in such a way as to leave the practical moral judgment in a vacuum. If God alone can bring the kingdom, if we are living in the "time between the times" in which God's kingdom is not yet manifested among us, if we live only in hopeful expectation of that entirely future consummation—then the issue is sharply before us of whether and why the concrete judgments of the here and now truly and ultimately matter *at all.*

To be relevant to the moral life, then, theology must provide us with some account of what is at stake in the structures of human existence in this present world. Contemporary theological ethics has sometimes been suspended between two extremes: On the one hand there are those who speak of human betterment or liberation in such a way as to imply that the conditions and structures of human existence in this world are the locus of God's whole intention and of our entire fulfillment.[18] On the other hand there are those who seek to establish the absolute discontinuity between the physical world and the world of the spirit. Their tendency has been toward complacency concerning the physical distress and injustices that activate the liberationists. Neither of these extreme tendencies can be held without doing violence to whole segments of Christian scripture and tradition, but Christian ethics must account for the truth represented by each of the extremes while also avoiding their errors.

Dietrich Bonhoeffer's concept of the "penultimate" furnishes us with at least a provisional approach to the problem. His point is that while the physical and social structures of our worldly existence are not the "ultimate," they are necessary to it. The penultimate is not self-validating. It depends for its meaning upon the ultimate—which to Bonhoeffer is our redemption and justification through the grace of Jesus Christ. Bonhoeffer illustrates his point concretely:

> If, for example, a human life is deprived of the conditions which are proper to it, then the justification of such a life by grace and faith, if it is not rendered

impossible, is at least seriously impeded. . . . The hungry man needs bread [he continues], and the homeless man needs a roof; the dispossessed need justice and the lonely need fellowship; the undisciplined need order and the slave needs freedom. To allow the hungry man to remain hungry would be blasphemy against God and one's neighbour.[19]

Attending to such things is not the ultimate, but to Bonhoeffer it is the "preparing of the way." The way these penultimate problems are dealt with can make a large difference: It can either aid or impede the full manifestation of the transcendent ultimate. God's purposes can be helped or hindered in the temporal sphere.

In theological terms, the doctrine of creation may finally prove decisive as the foundation for ethics. This is so because through a doctrine of creation we express our understanding of how it is that God is concretely related to the actual events and structures of this world. Terms such as "covenant" or "justification" or "redemption" express a theological understanding of how God is related to human life. But "creation" expresses our understanding of how God relates to human life in the actual setting of our earthly existence.

Karl Barth's formulation of this problem has proved especially helpful. Barth speaks of "creation as the external basis of the covenant" and of "the covenant as the internal basis of creation."[20] If we understand by "covenant" the full gospel proclamation concerning God's gracious redemptive relationship with human beings, which alone finally affords meaning to human life, one may also understand by "creation" the biblical idea that God is also the creator of humanity and the world and that this act of creation is a necessary (but not sufficient) condition of there being a covenant at all. Thus, Barth writes,

Creation is the external—and only the external—basis of the covenant. It can be said that it makes it technically possible; that it prepares and establishes the sphere in which the institution and history of the covenant take place; that it makes possible the subject which is to be God's partner in this history, in short the nature which the grace of God is to adopt and to which it is to turn in this history.[21]

Without creation, all that we mean by Christian faith could exist only as an idea in the mind of God. In any event, we do not exist as ethereal spirits of some sort, floating in a vacuum. Any presentation of Christian faith that tacitly assumes such a conception of the "spiritual" lacks foundation, either in reality or in Christian scripture and tradition. The Barthian approach to creation affirms the value of the natural and the physical while also locating moral value in specific aspects of the created world. But it avoids the naturalistic fallacy by viewing the whole of that created world as instrumental to the transcendent covenantal reality revealed most fully in the person of Christ.

If this conception of creation clarifies why issues and problems in the world really do matter, it also reemphasizes the inner reality of covenantal faith. That faith is partly a shared faith, for we are social as well as individual by nature. But it is also deeply personal. If faith is not held by us as individuals it can hardly be said to exist at all. And in the expression of that faith through decision and action, the importance of personal character is similarly crucial.

In the next chapter, I wish to take up this personal aspect of the moral life.

2

Christian Character
and the Virtuous Life

The only thing, according to Immanuel Kant, that can be regarded without qualification as *good* is the good will itself.[1] Whether or not that is an adequate summary of the beginning point of moral truth, particularly as it is stated in Kant's ethical system, is disputable. But could there be an ethics without a moral person?

It is possible to question the extent to which human beings are truly free moral actors. Behavioristic forms of psychology and philosophy think we are not. Their tendency is to regard human moral behavior as if it were altogether determined by causes arising outside ourselves.[2] We may experience competing claims of good and evil and the need to make decisions among alternative courses of action. But, according to those who question human freedom, what we will actually believe and do has already been programmed into us by our genetic constitution and the environmental forces that play upon us. The question is an engaging one, not least because it suspends the mind between two contradictory but apparently unavoidable certitudes: the clear experience of freedom of choice and the fact that all actual decisions can be analyzed, without remainder, into the causal elements determining them. Thus, both the case for freedom and the case against freedom appear overpowering.

It remains true, however, that without *some* degree of freedom there would be no point in pursuing ethics; our lives would be essentially meaningless. On the other hand, even freedom itself would be meaningless if there were no determining structures in human existence to provide continuity. Both points underscore the central importance of the individual actor in the moral life and the things that go into providing that actor with identity and character. All ethics presupposes the moral person.

This is not a new point to raise, of course. In all periods of Western ethical history the consideration of the character of the moral person has been central. But a number of contemporary Christian ethicists have given this

new emphasis.[3] Some have insisted that all questions of ethics come down
to issues of personal identity and character. Others, among them Bruce C.
Birch and Larry L. Rasmussen,[4] have sought some balance between the
ethical analysis of personal character and the decisions with which one is
confronted in the realities of a complex world. But in any event, some
emphasis upon personal character in ethics is absolutely indispensable.
Even among those who think of ethics primarily in terms of institutional
structures to be evaluated and decisions to be made, it is necessary to
presuppose the existence of people who make the evaluations and decisions.
Such people must have some degree of freedom, as we have said, but they
must also have some character defining the way in which that freedom is
exercised.

We may think of character as our disposition to exercise moral freedom
in particular ways. Character is what makes us at least somewhat predictable to others. When we say that people are or are not acting "in character,"
we mean that there are aspects of their nature and nurture predisposing
them to behave in recognizable ways. Even those who behave capriciously
or inconsistently may often be recognized as having a predisposition or
tendency to do so. Some may object to including purely natural endow-
ments—such as our inherited genetic makeup—in the definition of character. I do so partly because our inherited physical nature has a lot to do with
continuities of behavior, even though behavior that is altogether *determined*
by natural inheritance can hardly be said to be either moral or immoral
since it lacks moral agency. Socialization (or "nurture") is also obviously
important to the structuring of character. In practice, it is very difficult and
perhaps unnecessary to define precisely the extent to which our character
is determined by nature or by nurture; it is always some mixture of the two.
Wise parents, when attending to the upbringing of their children, know that
through nurture they can greatly influence the character of their children;
they also know that each child has a unique genetic and physical endow-
ment that will set limits and influence the outcome. Educators also participate in this process of the formation of character; so do all the other people
with whom one has meaningful interaction.

But if we all do have some degree of moral freedom, it also remains true
that we have a hand in the formation of our own character. The way we
exercised our freedom yesterday has some continuing influence on the way
we shall act today and tomorrow. Patterns of action that are initially, in
large measure, an expression of free will can become so ingrained that they
are, in the end, virtually involuntary. It is beyond our purposes here to
explore the psychological literature bearing upon this subject, but that
insight hardly had to await modern psychological and neurological studies.
In very large measure we are creatures of habit, and a good thing too, or
life would be an even more agonizing series of fresh new decisions to be
made for our every move. Behavior patterns that in the beginning require

considerable conscious thought and effort are largely taken over by subconscious levels of the mind, and we act without thinking.

This truth is most evident in our motor behavior. Once we had to learn to walk; later that became, as we revealingly say, "second nature." Highly skilled athletes and performing artists often appear to have splendid genetic inheritances that fit them for complex and graceful movement; but for most of them, at least, many years of exacting training go into the apparently effortless actions in the sports arena or on the concert stage. Still, much of the direction of the physical movements has been taken over at the subconscious level. How could an Olympic gymnast or figure skater possibly think consciously about all the pirouettes and midair somersaults in his or her program? How could a concert pianist continue to be conscious of each individual finger movement while playing a major piano concerto? As I type these words at my computer keyboard, the last thing on my mind is how to type! But initially, when learning to type, each move had to be thought about and drilled into brain and fingers.

Moralists from the ancient world to the present have been aware of the importance of habit patterns in moral behavior. (Paul even uses the analogy of athletic discipline in his characterization of spiritual life.) But moral behavior is not restricted to physical actions; it also includes the attitudes on the basis of which we are likely to act. That complex mixture of beliefs and values which comprises our attitudes is largely conferred upon us by our social environment. But we also have something to do with it ourselves, partly in our decisions of how to respond to those influences and partly in the way we set out to cultivate some kinds of attitudes and associations more than others.

So, if we are creatures of habit, it is not altogether true that habits are only things that happen *to* us. We have a hand in making them—and in making ourselves what we are.

Moral Virtues

A great deal of the literature in the history of ethics has been structured around discussion of moral virtues, and even in common speech particular moral qualities are often singled out for approval. Preoccupation with particular virtues or vices poses problems for theological ethics, which we will discuss below. But the concept of moral virtues is almost unavoidable.

In classical Aristotelian language, we may understand a virtue to be a disposition of the will toward a good end. It is a tendency to think or behave in accordance with goodness. Classical ethical literature emphasized the virtues of temperance, courage, and prudence, each of which represented a habit of the will to overcome a threat to our ultimate good. In the case of temperance, it was control of the appetites so that excessive indulgence would not threaten us. In the case of courage, it was control of fear, so that fear would not immobilize us in the face of physical or social dangers. In the case of prudence, it was the habit of making wise rational decisions. A person in whom such virtues could be found would be a person of good character—with the crowning virtue of justice, representing the harmonization of the appetitive, spirited, and rational aspects of life.

But that classical list far from exhausts the possibilities. One list, familiar to every Boy Scout in the United States, characterizes the good Scout as "trustworthy, loyal, helpful, friendly, courteous, kind, obedient, cheerful, thrifty, brave, clean, and reverent." Each of these twelve virtues has a history of its own. In fact, careful exegesis of those histories might provide an instructive entry into the cultural history of this society! Taken out of that historical context, of course, such virtues are simple abstractions into which one can pour meanings derived from one's own experience. Whether such "virtues" are really virtues, then, depends on one's moral assessment of the content given to the abstraction. The Boy Scout virtue of "thrift," for example, could represent a responsible conservation of resources and a willingness to defer immediate gratification for the sake of laudable long-term ends—or it could reflect a mean-spirited stinginess. "Loyalty" could mean dependability in friendship, faithfulness to important values, and responsible support of one's group—or it could mean chauvinistic forms of "loyalty" toward one's race, gender, or nation or a misplaced cronyism by public officials who tolerate corruption in their associates.

But even if we are supplied with the better interpretations, it is misleading to reduce the meaning of moral character to the sum of a person's accumulated virtues. To be a moral self is to be centered. It is always to be something more than one's various predispositions, whether those are a part of one's inherited nature, a product of one's socialization, or the results of prior moral discipline. It is to be a person of integrity, one who is capable of thinking and acting coherently on the basis of what one takes to be ultimate good.[5]

The word "integrity" is closely related to the word "integration," as both etymology and common usage suggest. Both words refer to a wholeness and unity of being. But some things are integrated without having moral freedom. A computer, for instance, is "integrated," but it does not have integrity. Arguably the same could be said of many animals, including human beings who live altogether on a sensuous level. But to have integrity is to be capable of choosing and to do so on the basis of a deeply unified commitment to good.[6]

Do individual virtues contribute to this? The wrong understanding of virtues can in fact detract from integrity, if the disparate virtues are inconsistent with one another or if any or all of them substitute for the centeredness of the self. But the virtues that have been named and cultivated and given intellectual refinement through human moral history are not merely abstractions. They express the immediate moral experience of vast numbers of people, and they often point toward moral meanings transcending immediate experience. To be a person of integrity is to have habituated predispositions toward the good in all its forms; it is to hold them and even to cultivate them as an expression of that central good in accordance with which the self is integrated.

Theological Entry Points Into Christian Character

Moral character is not exclusively a Christian subject. It is possible to discuss it, as we have thus far, without introducing theology. But the overall question of this book is the applicability of Christian faith to moral life, so we must now ask how different theological entry points contribute to better understanding of moral character.

The number of possible theological entry points is very large. I wish to highlight four, which I take to be especially important, both historically and logically, as we seek to ground our understanding of what it means to be a moral person in Christian terms.

1. The Imago Dei

The first such entry point in much of the literature of Christian ethics is the *imago Dei*. We are understood theologically to be created in the "image of God." That point has been interpreted in a variety of ways, but most of them emphasize that humanity was created by God and, in crucial ways, to be like God.

To be like *God?* Is it not the height of presumption for flesh-and-blood humanity to claim to be made in the image of God? To be sure, Christian theology has always recognized that humanity is less than God. We are not the source and sustainer of all being. We are not omniscient or omnipresent. We are not self-creating, except in the sense to which I shall shortly refer. Nor are we perfectly loving and good, as the doctrine of original sin makes clear. But having said these things, is there not a sense in which the *imago Dei* is implied in the personal metaphor for God, to which we referred in the first chapter? If God is (in important respects) like us, then we are (in important respects) like God. But what are those respects?

The theological literature on the subject has emphasized four things: human rationality, human freedom, human transcendence, and human creativity. As reasoning beings we, like God, are capable of grasping the interrelationships of ideas and pursuing truth. As beings with freedom, we are capable of choosing among alternative courses of action; we are not simply a product of forces acting upon us. (There is even a sense in which we are self-creating, for the choices we make greatly influence what we become.) As transcendent beings, we are capable of thinking about ourselves and of contemplating a universe beyond our immediate experience.

As creative beings, we are capable of bringing new things into being, actualizing potentialities.

But even these four points do not quite grasp the depth of the claim that we are created in the *imago Dei*. For to be in the image of God is not entirely a matter of rationality and freedom and self-transcendence and creativity. It is to be capable of caring relationship, of entering from the depth of one's own being into the depth of the being of another.[7] To be created in the image of God is to be given the capacity to enter into relationship with God, there to be recognized by God as fit for covenant. If the God we claim to know is truly God, the deepest aspect of our humanity is that we have been created to know and respond to God. Among people who believe this to be so, the ethical ramifications are obviously very great. For the conception of *imago Dei* suggests what human life ultimately is. When Paul Lehmann asserts that "what God is doing in the world [is] to make and to keep human life human," he recognizes that everything in ethics depends finally upon what it ultimately means to be "human."[8] The conception of *imago Dei* links our humanity to the character of God. We find our ultimate fulfillment in being what we are created to be in God's image.

2. Original Sin

The doctrine of original sin is an immediate reminder that our humanity has fallen short. How are we to account for the fact that we do not live out the implications of being in the image of God? The Genesis story of the Garden of Eden depicts the human act of rebellion against God's intended good in mythological form, and it is well to remind ourselves that the Christian doctrine of original sin is in no way dependent upon acceptance of the story as literal fact—or, for that matter, of sin as transmitted through sex. Like all profound myth, the story leads us to a deeper grasp of truth than factual detail. In this case, it suggests that something about our humanity leads us toward self-centered rebellion against God.

Probably no recent theologian has done more to recover a sense of the intellectual seriousness of the problem of original sin than Reinhold Niebuhr. Niebuhr relates the universality of sin to the universality of the anxieties engendered within us by our ability to understand our own finitude and by our tendency to place ourselves at the center of the universe we are able to comprehend.[9] Sin, according to Niebuhr, is inevitable but not necessary. It is not necessary because we remain free to resist sin. It is inevitable, however, because in our anxiety we are pushed deeply into self-centeredness, shoring up that self of ours in face of its apparent vulnerability. To be other than self-centered is theoretically possible. But the tendency toward self-centeredness is nearly irresistible. Could God have created us otherwise? Perhaps so, but only by depriving us of that freedom whereby we are able to enter into deep communion with the source of our being.

Much depends, obviously, on how pervasive one takes original sin to be. Has it totally effaced the *imago Dei* in humanity or has it only distorted it? Most theological interpreters consider original sin to have affected all of us to some degree, tainting all natural expressions of goodness with some self-centeredness. Some theologians, including Luther, are suspicious of any natural human goodness—any remaining evidence of the *imago Dei*—apart from the redemptive work of Jesus Christ. The most pessimistic accounts of original sin hardly seem to do justice to clear evidence of generosity and love expressed in distinctly non-Christian settings. But neither do the most optimistic accounts seem warranted, for sin is clearly a universal human reality.

Among other things, it means that the development of character cannot be an exclusively human achievement. We cannot overcome the effects of sin simply by trying harder to become good people. The problem is that our not being good people is rooted in our insecurity, not in our lack of effort. Our very effort to "be good" can in fact be an expression of self-centeredness. If we are training ourselves to be persons of good character who do good things, we may be doing so out of very selfish motives. And if, as we noted with Kant in the beginning of this chapter, motivation is the central point in ethics, the supreme irony may be that those who try hardest to be good are often the ones who fail most spectacularly. One recalls the anguished words of the apostle Paul, "I can will what is right, but I cannot do it. For I do not do the good I want, but the evil I do not want is what I do" (Rom. 7:18b–19). And one is reminded of the insightful lines of T. S. Eliot, "The greatest treason: To do the right deed for the wrong reason."[10]

3. Justification

The Christian doctrine of justification is, therefore, a very important theological entry point to a discussion of character. The theological literature on this subject is also vast, and we need not be detained over conflicting interpretations. From the standpoint of Christian ethics, the key point expressed by the doctrine is that we are enabled, as a result of the work of Christ, to accept the fact that we are accepted by God. We no longer have to prove anything to God or to ourselves. Secure in the faith that we belong to God, we no longer have to engage in a frantic quest for our own salvation.

Paul's discussion of this in Romans is particularly astute. Utilizing a first-century legal metaphor, Paul speaks of God's grace, a free gift of salvation offered to us despite our undeserving. We need only accept that gift of grace in faith for our lives to be transformed from self-centeredness (the "law of sin and death") into joyous confidence. Genuine love is now a possibility, replacing the futility of self-centeredness. We are free now to seek the good—God's good—for its own sake. We can now be fully human as God created and intended us to be. The doctrine of justification does not mean that human beings have miraculously become saints by the simple act of faith. It does mean that they experience a new moral security in spite of their imperfection; real moral growth is now possible.

The psychological insight contained in this theological statement is that the capacity to love is grounded in being loved and in being able to accept oneself. Fundamentally insecure people can improve in their ability to perform, but improved performance in conformity to a given set of moral rules and virtues is not to be equated with growth in love. We can obey rules and acquire "virtues" for the wrong—that is, selfish—reasons. From the standpoint of personal morality, this may be the supreme irony in the moral life. The deep truth is expressed by 1 John, where we are reminded that we are able to love because God first loved us, and where it is recorded that "there is no fear in love, but perfect love casts out fear" (1 John 4:18–19).

4. Sanctification

Justification is not the final word. It is not enough to be the recipient of God's grace, secure in the realization that we are valued at the center of our being by the source of all being. What we do about it and how we grow in love also matter. The traditional theological term for moral and spiritual growth is "sanctification," which literally means becoming more saintly. God's free gift of grace is the precondition, but grace by itself does not make saints of us.

Nurtured in a Lutheran tradition emphasizing grace, Dietrich Bonhoeffer warned against "cheap grace," the free-and-easy acceptance of a love that places no demands upon us.[11] Paul had also warned against the wrong interpretation of that freedom we have in the love of Christ: "For you were called to freedom, brethren; only do not use your freedom as an opportunity for the flesh, but through love be servants of one another. For the whole law is fulfilled in one word, 'You shall love your neighbor as yourself' " (Gal. 5:13–14). Here and elsewhere, Paul felt constrained to list a whole series of "works of the flesh" that are to be avoided if one is to "walk by the Spirit." We are saved by grace, not by "works," but what we do also matters.

Stating the relationship between grace and works is one of the most intricate problems of Christian ethics. If we place the emphasis on grace alone, we risk the excesses of "cheap grace" and the loss of all ethical demand. But if we emphasize works, we lose sight of the centrality of love—both the being loved, without which we cannot love, and our own growth as loving persons. As we have already seen, grace must be the basis of everything else, and for it to be *grace* it must be a total gift of God; it cannot be something we earn in any way. (In that sense, grace is less than cheap: it is free!) For grace to be grace we have to be able to count on it unequivocally.

But grace is a gift, not a command; it is an invitation, not a requirement. As gift and invitation, we have right of refusal. We can count absolutely on the steadfast love of God. But for that love, that grace, to take hold of us, we have to let it. To put this differently, we cannot accept the love of God unlovingly and inactively. Faith in God's grace is not a merely passive thing; it is not a thing to be absorbed in a self-centered way. In fact, to think of grace in passive, self-centered ways is not to escape the trap of original sin at all. It is to remain in our fundamental state of loneliness and insecurity, living out our days on the basis of idolatries of flesh and spirit.

Grace, in a word, is a free invitation into the life of love. It does not make us instant saints, but it sets us on the road to saintliness.[12] If this has a negative aspect, it is the realistic fear of the consequences of our neglect of the gift of love, for that gift is life itself. We need not fear that God will turn the divine "yes" into a divine "no" if we do not perform, for God's "yes" is altogether without qualification. But we do well to fear our own capacity to say no, lest we turn away from our own ultimate good.

How does one become sanctified?

In part, if we are fortunate, it is done "to" us. We take on the values, perceptions, and patterns of life of the groups into which we are born and by which we are nurtured. To become a good person it helps to be raised and surrounded by good people, just as it helps us grasp the love of God if we are loved by the people who are most important to us. Moral maturation is not a purely individualistic thing; as I shall maintain later, we are both individual and social by nature. The social part of our nature is deeply influenced, even to the point of being determined, by our social existence. Those theologians who emphasize the character-forming effects of the "stories" with which we are identified[13] are correct in citing the enormous influence of the communally remembered and interpreted past.

But we must not overlook the importance of personal response and self-discipline. Paul, employing an athletic metaphor, writes that "every athlete exercises self-control in all things. They do it to receive a perishable wreath, but we an imperishable. Well, I do not run aimlessly, I do not box as one beating the air; but I pommel my body and subdue it, lest after preaching to others I myself should be disqualified" (1 Cor. 9:25–27). This is not to earn God's favor but to make God's freely given grace effective. There is a point where our own disciplined response is indispensable.

Christian Virtue

At this point Christians can begin to discuss specific virtues without their being misunderstood as rungs on the ladder of salvation. The catalog of virtues and vices accumulated through twenty centuries of Christian moral thought is too extensive for detailed commentary here. Taken as a whole, the specific points can be understood as teachings, based on a vast reservoir of Christian experience, about what helps or hinders us in our growing responsiveness to God's grace. Thus, when John Wesley speaks of Christian perfection in his classic sermon by that name, he does not mean the abstract accumulation of virtues for their own sake; he means growth in love. To be perfect is to be loving, as God is loving.[14]

Viewed from this perspective, the various theological virtues referred to in Paul's classic "love poem" of 1 Corinthians 13 can be seen as aspects of the life of love. Cultivating these aspects quite intentionally can be a way of habituating ourselves toward loving response and away from self-centered response. It is worth noting that all the contrasting *vices* in that celebrated passage are forms of self-centeredness or denial of love: jealousy, boastfulness, arrogance, rudeness, insistence on one's own way, irritability, resentfulness, rejoicing in the wrong. For the sake of love, and in one's response to the gift of God's love, one intentionally resists the temptation to give in to those forms of attitude and behavior. And the more one resists such things, the easier it becomes to be loving by reflex—so that the virtues of patience, kindness, endurance, and hope can take hold of us and define our character.

Thus, to cite the virtues of patience and kindness, patience is recognizing and working with the development of good in other people and in the world, taking the time necessary to work with it and make it effective. In cultivating the virtue of patience, we intentionally resist temptations toward premature abandonment of important struggles or toward giving up on other people. (The virtue of patience clearly does not mean open-ended toleration of injustice.) Kindness is sensitivity toward the feelings of others and seeking what is best for others. In cultivating the virtue of kindness, we intentionally resist the tendency to inflate ourselves at the expense of others by arrogance or rudeness. All this is to recognize that we are creatures of habit and that our character is largely determined by the pattern of our previous actions and attitudes. It is possible to establish a certain momentum toward the good and to resist the drag of a momentum toward self-centeredness and evil.

In a sense, it does remain true that the terms referring to the various Christian virtues (or vices) are and remain empty abstractions apart from a communal context giving them definition. Even "love" itself is open to multiple interpretation and application—as a whole library of books on the subject makes abundantly clear.[15] But in the context of the Christian community, which is also a part of the context of God's loving action in human history, such virtues help us come to terms with grace and thereby grow in moral maturity.

Stages of Moral Development

Are there definite stages in this growth in moral maturity? Recent literature from secular[16] as well as Christian[17] sources suggests that there are
certain more or less definite stages through which people grow toward
moral maturity. Some developmental psychologists, such as Lawrence
Kohlberg, argue that such stages may be observed in any cultural setting
as a product of patterns of social interaction. According to Kohlberg, the
most elementary of these stages is that in which we derive our moral
judgments altogether on the basis of simple obedience to authority in order
to avoid punishment, while the highest stage is that in which we live by
universal principle.[18] Moral growth is here depicted as a natural process,
with the difference between higher and lower stages of development given
in the sequence itself. Once one arrives at a higher stage, one does not revert
to a lower one—although one may not progress to the final stage, and, in
fact, comparatively few people do. Kohlberg does not consider the differences between the stages to be established by moral argumentation but by
empirical observation and analysis. Thus, ethics appears to be reduced to
developmental psychology.[19]

The research underlying such a conception of moral development places
considerable emphasis on forms of cognitive development, and in that
respect it may well be true that there is a more or less universal pattern of
cognitive moral development among human beings. If that is so, it at least
means that we have a tendency to intellectualize moral concerns in accordance with particular stages. (Even that may be contested, however, as Carol
Gilligan has done in behalf of a feminist ethic. Gilligan argues that the
Kohlberg stages are basically male-oriented and that data derived from
women might show the highest stage to be more oriented toward human
interrelationships.[20])

There remain two problems with such an approach to moral development. First, we cannot really make normative judgments about the different
stages on the basis of observation alone. To establish stage six as morally
preferable to stage five or stage one requires more than the observation that
it is later—just as one cannot argue that senescence is a higher physical
stage than puberty because it is later and irreversible. We may agree that
a moral commitment to universal principle is a higher stage than the individualistic morality of stage two. But the point must be argued on moral
grounds.

The other problem is more basic: Character is not a purely cognitive
matter. Our moral conceptions may be considerably "higher" than our
pattern of character. Did not Paul write, "The evil I do not want is what
I do" (Rom. 7:19)? Is there not abundant empirical evidence of moral,
if not intellectual, regression? And is it not true, as well, that "higher"
forms of cognitive morality sometimes only provide us with more effec-

tive means of rationalizing attitudes and behaviors that are much lower?

The term "moral development" may still be useful as a bridge between research in developmental psychology and explorations of moral maturation that are more frankly based on religious values. But the excitement of discoveries in that research should not lead to more superficial conceptions of human nature. For moral maturity grows out of the depths of our encounter with the God who meets us with grace and out of our response in freedom.

Being Good and Doing Good

The point of this chapter is that it is good to be good. Good character is *intrinsically* good. It is not just good because it leads to some other good result. What, then, are we to say about that other side of ethics, the *doing* of good?

None of us exist only unto ourselves. We find ourselves in a universe created by God and in a world of fellow beings with whom we are linked in an exquisitely complex fabric of interrelationships. So we cannot just "be" good within ourselves. Our goodness must find expression in that world of interrelationships if it is to be real. That is why, ultimately, there can be no distinction between "personal ethics" and "social ethics," for every ethics is both personal and social. And being good and doing good are not ultimately separable.

That does not mean, as the next chapter will hope to demonstrate, that "being" good and seeking to "do" good lead inevitably to *knowing* the good that a good person will want to do. Our discussion of Christian character leads directly to the question: How can such a person arrive at dependable moral judgments in such a world?

We carry three basic points into a discussion of that question: first, a recognition that dependable moral judgments about that world will be theologically formed, for our theological perspective determines the value frame of reference in which we operate in all our judgments; second, an understanding that all discussions of moral judgment presuppose the existence of persons of character who are motivated by good will, for apart from such persons the quest for knowledge of the good is meaningless; third, a reminder that the analysis of character alone will not suffice as a guide to moral judgment and decision, for none of us exists as a character alone and the world beyond our own self is wondrously complex.

3

Moral Commitment
and Ethical Uncertainty

When it is said that the road to hell is paved with good intentions, the point is not that there is anything wrong with good intentions. The point is that there may be a difference between good intentions and knowledge of how to translate those intentions into actual good. Good intentions are often misdirected. "Love without knowledge goes astray." Even in a world populated entirely by good people, this would remain a problem as long as those people were capable of making honest mistakes. Good and honest people are often puzzled by the dilemmas they face in the real world.

This seems particularly true in our time. Scientists agonize over the incalculable possibilities and dangers of genetic engineering. Economists wrestle with the conflicting claims of free trade and protectionism in a world rapidly becoming a single economic community. Third World governments contemplate ruinous population growth rates and problems of economic development. Political leaders of the United States and the Soviet Union confront the awesome dilemma of preparedness for nuclear war, recognizing that no human values could be defended or advanced in such a war but fearing, all the same, that important human values might be threatened if nuclear deterrence were to be abandoned. Morally sensitive people in profoundly oppressive societies wonder how to achieve revolution without violence—or whether violence may be necessary and justified. Thoughtful people in many parts of the world debate the relative merits of Marxism, democratic socialism, and capitalism as they face an uncertain economic future, and the relative claims of democracy and authoritarian rule are much discussed. Young people everywhere face personal dilemmas involving sexuality, education, and career decision-making in a rapidly changing world. Older people wonder how to interpret and contribute to that same world.

Why is the task of moral understanding and decision-making so difficult? The usual answer is that this is, after all, a complex and rapidly changing world—which is certainly true. But the problem is deeper even than the facts of this particular time in history. Our age is plagued by so much uncertainty that we too easily forget that there has always been a gap between moral commitment and moral judgment. There has always been the possibility of the unintended mistake. The reason for this lies in a fundamental difference between the will and the mind. It is a nice thing when good people are also intelligent and wise, but that is an illusive combination. Sometimes, as Paul reminds us, we understand the good but do not have the will to do it. At other times, we have the will but lack the understanding. Sometimes good and loving people do evil things unintentionally. Sometimes evil people do good things by accident or for the wrong reasons. Most of us are a little bit of both and do a little of both.[1]

But without losing sight of the continuing importance of moral character, as discussed in the preceding chapter, our present problem is moral intelligence. Assuming that there is such a thing as good will, we must now address the question of how good people can come to recognize the good amid the complexities of life.

Christians will, in one way or another, want to reformulate the problem. They must ask, What are the implications of Christian faith for our actual moral judgments? What should the Christian attitude be toward sex, war, race relations, poverty, drug use, economic development, revolution, abortion, population control, political corruption, or any of the other areas where we confront dilemmas and confusions? There is both a subjective and an objective side to the question. The subjective question is whether I will commit myself entirely to whatever it is that Christian faith implies. The objective question is what Christian faith in fact does imply in relation to the circumstances of life. Having made the commitment (subjectively) we now must ask what (objectively) should be done about it. Our commitment may falter in face of the implications. But the question of judgment still remains distinct from the question of commitment.

We are thus led to a fundamental problem in the relationship between moral commitment and ethical judgment. Whether we do or do not commit ourselves, without reservation, to the God who is source of all good, we know we ought to. But we live in a greater climate of uncertainty about the objective world. Even if we believe it possible to arrive at relatively dependable judgments on the basis of relatively dependable knowledge and that we may one day arrive at total certainty in our moral judgments, the first thing the committed will confronts is uncertainty as to what it should do. This difference between will and mind is obscured by the fact that we often arrive at judgments without thinking about them. We assume that they express our commitment. But how can we be sure?

This problem of moral judgment is there whether we choose to think of the moral life prescriptively (as a matter of obedience to law) or teleologically (as a matter of creative efforts to achieve good ends) or relationally (as a matter of loving response to others).[2] We also face the problem of uncertainty whether we view morality as doing God's will or as our own free creative response to a multiplicity of possible ways of expressing our good will. All these ways of conceptualizing the moral life depend on a distinction between the good and that which frustrates the good, and thus all require us to arrive at judgments from a situation of uncertainty in the actual world. As Paul said, "Now we see in a mirror dimly" and "now I know in part" (1 Cor. 13:12).

The emerging question, then, is how we are to go about judging so that our ethical uncertainty will not frustrate our moral commitment. For if we cannot know the good at all, our commitment—however real and good subjectively—is incapable of dependable fulfillment in the real world.

The Loss of Moral Authority

There is a worldwide crisis of confidence in specific sources of moral authority in our time. Individuals and societies have always faced some uncertainty in arriving at moral judgments. But for a number of reasons, twentieth-century humanity has lost confidence in the social and cultural authorities that have traditionally provided guidance in making specific decisions. In many parts of the world, this reality is masked by the emergence of fanaticisms and fundamentalisms of various kinds. But fanaticism and fundamentalism are evidence of a crisis of faith, not of moral self-assurance.[3] People turn to one-sided, irrational values and creeds in an effort to shore up their anxieties, not to express a holistic vision of life. Christians have not escaped the general problem; in some respects their own crisis may be particularly acute. Previous generations of Christians have often been able to follow four interrelated sources of moral authority without having to examine them very much. They often struggled with uncertainties and disagreements as to the facts, but basic sources of authority could often be accepted without much question.

First, many generations of Christians were able to accept the Bible quite uncritically. The simple fact that the Ten Commandments or the Sermon on the Mount or Paul's ethical teachings were in the Bible made them almost self-evidently authoritative. There could be spirited disputes as to the meaning of a particular passage of scripture or its precise applicability to a problem at hand, but people on both sides of a dispute would accept the common presupposition of the Bible's authority. Nineteenth-century slaveholders and Christian abolitionists disagreed on the meaning of the Bible, but both quoted it as decisive moral authority.

This kind of confidence has now been eroded by more than a century of careful biblical criticism. The internal inconsistencies, the problems of canon and translation, the human authorship and historical situations underlying parts of the Bible have been scrutinized with care. The net result has been to show that, whatever their sources of inspiration, biblical writers were all flesh-and-blood human beings writing in quite human circumstances. Inevitably, the moral authority of the Bible as the unvarnished word of God has come in for reexamination. Appreciation for biblical insight has often been increased by this process, and in many respects the Bible has been made more available for sophisticated theological reflection. But uncritical and specific use of biblical injunctions as moral authority has been weakened.

A second authority was the church. Roman Catholicism, with its pope and hierarchy, has traditionally held a high conception of ecclesiastical authority, but Protestant Christians have also had much confidence in the moral authority of the church. Among some Protestants this has been a group matter: the "sense of the meeting" or the judgment of the "gathered congregation." Among others it has been more a matter of high respect for the minister's Sunday sermon. Pronouncements and declarations by Protestant church bodies have sometimes enjoyed high prestige as sources of moral teaching. But the moral authority of the church has been weakened by the demonstrated fallibility of church leaders and members. The moral authority of Protestant churches in American culture was badly weakened by their haste in baptizing Prohibition and World War I as absolute moral causes,[4] by their reluctance to support some obviously humane causes, by their intense competitiveness and racism, and by highly publicized scandals involving previously self-righteous religious figures. Disputes over sexist language in hymns and liturgy, while pointing toward deeper theological integrity, have undermined confidence in basic religious symbols among numbers of Protestant Christians.

Roman Catholicism has been shaken by anticlericalism in many European and Latin American countries over the course of the past century and by forces unleashed by Vatican II. (Ironically, this last event, while increasing respect for Catholicism enormously among non-Catholics, undermined faith in church authority among many Catholics by relativizing the role of pope and hierarchy.) Continued papal condemnations of the use of artificial contraceptives and papal unwillingness to ordain women to the priesthood contribute to the crisis of confidence among many Catholics who regard these as flatly irrational positions.

The relativizing of church authority, both Protestant and Catholic, has probably been made irreversible by the social sciences—particularly by sociology and psychology of religion and by anthropology. Such studies have demonstrated the continuities between religious and other kinds of institutions and the similarities between Christian institutions and those of other religions. Moreover, the "religious" motivations of churchgoers have sometimes been exposed as camouflage for status-seeking, economic self-interest, and neurotic illnesses. Much of this may have contributed greatly to the long-run health and integrity of the church, but it has clearly eroded any simple, unthinking respect for its teaching authority.

A third authority was natural law. Natural law is based on belief in understandable universal moral principles that can be applied definitively to particular issues. It presupposes considerable confidence in human reason and, more to the point, in the proposition that equally rational people will arrive at the same conclusions on the same moral dilemmas. Roman Catholics have generally considered Thomas Aquinas the best exponent of natural law. Aquinas also had considerable influence among Protestants, though Protestant theologians from Luther to Barth have been more skeptical of the claims of natural law. Many Protestants, however, have given similar status to the "inalienable rights" of the Enlightenment, to the Kantian categorical imperative, and to such ideologies as laissez-faire capitalism or socialism or the democratic creed. Where natural law has restricted itself to a purely rational analysis of the moral will, thus affirming that we are bound morally to choose the good and avoid evil, it may be questioned whether it has been affected negatively by twentieth-century experience. But the formal principle of the good will merely poses, without answering, the problem of moral judgment.

Where natural law has been used to provide authoritative guidance in forming specific moral judgments, and where it has treated aspects of physical nature as normative, it has also been weakened for modern life. Too many assertedly self-evident natural-law judgments have failed to persuade rational people. When Paul asks, in natural-law fashion, "Does not nature itself teach you that for a man to wear long hair is degrading to him, but if a woman has long hair, it is her pride?" (1 Cor. 11:14–15), it is quite clear to many people now that his "natural law" has fallen captive to transitory custom. Similarly, when Pope Pius XI writes concerning contraception that "since . . . the conjugal act is destined primarily by nature for the begetting of children, those who in exercising it deliberately frustrate its natural power and purpose sin against nature and commit a deed which is shameful and intrinsically vicious,"[5] non-Catholics and increasing numbers of Catholics suspect that something other than the pure gift of reason has intruded to dictate the moral conclusion. What has intruded is the notion that identifiable aspects and processes of physical nature are necessarily a reflection of universal moral principles.

All this is not necessarily a revolt against nature or against reason. A dawning awareness that we cannot take unlimited liberties with the natural world has begun seriously to chasten our pride of technological mastery. Nevertheless, our very great control over the natural world has made it impossible to view any specific aspect of the natural world as normative in itself. Far from being a revolt against reason, this kind of skepticism can be shown to have highly rational roots. Our appreciation for nature and our respect for its complexities may be increasing, but it is certainly more difficult for us to use the natural as a specific norm for moral judgment.

A fourth authority was custom or tradition. Patterns of behavior and attitudes become ingrained through the years and their authority is accepted without question. Some of the customs of Christians have been rooted in scripture and church teaching, though customs deriving from other sources may claim the same authority of assured rightness. But the authority of customs has also been dissolved by the social sciences and by the increased contact of persons from different cultures with one another.

The four types of moral authority were usually woven together into some general conception of rightness, and the individual Christian could use them in situations demanding moral judgment. But this sense of self-confidence is now largely gone.

Many Christians have deplored this loss of moral authority. They have, in one way or another, attempted to counteract the relativizing tendencies of modern life—but usually to no avail, for basic attitudes and values cannot be reestablished by tours de force. Other Christians have attempted to understand these relativizing currents from a deeper perspective.

Twentieth-Century Theology as a Source of Relativism

Many have concluded that the most subtle and powerful undermining of specific moral authorities is implied by Christian theology itself. Such twentieth-century theological giants as Karl Barth, Paul Tillich, and Reinhold and Richard Niebuhr have deeply relativized the moral claims made for particular cultural absolutes—Barth by emphasizing the transcendence of God and the covenant whose gracious character is revealed in Christ and not in any cultural values or norms as such, Tillich by emphasizing the "Protestant principle" of criticizing "any absolute claim made for a relative reality,"[6] Reinhold Niebuhr by ruthlessly dissecting the self-centeredness at the root all human life,[7] and Richard Niebuhr by questioning all relative values except insofar as they are grounded in the transcendent God as center of value.[8] In the work of such theologians we are left with a radical gap between the transcendent God and the specific aspects of human existence.

Other twentieth-century theological movements such as the "death of God" and "secular theology" movements of the 1960s have obviously had an even more strikingly relativizing effect. And while such later tendencies as liberation theology, process theology, and feminist theology have made strong assertions about particular moral imperatives, even they have effectively criticized the moral pretensions arising from the "social locations" occupied by people; in the case of process theology, the very possibility of any final claim made for a particular historical moral conclusion is effectively collapsed.

A new freedom—freedom to judge, freedom to decide, freedom to act—has been emphasized in one way or another by twentieth-century theologians. With many, this freedom is rooted in some understanding of the transcendence of the divine and in the dependability of grace.

Yet such freedom is paradoxical. While it liberates one from many traditional values and authorities, it also seems to lack particularity. Freedom from cultural absolutes permits wide latitude for creative expression. But now what are we to express, and how are we to express it? Our loss of guidelines may permit us to judge *everything* for ourselves. But then, what is the basis on which we are to judge *anything?* Moral authority has been purified of earthbound idolatries. But it is not immediately evident how the transcendent God is to be related to the particular aspects of experience without a return to the old cultural idolatries—or to new cultural idolatries that can also appear in theological form. The issue is unavoidable, for, as Gabriel Vahanian has said, "Without a cultural vocation there can be, insofar as Christianity is concerned, no faith in God."[9] Unless faith in God can find specific cultural expression it is literally nonsense. So the issue is not merely whether or not Christian faith can help us with our moral decisions; it is whether there can be such a thing as Christian faith.

The Response of Situation Ethics

The problem of ethical method resulting from this theological situation has been posed strikingly by what is loosely termed situation ethics or contextual ethics. This approach has important implications for our method of arriving at moral judgments, even though its intellectual influence has waned to some extent since it emerged prominently in the 1960s.

It offers a seemingly clear negative answer: We are *not* to make our judgments on the basis of any moral rules that assume the intrinsic goodness or evil of particular kinds of acts, practices, or institutions. Joseph Fletcher made the point characteristically that "in Christian situation ethics nothing is worth anything in and of itself. It gains or acquires its value only because it happens to help persons (thus being good) or to hurt persons (thus being bad)."[10] The only intrinsically good thing, in his view, is love itself: "No law or principle or value is good as such—not life or truth or chastity or property or marriage or anything but love. *Only one thing is intrinsically good, namely, love: nothing else at all.*"[11] Paul Lehmann, whose position we shall examine shortly, is also at pains to establish that no moral rule is intrinsically valid and thus universally applicable apart from the transcending theological basis of morality. While Fletcher and Lehmann are sharply different in their formulation of the basic norm of Christian ethics, they and other situational or contextual ethicists agree upon the negative proposition: There are no universally applicable rules that provide a basis for moral judgment.

How, then, are we to decide? Here the term "situation ethics" is itself a bit misleading—at least so far as the intentions of Fletcher and Lehmann are concerned. Situation ethics is not sheer relativism, or it would not be ethics but a denial of the moral life. Nor is it a brash hedonism of the *Playboy*-philosophy sort. More is involved than the situation and our pure subjective inclinations. Fletcher carefully insists that his ethics can make use of principles of rational calculation (he speaks, for example, of a coalition between Christian situation ethics and utilitarianism in acceptance of the principle of "greatest good of the largest number"), and he speaks appreciatively of the collective moral wisdom of this and previous generations as a resource to enlighten our judgments.[12] Still, we ourselves must judge, and if necessary we must know when to set aside the rules.

What precisely do the rules mean, then? This is a difficult question for Fletcher, and it suggests that a whole level of analysis has, perhaps inevitably, been neglected. This is the level of accounting for the relationship between *agape,* the only intrinsic good, and the specific ends sought in relation to the world of nature and of human institutions. Surely these ends are not validated morally solely as "a function of human decisions" made in love.[13] How is love to know what difference any decision makes? It helps but little to say, as Fletcher does, that the decision is good if it increases the sum total of loving-kindness,[14] because we still do not know the relationship between the structures of human existence and loving-kindness. The collective wisdom of humankind is helpful, to be sure; but an appeal to *consensus gentium* in the form of inherited tradition or summary rules only pushes the problem back one step, particularly since the consensus may be set aside if necessary for the sake of love. What relationship has humankind, through its moral traditions and summary rules, perceived between love and the structures of existence? If there is not any objectivity to the structures that stand over against love, Fletcher has surely surrendered to antinomianism, notwithstanding his protestations to the contrary.

As it is, Fletcher's ethics contributes a striking reaffirmation of the importance of moral (that is, loving) commitment, but we are not greatly helped with our ethical uncertainties. As Paul Ramsey has shrewdly observed,[15] even in his own illustrative cases Fletcher demonstrates the inability of his method to provide insight. For "love" in some of Fletcher's case illustrations seems to require actions diametrically opposite to those in other quite comparable situations. Without our pausing to argue the merits of such cases, it is evident that *agape* is at work only as a possible *motive*—not as a source of insight into what should be done if love is well directed. It is difficult to escape the conclusion that so far as judgment is concerned we have been left with a basically intuitive ethics.

Paul Lehmann also rejects any universal claims for moral rules, and in this respect his position is similar to that of Joseph Fletcher. His rationale is, however, strikingly distinct. The fundamental problem of Christian ethics is not, according to Lehmann, how to comprehend the good to be sought through our actions. Rather, it is that of analyzing the new life, the new maturity of those who have been transformed by God's action in Jesus Christ: "The main concern throughout these pages is with the concrete ethical reality of a transformed human being and a transformed humanity owing to the specific action of God in Jesus Christ, an action and transformation of which the reality of the Christian *koinonia* is a foretaste."[16] Christian ethics, therefore, is to be considered indicative, not imperative. The question is not what I *ought* to do but rather what I *am* to do.[17]

Lehmann's meaning can easily be misunderstood. He does not deny that all people, including Christians, confront alternative action possibilities and that it matters, ethically, which actions are chosen. One may restate his argument along somewhat Kantian lines by acknowledging that it is the will that is decisive, not the specific choice. The ethical problem is in the will, not in the alternatives.[18] Thus the specific analysis of the situation of choosing must be subordinated to analysis of the person who does the choosing. The "ought" therefore has to do with what a person ought *to be:* one "ought" to be *good.* The further question of one's specific actions becomes (if one *is* good) not an imperative but an indicative question: that is, a question of what a good person will *in fact* do. One does not, in the moment of choosing, decide whether or not to be good. That question is already, as it were, settled. Since it is settled already, the only remaining question is which of the possible actions best expresses the goodness that one is. That question can be regarded as "indicative."[19]

The issue for Christians is settled by faith in God's action in Jesus Christ, which has established in human history a "new order of humanity, in which and by which the Christian lives." The essential nature of our humanity having been revealed in Jesus Christ, there is, in the church—the *koinonia* of faith—a foretaste of the fulfillment of this new humanity. In a formal sense, the Christian ethic involves doing the will of God. But the will of God is revealed only in what God has actually done and is actually doing in human history "to make and keep human life *human* in the world." Christians grow in maturity as they live in this reality in the *koinonia.* Their actions, then, are simply an expression of their mature humanity. They are to do what they are: "To do what I am is to act in every situation in accordance with what it has been given to me to be. Doing the will of God is doing what I am."[20]

But how are we to *know* the will of God? Can we simply rely on direct perception of God's humanizing activity in the world and on our ability to relate to it effectively? How are we to interpret differences of perception among Christians? When Christians experience dilemmas as troublesome, does it mean they are not sufficiently attuned to God—not sufficiently Christian?

"Understandably," Lehmann writes, "such an ethic will be puzzling, even ridiculous, to those who have no eyes to see the signs of the times, who do not know what belongs to their peace. Such knowledge comes by insight, not by calculation. It is the gift of faith available to those who are willing to take seriously what faith knows about the doing of God's will in the world." To be sure, Lehmann acknowledges at the same time the "complexity of the actual human situation" which "is always compounded of an intricate network of circumstance and human interrelationships."[21] But it would appear that Lehmann, like Fletcher, places a very heavy burden upon sheer intuition. We are left without specific intellectual resources to help us in arriving at dependable moral judgments.

I must confess I do not simply and intuitively *know* what is to be done in relation to modern war, the environmental problems, racial tension, allocation of economic priorities, abortion, or any number of other complex issues humankind faces! Intuitive judgments are more likely to reflect Christian faith accurately in the immediate face-to-face relationships characteristic of small groups or communities, though even there sheer intuition often fails. The truth is that Christian ethics, while presupposing much of what Lehmann has said concerning Christian motivation and God's activity to humanize humanity, must involve more personal and collective *thinking* about the implications of this faith in the world of decision-making. When Christians find themselves espousing opposite sides in public policy debates, the differences of insight cannot be attributed simply to differences in maturity of faith or of intuitive perception of God's actions in human history. We need some basis for rational assessment of situations. Rational assessment, for Christians, must involve faithfulness to basic theological insights and recognition of regularities and continuities in God's humanizing action. It also involves the possibility of meaningful communication among Christians concerning the implications of their faith.

By asserting that intuition is not enough, we should not think of it as being unnecessary. That flash of insight we label intuition is bound to play an important role in most actual moral judgment, partly because we often have to make decisions in a hurry and partly because the complexities of actual moral problems are often too great to organize with conscious rationality. In real life we cannot be rational deliberating machines—human computers—coldly dissecting and reconstructing the moral dilemmas we face as systems of ethics sometimes curiously imply we should do. Still, a rational method of moral judgment can at least serve us before and after the fact of intuition. Before, it can prepare us for more faithful, loving, dependable intuitions, so that when we move instinctively it will be instinctively in the right direction. Afterward, it can help us analyze our intuitions, assessing their adequacy, correcting our errors. Situation ethics does not provide us with a sufficient basis for either of these important functions of ethical reflection, just as it does not afford a more-than-intuitive approach to decision-making in the situation itself.

Beyond Situation Ethics

A number of Christian thinkers are uncomfortable with the intuitive method of situation ethics, even while remaining fully cognizant of the difficulties of ethical legalism and of most of the traditional sources of moral authority when these are treated as absolutes. John C. Bennett, for instance, has sought to restate natural law doctrine more acceptably and to make use of "middle axioms" as a way of conveying the demands of the gospel in universal form without force of treating them as absolute rules binding for all time. He understands a middle axiom to be "more concrete than a universal ethical principle and less specific than a program that includes legislation and political strategy." They are "the next steps that our own generation must take" in fulfilling the purposes of God.[22] In respect to natural law, Bennett has argued that "there is a moral order in the world that can be known with varying degrees of clarity apart from revelation." Illustrating natural-law perceptions, he lists the widespread moral convictions "that the human race is one in the sense that there are no permanently superior and inferior human groups . . . ; that society should be open to free criticism from within; that men and nations should be true to their pledged word; that justice on the corrective side should be administered with impartiality and that on the side of the distribution of wealth it should be so administered as to provide equal opportunity for all."[23]

Paul Ramsey has also been concerned to incorporate moral principles in Christian ethical reflection, although he has done so from a more specifically theological point of view. Departing from an earlier period in which his views were somewhat situationalist,[24] Ramsey came in his later years to emphasize moral principles and rules in areas ranging from international relations to medical ethics. One of his most striking contributions was an analysis of how rules can express and implement Christian love.

In his essay "Two Concepts of General Rules in Christian Ethics," Ramsey suggests three ways in which rules can express and implement Christian love. First is through summary rules—rules that are a summary of previous experiences of attempting to judge and act on the basis of love. "*Summary rules* are reports that cases of a certain sort have been found to be most love-fulfilling."[25] Summary rules are more than an expression of individual experience. They can embody the wisdom accumulated through centuries in the traditions of a community which has attempted to live on the basis of Christian love. Nevertheless, the status of summary rules is only provisional. They are rules of thumb, which can be set aside for the sake of a more direct expression of love whenever the situation demands. One must be prepared to violate them "in situations in which to follow them would conflict with what love dictates in that situation."[26]

To Ramsey this is not enough. A Christian, he believes, ought not to reject "the possibility that Christian faith and love affords mankind more than *probable knowledge* into ethics." The basic theological ground for this possibility is in the faith that God has chosen to be bound absolutely, in love, to humanity. God's binding covenant is the basis for all (binding) covenants among human beings. Therefore, "love seems to have only a dissolving or relativizing power when the *freedom of agape* is taken to mean love's *inability* to bind itself one way and not another or in no way except in acts that are the immediate response of one person's depth to another's depth." There are, he concludes, "some things that are as unconditionally wrong as love is unconditionally right."[27] The unconditional rightness of love can be embodied in rules as well as in acts, at least in the negative sense that some things may be defined as generally (always) unloving. It follows that there are general rules which are more than summary rules.

Can such rules be known? Ramsey's position would seem to be that they can *become* known. Whether or not any particular supposedly general rule (such as the rule of promise-keeping or rules against cruelty or rape) is in fact properly so regarded is an important part of the subject matter of ethical reflection. It is the business of Christian ethics to seek out those general rules which embody Christian love. The difficulty of this task is insufficient ground for saying (with the situationist) that Christian rule morality can go no further than summary rules or "rules of thumb." Ramsey insists that such possible general rules are not a form of legalism. It is an altogether different thing to speak of rules for the sake of love than to speak of rules for the sake of the rules themselves.

But following John Rawls,[28] he also suggests yet another basis for love-embodying rules in what are called "rules of practice." A "practice" can be understood as a societal rule, or custom, or institution—it is a system of mutual human expectations governing behavior. If one is involved in the system it is expected that one will observe the rules of the system, just as the participant in a game must observe the rules of the game. The question of whether one will observe the practice and the rules of the practice are not separable. By violating one of the rules, a person simultaneously rejects the practice in which the rule is embedded. Thus, if promise-keeping is accepted as a social practice, one cannot break any of one's own promises without also weakening that general practice of promise-keeping. Similarly, marriage as a generally accepted social practice or institution is weakened by infidelity, regardless of the specific claims of Christian *agape* that may be made in a particular situation to justify the deviation. If some practices (or institutions or customs) embody love so that Christian love has a stake in the continuation and strengthening of the practices, it is an act against love to violate a rule implicit in such practices. "Rules of practice," he argues, "necessarily involve the abdication of full liberty to guide one's action case by case by making immediate appeals to what love (or utility) requires in each particular case." The point is not necessarily conservative. Practices can be *challenged* for the sake of love. But "there cannot be exceptions [to practices] that depart from them by direct general appeals to *agape* overriding the rules in particular cases in which the agent does not take the weighty responsibility of criticizing the practice as a whole and attempting to replace it with another. *Agape* justifies no exception within a practice. One must rather undertake to reform the accepted practice as a whole [to] render it generally a more loving practice."[29] The point can even be revolutionary if, in fact, it is one's judgment that existing practices or institutions violate rather than embody love. But one cannot sever the connection between particular actions and their relationship to the broader coordination of human actions and expectations and do this in the name of particular case-by-case decisions as to what is the loving thing to do.

Both Bennett and Ramsey have made enduring contributions, but it is questionable whether either has finally solved the basic underlying problem of moral judgment. It is one thing to affirm the existence or value of middle axioms, general rules, or general practices; it is quite another to identify *particular* axioms, rules, or practices that assuredly *do* embody love or goodness. It is still another thing to relate the axioms, rules, or practices to the actual facts at hand. At both these latter points, neither Bennett nor Ramsey has provided us with a sufficient basis of judgment. What both have done is to help locate the thing to be judged and, in particular, to see that the problem of judgment cannot be merely a matter of case-by-case intuition. Life *is* interconnected. There *are* regularities in human social and historical experience. Generalizations *can* be made about what it means to love in society in a broader historical frame of reference than that suggested by the situationalists. But this level of insight does not offer us as much methodological help as we need.

It may be questioned, moreover, whether either Bennett or Ramsey has in fact gone beyond a summary-rule ethic. To do so it would be necessary to validate a rule claim on some basis other than the experience of oneself or of one's community or of tradition. It is particularly evident that Bennett's middle axioms and Ramsey's practices would in most cases be validated in respect to human experience. It is not so clear, however, with respect to Ramsey's love-embodying pure general rules. Here the question is whether or not it is the case that some rules can be found that categorically express love's demand on the basis not of a summary of particular experiences but of an analysis of what it means to be human. Are there some general rules pointing to things that love cannot *ever* permit to be done? Ramsey suggests in passing that some things, like cruelty and rape, "are inherently wrong, wrong in themselves, because of the lovelessness that is *always* in them."[30] Similarly, he suggests that "promise-breaking" might be considered to be wrong by definition. But such asserted general rules are not to be taken as classes of acts alone but as classes of acts undertaken from unloving motivation. It is not, for instance, physical suffering per se that is objectionable to Ramsey when he speaks of cruelty as something so inherently unloving that it can be proscribed by a general rule. It is suffering deliberately caused. It is not intrinsically immoral, in Ramsey's estimation, to cause suffering in war. Even innocent bystanders can be made to suffer if the suffering was not intended and was only a consequence of necessary and justified measures to conduct a justified war.[31] But if it is the *motivation* that justifies calling a given act "cruelty," Ramsey has only expressed a truism (however helpful the truism may be)—that is, the truism that unloving acts are intrinsically and generally loveless.

Still, it remains that more than our loving commitment to God is implied in Christian faith. God's own commitment to us surely does have important implications for our concrete choices, as Ramsey has attempted to express in his view of general rules. But a margin of uncertainty remains to plague the application of any ethic, for the problem remains of how we are to relate our commitment to the empirical world. How are we to know that world so as to relate it fittingly to whatever ethical principles we feel we can derive from Christian faith? And if, as one may suspect, our knowing of that world and its relationship to Christian faith is always somewhat problematic, how are we to deal simultaneously with the truth that is present to us and the truth that is veiled behind our ignorance?

A third significant recent thinker, Walter G. Muelder, has also attempted to find and apply ethical principles. The starting point of Muelder's ethics is the moral law formulation first developed by Edgar S. Brightman and later refined substantially by L. Harold DeWolf and by Muelder himself. The "moral laws" developed in this tradition are based on philosophical analysis, not specifically on Christian faith claims. The moral laws can therefore be understood as a reformulation of natural law. The table of laws themselves is intricately developed, and it is beyond our purposes to discuss them in detail here.[32] Several things about this formulation are significant, however. It is, in the first place, structured on a Kantian analysis of the moral will. The moral will is universal and therefore free of self-contradiction. As the will confronts the real world, it always relates to it through affirming the good as it can best be understood. One must accept as binding one's own ideal values and regulate all particular value experience on the basis of what one considers to be the universal good. In the real world, our conception of the universal good may often be frustrated. But if we are to avoid self-contradiction we cannot settle for less than the "best possible" good in the situation. The total range of consequences of projected actions must be calculated as far as possible, and in this sense we have here a prudential ethic. But it is important to note also that no conceivable consequence could justify self-contradiction or a violation of the ideal values on the basis of which consequences are themselves evaluated. That would be literal nonsense.

The original Brightman formulation of this system defined the material good in terms of personality: It is our ideal of what we and other persons ought to be and to become that ultimately defines the nature of the good. Subsequent formulations by L. Harold DeWolf emphasized the importance of human interaction in community and of our understanding of the metaphysical unity of reality. Both DeWolf and Muelder stress that Christian theology establishes, for the Christian, the content of the regulative terms "person," "community," and "metaphysical reality." For the non-Christian, the moral laws are equally binding, but for them the particular content will be different. Thus an attempt has been made here to restate the natural law on a Kantian and personalistic rather than Thomistic basis and to define the relationship between this ethic and the Christian faith that supplies it with concrete meaning. As the moral laws themselves stand (apart from the theological content utilized by particular Christian thinkers), they have the appeal of almost self-evident logical clarity. It is unthinkable to say that we may do anything less than the "best possible," or that our acts ought not to be relevant to the context of action, or that we ought not to be concerned about the consequences of actions. Moreover, one can defend the centrality of the categories of "personhood" and "community" and of the problem of understanding the metaphysical context in which moral action is ultimately to find its meaning. But our problem is how we are to locate this meaning in other than formal terms, on the one hand, and how we are to discover in the real empirical world what it means to be an actually existent person or to have an actually existent community, on the other.

It is here that Muelder's peculiar contribution takes shape in his understanding that social ethics is an intersectional discipline, mediating between normative disciplines (such as theology and philosophy) and empirical disciplines (including the natural and social sciences). What can the one know about the other? Since all disciplines are constantly developing, there is no possibility of a final, once-for-all synthesis. There is, rather, the prospect of what Muelder calls "emergent coherence": a constantly developing state of synthesis as the different divisions of human knowledge themselves develop and interact in dialogue.[33] More than the other thinkers we have considered, Muelder takes seriously the contributions of the sciences as providing a basis of dependable knowledge about the actual world. The question posed by science to the moralist is whether or not our approach to both natural and social phenomena will be casual and impressionistic (and intuitive) or whether it will be orderly, thoughtful, and disciplined. How shall we understand, for instance, the rules of practice of which Ramsey speaks? Can a disciplined examination of the family or economic life or particular forms of government contribute anything to our understanding of morality in the real world? Clearly we cannot say that analysis of facts alone is the same thing as moral judgment. But if facts enter into moral judgment, as surely they must, then a more refined understanding of what the facts really *are* contributes significantly to the accuracy of moral judgment. Among the not-inconsequential results of taking social sciences seriously is an increasing appreciation of the factual interdependency of all life and of the greater complexity of so loose a term as "situation" or "context."

But, of course, the emergent coherence of which Muelder speaks does not relieve us of the difficulties and uncertainties of judgment. As with Bennett and Ramsey, we still must face the problem of how we are to act with conviction despite our knowledge that we shall never know for certain that our actions and judgments are truly the faithful expression of goodness we intend them to be. It is unlikely that we shall be able to think our way out of this basic problem to a position of absolute certainty, but we may hope to find grounds for clarification and for acting with relatively greater confidence as Christians.

The Pure Ethic of Jesus

All this may seem too limited and too relativistic to a group of Christian thinkers who have sought to translate the gospel more directly into relevant social decision-making. A kind of evangelical renaissance has emerged in recent years to challenge the marriage of conservative theology to conservative politics and, at the same time, to challenge what is perceived to be the sterility of the combination of liberal theology and liberal politics. In one way or another, these thinkers are convinced that the gospel of Jesus Christ provides direct, unambiguous moral guidance. They are also conservative in their use of the Bible, although they do not necessarily believe that every moral injunction in the Bible is of equal significance.

John Howard Yoder is a particularly striking leader in this movement. In his *The Politics of Jesus,* Yoder argues that Jesus is himself the norm for Christian ethics and that the perfection in love enjoined by the life and teaching of Jesus is fully relevant to human existence. We should therefore reject the false choice between compromising Jesus as the true norm of our actions in order to be "effective" in the social world and withdrawal from the world in order to preserve our Christian perfection. Yoder regards Troeltsch's famous "church-type" and "sect-type" as equally unacceptable options:

> In the tradition of Ernst Troeltsch, Western theological ethics assumes that the choice of options is fixed in logic and for all times and places by the way the Constantinian heritage dealt with the question. Either one accepts, without serious qualification, the responsibility of politics, i.e. of governing, with whatever means that takes, or one chooses a withdrawn position of either personal-monastic-vocational or sectarian character, which is "apolitical."[34]

The choice between these two options is a false one, however, if one considers Jesus to be the Messiah of God. To say that Jesus is Messiah is to say that Jesus' approach to the realities of social and political life is the approach that ultimately has God behind it. We do not need to take responsibility for managing history; ultimately that is God's responsibility, not ours. Nevertheless, we can be sure that in obedience to Jesus' way we shall be most relevant to the historical process, not in retreat from it.

It may be accurate to say that Yoder provides a categorical answer to the problem of moral judgment only in the negative sense of defining what is always and in every circumstance to be avoided. We can be sure in our moral judgments insofar as they involve a rejection of the use of evil means, such as violence. In every case where we are presented with the prospect of such moral compromise we are to reject it: about that we can be very clear, and to that extent Yoder seems sure that there need be no uncertainty in our judgments. He does not conclude from this that "for any question of social ethics a direct solution can be sought in the casuistic teachings of the New Testament."[35] In order to arrive at judgments concerning the complex ethical dilemmas of modern society, we could not do without "broader generalizations, a longer hermeneutic path, and insights from other sources." Yoder is not a biblical perfectionist in the sense of affirming "a specific biblical ethical content for modern questions"—except in the renunciation of violence and other uses of what we ourselves know to be evil. When we cannot reasonably predict "success" as an outcome of this kind of radical obedience to Jesus, we should remember that our obedience is to something deeper than immediate success and that Jesus, as God's Messiah, is Lord of history.

The British pacifist writer John Ferguson echoes the notion that our ethic should be patterned as directly as possible on that of Jesus. The right question, writes Ferguson, is "What will Christ do—in me?" Ferguson is confident that "he will have no part in war; he cannot do so and be true to his nature, to his very being. His way is the way of nonviolent, suffering love, and if I do not put my worldly wisdom as a barrier to shut him out, this is the way he will continue to take in me." Thus, he continues, "Christ showed us a new way, a way of life, a way of changing the world. It was *in its own way* revolutionary. It was the way of love, the way of the Cross, the way of non-violence, the way of Truth-force, Soul-force, Love-force."[36] So Ferguson also is convinced that a clear, unambiguous answer can be given to the question of moral judgment, at least insofar as we are tempted to use evil means to advance good ends. In chapter 6, we shall return to the problem of compromise with evil. Thinkers like Yoder and Ferguson believe there is greater clarity in the negative than in the positive side of social judgment. Certain things are rejected, more or less absolutely. But there may be some continuing uncertainty among the various positive options. Such thinkers do not attempt to give us absolute guidelines for moral judgments in situations where we have to choose between alternative positive strategies of witness and action. It is evident that we have not here been provided with an adequate solution to the problems of translating love into intelligent action.

Christian Character and Moral Judgment

It remains finally to note that a number of Christian ethicists would say that this chapter has defined the problem of Christian ethics in altogether the wrong way. By focusing on moral judgment in an uncertain world, these ethicists would hold, we have displaced the proper subject matter of Christian ethics, which is the Christian character and way of life as disclosed in the Christian story and community. We have replaced it with a "decisionism" that reduces Christian life and story to actions and decisions by abstract individuals in an abstract world. Our real identity as Christians is supplied by the narratives (or "story") of the Christian community, of which we are a part. The ethical problem is how, as Christians, to be faithful to that story, to allow that story to shape our very being—our character—so that in all we do or say we are "truthful."

In a book emphasizing such themes, Stanley Hauerwas is specifically critical of the earlier *A Christian Method of Moral Judgment* as subordinating the story of Jesus to ethical propositions requiring "little reference to who Jesus was or what he did for their meaning or intelligibility." But Jesus did not *have* a social ethic, Hauerwas argues; "his story *is* a social ethic" and "the form of the church must exemplify that ethic."[37] Echoing that theme, James W. McClendon is sharply critical of "decisionism," which focuses on decisions as the substance of morality. McClendon grants that "there are perplexities, there is surely temptation; our minds are sometimes divided." But "decisionism with its entailed voluntarism and interiorization cannot be an adequate or full account of the moral life." He considers this point to be underscored by the Parable of the Last Judgment (Matthew 25), in which the righteous are rewarded for deeds of love and mercy that were "far from having been deliberate and calculated acts of moral decision" but rather "deeds that unconsciously registered their character and their faith."[38]

Such accounts of the Christian "story" and of the importance of Christian "character" and way of life are useful reminders that Christian ethics must be grounded in the traditions of the Christian community and that the character of Christians is basic to anything else one might wish to say about their attitudes, behavior, and decisions as human beings in community.

But where does that leave us in respect to the problem of moral judgment? Writers like Hauerwas and McClendon acknowledge that Christians do have to decide and act in a world outside themselves and their communities of faith. But are we to suppose that people whose character is well grounded in the Christian "story" will, more or less intuitively, arrive at the most faithful solutions to the perplexing dilemmas we all face? If so, what we have here is simply another version of the situation ethics of a Fletcher or the contextual ethics of a Lehmann. Or are we to suppose that there is enough content in the Christian "story" to sustain dependable conclusions about what we should do? Both Hauerwas and McClendon are particularly concerned to emphasize that Christian faith is not consistent with doing evil that good may come. And if that is their serious message about Christian ethics, what we have here is another version of the evangelical position of a John Howard Yoder—which is clear only in its negative disavowal of actions regarded by them as inconsistent with the gospel.

Hauerwas and McClendon are ambiguous enough about such questions to leave us unsure of exactly how they would counsel Christians (of good character and well grounded in Christian story and community) to *think* about the moral problems and dilemmas facing them in the world. Part of the problem is that they are reluctant to move from a narrative mode of moral discourse to a conceptual one, as critical thinking requires us to do. Their own books move back and forth between narrative and abstract conceptual thought, and there is probably a good deal more "decisionism" in their work than either would care to acknowledge. But they have not provided us with clear methodological guidance about how to express Christian faith with faithfulness and intellectual integrity.

The Problem of Ethical Methodology

We should remember again that the twentieth century has placed an unusually heavy strain on our search for clarity in judgment. Two great wars, instant communication techniques linking previously insulated cultures, the rise of communism, the struggles for the independence of colonial peoples, racial strife, space travel, contraception, technological expansion into automation and cybernation, the environmental crisis, the population explosion, nuclear stalemate and nuclear proliferation, the emergent prospect of the collective suicide of the human race—such things tax the maturity of our ethical judgments to the limit. "New occasions teach new duties; time makes ancient good uncouth." Surely this is not so of the center point of ethics, the good will. Love does not become obsolete. But it is an accurate statement of the problem each new generation, and particularly this one, encounters in trying to locate the good in the real world. If, as we have seen, we are not likely to discover a method of arriving at *certainty* in our moral judgments, we may at least hope to clarify the bases of those judgments. A method of moral judgment must at least help us to minimize the morally weakening effects of uncertainty. It must permit us to act with certitude, if not with certainty.

This discussion may be concluded by suggesting some criteria for an adequate Christian ethical methodology:

1. It must be *tentative* with respect to particular moral judgments. It must remember that no one's perceptions of God (and therefore of the full meaning of the good) are ever complete. We are all finite beings. Even were this not so, our judgments would continue to be distorted by our own self-centeredness. And even were that not the case, our perceptions of the actual world would remain incomplete. The data are never all in. An adequate methodology of Christian moral judgment must therefore always be open to the possibility that particular judgments arrived at with the best of intentions may be mistaken.

2. It must be *faithful* to the central affirmations of Christian faith. A methodology of Christian moral judgment is rooted in Christian faith. That is its starting point. The center of value, the ultimate source of norms, cannot be derived from other sources. Christians may and do differ widely in their interpretation of what Christian faith really means. But a methodology of Christian moral judgment will always be some kind of interpretation of what it means to act in faithfulness to the Christian faith commitment.

3. It must provide a basis for investing judgments and actions with *wholehearted commitment and seriousness* without abandoning tentativeness. Commitment itself cannot be tentative, though the particular directions to which commitment is directed must be tentative. Our problem is how to act and judge in the real world so as to preserve the wholeheartedness of commitment without closing off the intellectual openness required by our actual uncertainties. How can we judge tentatively in such a way that the tentativeness of our judgment does not paralyze the will? How can we act with "singleness of heart," even though we know our actions may be mistaken? An adequate methodology of Christian moral judgment must provide a way of doing so.

4. It must provide a basis for *clarifying moral dialogue* as to why particular actions have been chosen. We may never have certainty, but it would be a useful service to Christians if better forms of moral communication could be discovered. If the debates raging within the churches regarding homosexuality, or abortion, or preparedness for nuclear war, or economic and racial dilemmas could have clarified the *Christian* grounds for the particular stances taken, this would have been a noteworthy service in and of itself. Moreover, as Christians relate themselves to non-Christians and to policymakers (who may or may not be Christians), there is need for greater clarity of statement as to why it is that a given Christian or Christian group supports or opposes a particular position. Clarity in moral dialogue is not in itself a sufficient end for ethics, but it is an important service to those who are honestly groping for new insight.

4

Initial Presumption
and the Burden of Proof

There is a tendency in ethics to deal with moral judgments in one or the other of two opposite ways. Ethical perfectionists of various kinds may treat a moral problem as though we can know the one correct solution with certainty. A given moral tradition is believed to supply the right answers. A casuistry may need to be developed to clarify the implications of that moral tradition for cases not clearly anticipated in the tradition itself. But we may have confidence that moral judgments can be made without uncertainty. The ethical perfectionist is, in fact, likely to regard uncertainty as evidence of moral failure, not intellectual failure. We have already seen the impossibility of this as a general stance. The actual content of our judgments simply is not immediate to us. Ethical perfectionism has the virtue of preserving the seriousness of moral commitment in the face of the judgments we are called upon to make in the real world. But it has the drawback of possible self-deception. By holding fast to perfectionist standards or prejudgments with intellectual rigidity we may unwittingly cause great evil, and the purity of our moral commitment may itself become clouded by self-righteousness.

On the other hand, situationalists and realists have a tendency to weigh the available evidence in moral decision-making without sufficient precommitment as to what is *probably* the best course to follow. To Joseph Fletcher, love must decide "then and there" what is to be done from among the existing alternatives. There is no such thing as a moral exception or a necessary evil,[1] for such concepts imply that there may be something suspect about what one must do in obedience to love alone. To Reinhold Niebuhr, moral judgment is the sorting out of the most realistic means to attain the most defensible proximate ends—without precommitment to some means as inherently more moral than others. Both situationalists and realists are committed only to what the preponderance of the evidence seems to require. Both have the virtue of openness and a certain quality of humility. Both have the drawback of neglecting to enter prior moral commitments, other than to love itself, into the method of judgment. A preponderance-of-evidence approach to moral judgment tends to treat different *kinds* of evidence without sufficient discrimination.

To be of greatest use, a Christian method of moral judgment must steer between perfectionism on the one hand and situationalism on the other. It must seek to combine the moral seriousness of the one with the flexibility of the other.

The Moral Burden of Proof

The most productive way to do this is by frankly admitting certain initial biases or presumptions into our decision-making. Among the available options, we should look first to the ones with strongest apparent support in our ultimate value commitments and give them our tentative approval. The others should be required to bear the burden of proof. We thus arrive at judgments despite uncertainties by making an initial presumption of the superiority of one set of conclusions and then testing that presumption by examining contradictory evidence. If, after examining the contradictory evidence, substantial doubt or uncertainty remains, we decide the matter on the basis of the initial presumption. We *presume* a certain kind of decision or a certain course of action to be the right one morally, unless it can be shown beyond reasonable doubt not to be.[2] Such an approach seems peculiarly useful in approaching moral judgments in the face of continuing uncertainty. If we can establish in advance what is *probably* the best line of decision in the light of our most basic moral commitments, we have a clear basis for proceeding—even though this method will by no means banish uncertainty altogether. Such a method gives us more guidance than sheer impulse or intuition. It offers more help than calculation of consequences from scratch without a strong initial preference for certain means over others.

This use of initial presumption is important in two areas of human decision-making. In both these areas people have learned to live with uncertainties while still arriving at the kinds of judgment that permit unambiguous action.

The first area is jurisprudence. In the legal process matters are constantly in dispute, and doubt often exists about the facts of a case or the relevant interpretation of the law. The concept of legal presumption has been developed not to settle matters infallibly but to organize the process of decision-making along the lines of greater or lesser probability so as to safeguard the most basic community values.

A good illustration is the principle in Anglo-Saxon law that the accused is presumed to be innocent until proved guilty. The state must prove the guilt of the accused beyond a "reasonable doubt," or acquittal will result.

This principle assumes that all citizens are law-abiding. It protects them from arbitrary detention and frivolous or malicious accusations. The presumption of innocence establishes the method by which both sides will proceed. The prosecution must construct a plausible interpretation of the facts to show that a violation of law has been committed by the defendant. The defendant's lawyer, on the other hand, need only show that the state has failed to make its case. If a reasonable doubt persists, the state loses and the defendant is acquitted.[3] Doubt itself has not been abolished by this kind of procedure, but a method of handling doubt has been put into practice.

Another legal illustration, also with ancient roots, is the principle that the actual possessor of property is to be presumed to hold that property rightfully. The burden of proof rests with any challenger to show that the property was gained unlawfully.

Fixing the burden of proof does not end the juridical process. Indeed, the burden may shift in an appellate proceeding. For instance, a defendant who has been found guilty will find that in an appeal to a higher court the latter tends to presume the legal propriety of the lower court's proceedings—hence the burden of proof must now be borne by attorneys for the one who has been convicted. Similarly, a higher court will presume the legality of an act of legislature or Congress or chief executive and require those challenging the constitutionality of legislative enactments and executive policies to bear the burden of proof. Such presumptions help to structure the decision-making process and make it easier to cope with uncertainty. Such a process enables society to define in advance the kind of conclusions that, on the whole, can best form the basis for resolution of disputes in case a full review of the available evidence still leaves considerable doubt. In law, as elsewhere, we have such approaches to decision-making in mind when we speak of the "benefit of the doubt."

The second area in which the use of initial presumption is illustrated is that of decision-making by executives. An executive in modern society is a generalist, often confronting doubt or uncertainty about which policies to pursue. He or she must depend on expert advice from many specialists who know far more about the various aspects of the problem than a typical executive possibly could. Who is to be trusted? An executive also must establish certain presumptions. Some of these presumptions may be theoretical or traditional in some sense, but others will relate to the kinds of persons whose information or advice can be depended upon. The executive will tend to place the burden of proof against those whom he or she regards as laypersons or amateurs. Faced with a new kind of problem, a competent executive will normally cast about for the generally recognized experts in the field. The advice of such experts may be disregarded if, upon closer scrutiny, it appears flawed. But the executive will tend to take their word first. Of course, the burden of proof may well be placed *against* those particular "experts" who have let the executive down in the past.[4] But the executive cannot avoid the question of what sources of expertise and advice are to be accorded presumptive rightness.

I believe we all actually tend to do our thinking on the basis of initial presumptions, though we often do it quite unconsciously and therefore unclearly. We have instinctive points of reference that constitute initial presumptions. Many of our presumptions have been instilled in us very early in life, though this is not always the case. The point is that we place a conscious or unconscious burden of proof against apparent deviations from what seems to be right. Our presumptions are our basic prejudices; and to say this, in light of the usual connotations of the word "prejudice," is to take note of the fact that our presumptions can be quite evil in effect. Racial prejudice, with its attendant evils, is a matter of placing the burden of proof against the full moral humanity of persons of a different race. A specific person of the other race may meet that burden by possessing outstanding personal qualities. Then, if we are really prejudiced, we will carefully mark that person off as an exception to the usual rule! We may place the burden of proof against the intelligence of a poor person or in favor of the competence of the rich. A new book or a new idea from an unknown person is likely to confront a much heavier burden of proof than the same from a person of established reputation. Historically, women have often had to face a heavy weight of prejudice in male-dominated societies. This is what prejudice means; it is a prejudgment of the facts. But despite the evil possibilities in prejudice, it is inevitable that we shall form and judge things on the basis of presumptions.

This is as true of our moral judgments as it is of factual ones. To illustrate, many people tend to think about political issues with a moral presumption in favor of political democracy. They may agree that in some circumstances (such as the incipient anarchy of the period following the breakup of colonialism in Africa) political democracy may not be the best immediate answer. But they tend to retain democracy as the moral standard for political organization, and any deviations from democracy must bear the burden of proof. Similarly, in the Western world some persons have a strong initial presumption in favor of laissez-faire capitalism. Any form of governmental involvement in economic matters must bear the burden of proof, as far as these people are concerned. But there are also people who have a strong initial presumption in favor of socialism, and for them free-market institutions can be tolerated only to the extent proven necessary. Economists like Milton Friedman clearly place the burden of proof against governmental involvements in economic life, while the reverse would be true of a Michael Harrington.[5] Presumptions in favor of monogamy and the nuclear family and against extramarital sexual relations and homosexuality continue to influence moral judgments powerfully in most contemporary human societies, although exceptions are more frequently accepted today than in previous years.

The real question is not whether we have prejudices and presumptions but whether we are able to clarify and modify our initial presumptions on the basis of our ultimate value commitments. Do our presumptions reflect our deepest moral integrity, or are they rather an evidence of a morally split personality? For the Christian, the issue is whether our presumptions are or can be in any authentic sense *Christian* moral presumptions.

Christian thinkers have indeed illustrated this use of initial presumptions quite clearly. Sometimes they have done so consciously; at other times they have seemed unaware of the sources of their actual judgments or of the fact that these judgments had little relationship to the theological foundations upon which they supposedly rested. An example of the latter that might occur to any student of twentieth-century Protestant ethics is Emil Brunner. While Brunner's theological writings have made seminal contributions to Christian ethics, his own judgment of concrete issues (such as woman suffrage, which he opposed) sometimes seemed more a product of Swiss conservative culture than of his basic theological position. Or one could take the case of Paul Ramsey, whose published judgments on foreign policy issues rather consistently supported American military commitments and interests even when U.S. policy seemed inconsistent with Ramsey's own ethical methodology.[6] In such instances one might legitimately ask whether the operative presumptions were provided by Christian ethics as such or by other cultural values held more unconsciously. To some extent that kind of question can doubtless be asked of everybody who has written in ethics. All of us are influenced by background impressions or loyalties of which we may not be wholly aware. This does not mean that moral thinking is, after all, only a rationalization of inherited interests and prejudices. If it were, we would have no rational basis for exposing any rationalizations. But we are more likely to make good judgments if we are *conscious* of our initial presumptions and if we apply them rationally and clearly in relation to our deepest moral commitments.

Christian moralists have often attempted to do this. A very old example is the just-war tradition. In essence this tradition represents the effort of successive generations of Christian thinkers, from Augustine on, to define the circumstances under which a Christian can properly approve of war. The immediate impression created by this way of thinking (and by the nomenclature of "just" war) is that it is a militant, nonpacifist viewpoint. Indeed, for Christians to accept the notion that any war *could* be justified represented a major shift from the predominantly pacifist stance of much of the pre-Constantinian church. Nevertheless, as stated by Augustine and as refined by later Catholic thinkers, the just-war tradition was based upon a strong Christian presumption *against* war. It could almost be termed a crypto-pacifist position. Just-war doctrine has said, in effect, that only under certain exceptional conditions (specified and refined by thinkers dealing with the problem) could a Christian approve of war. Peace, on the other hand, is to be regarded as normal. The burden of proof must be borne by every particular war. In case of continuing doubt as to whether a war is justified, the Christian must withhold approval and participation.

Another Roman Catholic illustration of the use of initial presumption is the doctrine of subsidiarity, a principle that has been developed in a number of twentieth-century papal encyclicals. The doctrine was stated by Pope Pius XI in the encyclical *Quadragesimo Anno* in the following way:

> It is a fundamental principle of social philosophy, fixed and unchangeable, that one should not withdraw from individuals and commit to the community what they can accomplish by their own enterprise and industry. So, too, it is an injustice and at the same time a grave evil and a disturbance of right order, to transfer to the larger and higher collectivity functions which can be performed and provided for by lesser and subordinate bodies.[7]

According to this principle, the more inclusive or universal levels of social organization would have to bear the burden of proof in relation to the more immediate or local levels. Putting aside the question of whether this is good doctrine, we may note that it is a clear attempt to locate the initial presumption. In a later encyclical, *Pacem in Terris,* Pope John XXIII made use of the same principle in calling for a strengthening of "the public authority of the world community" in view of the fact that lower levels of collectivity are not able to deal with urgent problems now facing humankind as a whole.[8] He thus held that the burden of proof posed by the principle of subsidiarity had been met by those calling for a strengthening of international institutions in view of the actual relations of modern nation-states.

Roman Catholic moral theology has doubtless wrestled with such methodological issues more carefully, by and large, than has Protestant ethical thought. This may be a result of the former's more typically prescriptive approach, although methodological use of presumption is quite as appropriate to other ways of posing ethical problems. Nevertheless, Protestant moral thought has also provided illustrations of more or less conscious methodological use of presumption. An example might be the Message of the First Assembly of the World Council of Churches (Amsterdam, 1948), which asserts that "we have to make of the Church in every place a voice for those who have no voice." Those who "have no voice" are presumed to have the strongest moral claim on the active support of the church—that is, the church should be biased in favor of such people. That, of course, is exactly the point upon which liberation theology insists, in its expression "the preferential option for the poor." The question of the merits of such a presumption in favor of the underdog will occupy us in chapter 6. Now we may simply note that this is a case of arriving at moral judgments locating the initial presumptions of greatest moral weight.

Many further illustrations of the use of presumption could be brought forth. This is not a startlingly new approach to moral judgment.[9] But it is a method that needs further analysis and development in the light of Christian ethics so that it can be of maximum use as Christians approach their moral decisions.

The Testing of Moral Presumptions

The methodological use of initial presumption implies a combination of commitment to an initial viewpoint with an openness to changes or exceptions. But a practical problem emerges in the actual process of judgment. It is that while we may be willing enough to clarify and follow our initial presumptions, few of us will go out of our way to give the possible exceptions their day in court. We are convinced the basic presumption is right and any exceptions ought to have to bear the burden of proof. Therefore, is it not the responsibility of those who favor the exception to convince us that in at least this or that one case we should deviate from our presumptions? The practical problem is that we may not be willing enough to expose ourselves to the contrary evidence. Why should we?

Often, of course, we can simply follow our initial presumptions with a high degree of confidence when they are under no apparently serious challenge. Presumptions in favor of peace, or faithfulness in marriage, or truthtelling can simply guide us where there is no substantial uncertainty. The moral life largely consists of the attempt to build one's whole lifestyle around faithfulness to such presumptions, and one surely need not feel troubled or closed-minded about such faithfulness.

But serious truth-seeking does force us to be honest about our doubts as well as our convictions. It requires us to examine serious alternatives. On occasion it may even require us to go out of our way to test our presumptions against possible alternatives.

Another legal analogy may be useful. Although in a criminal prosecution a person is presumed to be innocent until proved guilty, the accused *is* brought to trial if there is "probable cause" to believe he or she may have committed a crime. The burden of proof is on the prosecution to show that probable cause does exist, but the state has the responsibility to bring this to a test in court if a serious complaint of law violation has been lodged, backed up by substantial evidence. The courtroom thus is a testing of the presumption of innocence versus probable cause of guilt. Normally, a preliminary hearing before a lesser magistrate or grand jury will be required to establish that there is enough probability to justify a full legal inquiry. Trivial matters can be dismissed at this stage, as can cases that could not, on the face of it, bear the burden of proof. Something like this establishment of "probable cause" must also occur in the factual situation of moral judgment. It may become apparent that simple adherence to our presumptions will be impossible or, if not impossible, that it will yield obviously undesirable consequences. In an actual situation it may also appear that some of our basic presumptions are in conflict and thus that some kind of exceptions may be advisable.

Of course many people may be unwilling to examine their basic presumptions (or prejudices) at all; their thinking is clearly not accessible to influence on moral matters. But this is evidence of a lack of genuine moral seriousness or lack of awareness of the actual limitations of our moral understanding. And that does not lessen the potential usefulness of a method of moral judgment making explicit use of initial presumption.

Criteria of Exception

The actual process of determining whether an exception to a moral presumption is able to bear the burden of proof requires some clarity in determining what "proof" could mean. The problem is one of defining what kinds of reasons have sufficient weight to justify a moral exception.

The just-war tradition provides a useful model of the possibilities. Depending on the particular formulation, this tradition specifies six or eight factual conditions that must be met if we are to consider a breaking of the peace to be justified.[10] These conditions represent the criteria of exception; all of them must be met if the exception is to be approved. All but one of the traditional rules (the principle of discrimination, which prohibits any direct breaking of the moral law in war) can be described as summary rules. They embody a summary of previous human experience with war and an attempt to relate that experience to the good as it is ultimately understood. No attempt to define meaningful criteria of exception can evade this task of reflecting upon actual experience in the area of human life concerned. This is so because the *need* for exceptions is itself only borne out in actual experience.

One general criterion is involved in all thought about exceptions. This is that more good is ultimately gained by making an exception than by remaining faithful to the presumption itself. For example, in his interpretation of the doctrine of "strange love" of Martin Luther, Paul Tillich speaks of love taking negative forms in order to preserve the true intention of love itself: "It is the strange work of love to destroy what is against love. . . . Love, in order to exercise its proper works, namely charity and forgiveness, must provide for a place on which this can be done, through its strange work of judging and punishing."[11] The ethical issues raised by a doctrine of the "lesser evil" are serious and will occupy us in subsequent chapters. But for now it must be marked off that if there are sound reasons for holding a particular presumption, there must be even weightier reasons for setting it aside. The general criterion must at least be that more good will thereby follow.

Secondary criteria can be developed out of experience relevant to the presumption. For instance, a presumption in favor of economic equality (if such a presumption could be shown to be good) might be set aside by finding that economic equality greatly undermines productivity (if *that* can also be shown to be good). One criterion of exception could thus read that exceptions to the moral presumption of economic equality can be made in cases where economic equality will undermine production to an unacceptable degree. The burden of proof would fall upon opposition to economic equality, and deviation from the presumption for equality could not be greater than that justified by the probable threat to productivity.

Sometimes apparent exceptions to a moral presumption must be made for the sake of the presumption itself. Thus, for the sake of economic equality certain *apparent* inequalities might have to be tolerated. Persons with greater objective need (such as a difficult medical condition) must have more income in order to be equal to people who do not have as much need. An apparent exception in this case would not be a real one, although the burden of proof would still apply to those attempting to show that it is not a real exception. Criteria of exception can be expressed either on the level of setting aside the presumption for the sake of that which ultimately justifies the presumption or on the level of a proper understanding of the meaning of the presumption itself.

Resolving Conflicts Among Presumptions

This last point must be emphasized. Some readers of the first edition of this volume raised the question of how the method of judgment works when our presumptions are in conflict. Clearly that possibility is not remote in light of the very large number of moral values and principles having a claim upon us.

Sometimes careful thought leads to a logical ordering of our operative moral presumptions in which conflicts among them are minimized, but obviously that is not always the case. Sometimes one presumption must simply override another.

It is well beyond the possibilities of a book of this kind to establish an intricate ordering of priorities among all conceivable moral values so that such decisions will be clear, in advance, to everybody! The computer age might provide us with technical support for such an ordering of values and principles,[12] but it could hardly do justice to their ultimate source. And that is the crucial point. For ultimately the conflicts in presumptions must be referred to that source, our ultimate "center of value," but our *perceptions* of that source, based as they are upon faith and metaphor, can never be as exact as we would like them to be.

Moral judgment therefore requires rigorous thinking, for which general works on the subject can never fully prepare us. The best that writings on ethics can hope for is to equip individuals and communities to engage in such thinking more productively.

Significant Forms of Presumption

We may conclude this chapter by listing and briefly characterizing some of the main forms of presumption that have significance for the problem of moral judgment. A number of these will be discussed more fully in subsequent chapters, but their mention here may help fill out a preliminary understanding of how we can make use of presumptions in a method of moral judgment.

Procedural presumptions represent a bias in favor of decisions reached as a result of certain procedures rather than others. This may be quite apart from the merits of the decisions themselves. We might decide, for example, that a policy adopted within a group by majority vote should be presumed to be right simply because that is how the group reached its decision. The basis of such a presumption could be rather pragmatic, with social peace as the governing norm and with the belief that majority rule is less conducive to disorder than the reverse since a majority, when it governs, confronts only a minority in opposition. Or its basis could lie in a morally principled view of the meaning of covenant in which one wishes to honor one's prior agreement to abide by the wishes of the majority. Here the sanctity of promise-keeping and the importance of personal integrity would be stressed. For the sake of keeping one's pledge to the group, one would be willing to presume the rightness of the actions of the group even when those actions appear to be wrong. Such considerations are, of course, very important in the social contract theories of the past few centuries.

Not all procedural presumptions are based upon a process of consensus formation. I might decide that I would place the burden of proof in any of my judgments against whatever appears to be opposed to my personal self-interest. This presumption of outright selfishness would be procedural in the sense that it could be adopted before any consideration of what my own personal interests in fact are. Or one might adopt a presumption *against* one's own self-interest, perhaps on the theory that one needs to compensate for selfish tendencies in judgment. Or pure chance could be employed in a procedure. When confronted by a particularly difficult decision, all of us have at some time or other been advised to flip a coin between the alternatives and then see whether we are happy with the way the coin landed. What this procedure does, in effect, is to make a choice for us outside our mental processes, placing the burden of proof against those of our inclinations that are contrary to the choice fixed externally by chance. Even such an arbitrary method may sometimes help us sort out our mental processes, but the point is that in using such a method one has devised a form of procedural presumption.

Usually, of course, a procedural presumption will itself rest upon other and more basic values. If we ever feel we should choose a procedural presumption over a substantive presumption, it can only be because of those more basic values that are at stake. If, for instance, we feel we should accept some unjust policy that has just been adopted by democratic process, it can only be because some fairly substantial values are at stake in the preservation of that democratic process. Some of the worst dilemmas in ethical judgment doubtless come about in this way.

Presumptions of principle are substantive, not procedural, but they are also general. They abstract from human experience and religious tradition certain qualities and values deigned worthy of preservation or enhancement in the organization of life. Morally, their status derives from some understanding of what is ultimately at stake in human life—a point we shall survey more closely in the next chapter. But they are meaningless unless they are capable in some fashion of organizing actual experience. Examples of such presumptions are "freedom," "equality," and "unity." Obviously such abstract principles are capable of being used in diverse and even contradictory ways. But where the meaning of such a presumption of principle has been established clearly, it can be used with methodological effect. Much depends on who is speaking of "freedom" or "equality" and out of what kind of cultural or religious tradition. For a Marxist and a laissez-faire capitalist to use the term "freedom" clearly in conversation together, each would find it necessary to define the term in relation to what is considered to be the source of freedom.

Ideological presumptions depend on presumptions of principle, but they also represent a model of the world or of human relationships that we consider to be implied morally by our basic norms. Democracy, fascism, Marxism, capitalism, feudalism, democratic socialism—all represent complex systems of values and perceptions of reality. The terms themselves have been employed so loosely as to diminish their ideological precision. Nevertheless, to cite such terms is to recall that people do employ them with quite specific mental pictures of what it is that they would regard as good social arrangements. These mental pictures become tools for judgment when they organize our weighing of alternatives. We place the burden of proof against deviations from these pictures, regardless of whether our model is of a status quo we wish to preserve or of a revolutionary future we wish to hasten. The problem of Christian ideological thinking will occupy us in chapter 9. For now, it may simply be asserted that Christians, along with all other people, do much of their moral judging with ideological presumptions at least in the background.

An *empirical presumption* is a model of situations as they actually are. It is the only one of this list of presumptions that is not normative, although many people often do judge on the basis of preserving some empirical status quo. It is proper to refer to this as a form of presumption, however, because we must also act on the basis of our understanding of the factual situation.

We tend to form mental pictures (models) of the nature of situations, which reduce their complexities to manageable form. Alternative basic models must then bear the burden of proof.

Consider, for instance, the different empirical presumptions by which people conceptualize the contemporary international situation facing the great powers.

1. For some, it is a good-versus-evil confrontation between Christian capitalist democracy (the U.S.A.) and atheistic, expansionistic communism (U.S.S.R.). Relations between these superpowers and other nations are interpreted primarily as they bear on this grand historical struggle.

2. For some, it is the confrontation between prosperous industrialized parts of the world (the "north") and the poor, less developed parts of the world (the "south"), with the prosperous areas largely responsible for the underdevelopment of the poor. According to this model, the U.S.A. and the U.S.S.R. have more in common with each other.

3. For others, it is a vicious circle encompassing a ruinous population explosion, energy depletion, and environmental pollution, with political conflicts interpreted principally as effects rather than causes.

4. For still others, it is a vast period of cultural change as humanity struggles to digest the meaning of technological change and increased contact of persons of vastly differing ways of life.

These models (and others that could be constructed to interpret the international situation) serve as basic presumptions concerning empirical reality, quite apart from our moral presumptions concerning the values at stake. Facts or interpretations inconsistent with the basic empirical presumptions might actually bear the burden of proof, depending on the rigidity with which these presumptions are held. And most of us might acknowledge that there is at least some germ of truth contained in all such models of reality that are held by numbers of people. But the mind is simply incapable of absorbing *all* the facts and of arranging them into an indubitable presentation of reality itself. So we are prone to think on the basis of such constructs of reality.

Presumptions of authority can be both normative and empirical. These are the sources of moral guidance and of factual (or expert) information that we consider to be worthy of trust in situations where we cannot make a direct judgment for ourselves. Presumptions of authority identify the secondary authorities to which one accords the benefit of the doubt—secondary in the sense that they involve the judgments of other persons or groups. Most religious groups have institutionalized forms of human authority. Doubtless all of us have trusted friends or authority figures of one sort or another to whom we instinctively turn for advice when confronting problems that seem beyond our own resources. Our tendency is also to give the benefit of the doubt to their advice. Chapter 8 will be devoted to further analysis of this form of presumption.

Presumptions of priority represent our approach to the presumptions when they are in conflict with each other and we must choose among them. Doubtless such conflicts do occur, as we have already noted. But some presumptions are on a higher level than others. When conflicts occur we may sometimes locate "presumptions among presumptions." For instance, one presumption may be important because it serves another. When there is an apparent conflict, the initial presumption must lie with the higher or more intrinsic presumption, the burden of proof being borne by the lower or more instrumental one.

One particularly troubling conflict in contemporary Christian thinking is between peace and justice. In face of an actual conflict between the two, which should have to bear the burden of proof? Justice might be regarded as the more inclusive category, since justice includes the whole of our normative view of proper human relationships, rights, and duties within the community. Peace would then be seen as only a part of the meaning of justice. In an actual case, peace might have to defer to the broader interests of justice in bearing the burden of proof. But the problem could be stated differently as one of selecting those means that are appropriate to the securing of justice, and then the presumption might well be in favor of peaceful or nonviolent means. The burden of proof would be upon those asserting that in a given case violent means will better serve the ultimate causes of justice than will nonviolent ones.

The preceding discussion may help to clarify how we arrive at moral judgments by means of moral presumptions, which are then tested against alternatives that are required to bear the burden of proof. To some extent, all people probably structure their thinking by means of such an approach. But the usefulness of the method depends on our ability to identify basic presumptions that are grounded in our ultimate moral perspective. To this task we now turn.

5

Positive Moral Presumptions of Christian Faith

Is it possible to derive moral presumptions from the Christian faith itself? Are there moral presumptions that can meaningfully be described as "Christian" and that can also serve as helpful guides to moral judgment?

We have already noted, in chapter 1, the deep relationship between moral life and religious faith traditions. That relationship is so intimate that one can speak of the moral life as belonging to the *essence* of the Christian faith. We do not go far wrong in asserting that the gospel is *about* moral life. But in order to say this we must also reconstruct our understanding of moral life. Christian faith is a moral interpretation of the meaning of reality. It is an interpretation of reality through which one sees oneself in relationship with the ultimate, not as an objective observer but as an interacting, personal being.

The great themes of Christian faith open up many theological entry points into ethics that can be expressed in the form of presumptions. Obviously they cannot all be fully explored here. Our problem is the more modest one of locating the points where the content of the faith has greatest critical relevance to the methodological problems of moral judgment. A certain shorthand is called for, though such abstractions can never do justice to the full richness of meaning in Christian faith.

Positive Moral Presumptions

We are prepared, then, to take up the question of whether there may be positive moral presumptions, directly implied by Christian faith, that can serve to guide our judgments in such a world.

I wish to propose four basic presumptions that I believe to be implied by Christian faith. These four presumptions are affirmative. They state positive conceptions about humanity and the natural world to serve as a basis for initial attitudes. They will later be contrasted with certain negative presumptions, which point to limitations in the human situation and to some extent modify the full force and applicability of the positive presumptions. Such positive and negative presumptions can be restated in different linguistic or typological form. Indeed, the four positive presumptions overlap one another to a considerable degree, for they represent different angles of vision into the same reality—though they will prove useful in bringing different aspects of that reality to bear upon the judgment-making situation.

1. The Goodness of Created Existence

It is implied in all we have been saying about creation that it is good. Creation has its source in the activity of the same good God who intends good for humanity. Creation is to be viewed as intended by God to help in the fulfillment of love in the divine-human covenant. The goodness of creation is affirmed throughout the biblical tradition, beginning with the very first chapter of Genesis: "And God saw everything that [God] had made, and behold, it was very good." The creation narratives of Genesis and the great nature psalms specifically celebrate the goodness of creation. Elsewhere in the Old Testament there is a notable frankness about the necessity and goodness of the material conditions of life, and justice is largely understood as equitable provision for each person to share in those conditions.

The theme of the goodness of creation is not developed in a particularly polemical spirit in the Old Testament. The ancient Hebrews show little awareness of theological or philosophical alternatives to their optimistic attitudes toward nature. What polemic there is of this sort is mainly directed against the absurdities of polytheism in the face of the monotheistic conception, as in Isaiah 40, for example.

The New Testament is no less affirmative about God's creative role, but at points in their development the Christian scriptures show the effects of a death struggle against a spiritualistic dualism. It will be recalled that early Gnosticism pictured the actual physical world as evil. Christians with Gnostic tendencies (such as the second-century Marcion) tended to repudiate the Old Testament heritage and to speak of a spirit God and a spirit Christ at war with the alien material world. The world was sometimes pictured as the source of evil. Early Docetism sought to preserve the figure of Christ himself from any real connection with (or contamination by) the physical world. He was viewed as an appearance only. He was not actually born; he did not actually suffer; he did not actually die; he did not actually taste and touch and experience pain. In the New Testament there is evidence of struggle against this view that creation is evil or illusionary and that Christ had nothing to do with the created physical world. As we have already noted, the epistle to the Colossians states in the strongest language that God is not merely spiritual. The created world is to be attributed not to the powers of darkness but to the loving activity of God. Christ is vigorously identified with God on the one hand and with creation on the other: "He is the image of the invisible God, the first-born of all creation."

In the same way, the pastoral epistles reject a false asceticism with the exclamation that "everything created by God is good, and nothing is to be rejected if it is received with thanksgiving" (1 Tim. 4:4).

To be sure, both the biblical witness and subsequent Christian tradition are also well aware of the existence of evil within the created world. Moreover, it cannot be said that there is any one dominant Christian understanding of the precise nature of evil. The problem of sin (human rebelliousness against God's intention) intersects the problem of evil. It is arguable that there is no intrinsic evil in the created world apart from some sinful human will. It is also arguable that frustrations arising from natural causes (such as earthquakes, volcanic eruptions, disease epidemics, and birth defects) can properly be called natural evil—though a doctrine of natural evil needs to confront the question of whether a world in which accidents could not occur would really be so good. Clearly, a doctrine of natural evil that went so far as to regard nature as *essentially* evil would be a reversion to Gnostic dualism. A view of evil that attributes it to the fall has certain symbolic possibilities we shall examine in greater detail in chapter 6.

But even the doctrine of the fall implies that the original intention of the Creator in and through the creation was good and not evil. Moreover, the fall is not really to be understood as the fall of creation so much as it is the mythical or symbolic representation of the tendency of human beings, *in their freedom* and not through creation, to sin. The profoundest grappling with evil is at the point of human sin. Everything that exists on the physical plane as a frustration to the fulfillment of God's intended human life on earth properly challenges us to vigorous, creative action whenever possible. But when such frustrations arise from entirely physical causes, the word "evil" cannot unambiguously be used to describe them; this term might better be reserved for frustrations of the good that derive from malevolent wills. Natural forces are not intrinsically evil, although if we are to live with our vulnerable bodies in such a world we are liable to be injured or destroyed if we chance to be in the wrong place at the wrong time or if our bodies become the carriers of harmful viruses or genetic distortions. But if we were not thus vulnerable during our earthly pilgrimages could we be as sensitive? Could we experience the physical as an avenue of awareness and as a basis for creative activity in God's intended covenant?

Everyone who has known and seen suffering and has lost loved ones through the final earthly calamity of death will not be too glib about the problem of natural evil, yet the article of faith, the presumption, remains: God has created the world, and the creation is good.[1] How, exactly, can such a faith claim serve as a presumption to help guide Christians in their moral judgments?

In a general sense, the answer is that in any issue of judgment where the postulated goodness of creation is itself the matter in question, our presumption should always lie with actions reaffirming that goodness. Potential suicide is an obvious illustration. Excluding deliberate acts of martyrdom or heroism, which are not really suicidal, taking one's own life usually suggests that existence has become intolerable. The psychology of suicide is complex, and we cannot explore it here. Nevertheless, the presumption of the goodness of creation necessarily places a burden of proof against such a desperate act. To put this differently, our initial presumption must be that suicide is incompatible with Christian faith, since such an act always suggests that for the individual involved existence is no longer good.

Some forms of alleged suicide may be excluded from this assessment because they are in no sense based on suicidal intent (or on the conclusion that existence is no longer good). In war there have been reported instances of soldiers hurling themselves on live grenades in order to absorb the lethal impact of the explosion, thus saving the lives of comrades. An act of this kind is suicidal in the limited sense that the one who did it could be almost certain of death as a result of the action taken. Nevertheless, the *intent* is not to cause one's own death but rather to preserve the lives of one's comrades. Presumably the soldier would be overjoyed if the grenade, by some happy accident, were not to explode. The act is not based on loss of faith in the goodness of creation; exactly the opposite: It is motivated by a generous desire that others should continue to enjoy that goodness. (Of course, "unselfish" acts of heroism in war can sometimes be unconscious expressions of self-destructiveness, in which case they do represent that loss of faith in the goodness of creation which Christian faith does not accept.) The word "suicide" ought to be reserved for those actions that have the termination of one's own existence as their primary end—and not for actions that, while inevitably self-destructive in effect, are primarily designed to save the lives of others.

Still, the burden of proof ought to be against even generous actions that will inevitably result in personal loss of life. Among those who love life, who find created existence good, this presumption functions automatically and can only be overcome when some greater good than one's own continued physical existence is at stake. The burden of proof may then have been met.

A tragic incident illustrated these questions some years ago when a small aircraft crashed into the home of a Christian pastor who lived near an airport in a small California city. The house was quickly engulfed in flames. Miraculously, the minister escaped uninjured through the front door. Without his knowledge, his wife and his mother escaped through the back door, also uninjured. Frantically looking about in front for his loved ones, he dashed back into the burning house to save them. As a result of this unnecessary act of bravery he received severe burns, from which he later died. What should be said concerning such an instinctive act of self-sacrifice? Surely one could not fault the intent or the sacrificial courage displayed. Nor could one say that the man should have waited until the facts were more clear, since there was virtually no time. If his wife and mother *had* still been in the house, only that quick impulsive act might have saved them. It might be said that the burden of proof justifying this exceptionally perilous act had been met. However, the objectively needless waste of this good man's life should remind us that heroic self-sacrifice where there is virtually no hope of achieving the good sought must have a burden of proof placed against it. The instinctive feeling of one who is driven to a hopeless act *may* be that life would not be worth living without this or that loved one, and against this the presumption stands that existence will continue to be good, even despite the tragic loss. This is why more coolheaded bystanders do well physically to prevent hopeless and dangerous acts of heroism.

Euthanasia poses similar questions. How are we to judge in the case of persons whose existence apparently is *not* good, either to themselves or to society? How are we to assess an act terminating the life of somebody known medically to have no hope for anything other than a slow, painful death?

As generally proposed, euthanasia would involve the patient's consent (thus entailing a suicidal factor), though it would be an act in which society would also participate responsibly. Of course some kinds of suffering can be excruciating and, in terminal illness, hopeless. They can involve virtual disintegration of personality. In face of this are we to say that for such people creation continues to be good, and are we then to forbid release from existence?

Answers to this question cannot be given casually by those who have never experienced such suffering. I would not wish to exclude euthanasia categorically, but the burden of proof should be strongly against it. As long as a person retains consciousness, there are some *aspects* of existence that may be regarded as good. Despite suffering, one's physical existence still provides the condition necessary for one's continued interaction with loved ones—and that possibility of interaction, as such, is to be presumed good. One may find it possible to formulate and achieve some creative purposes as one's own contribution to the improvement of existence—and that possibility, too, must be presumed good. I once served as pastor to an elderly woman who was suffering from terminal cancer. She did outlive her doctors' prognosis by some months, but in a wasted-away condition accompanied by great suffering. Nevertheless, despite her suffering and her inability to do anything physically other than communicate, this woman's radiant spirit was obviously a great force for good within the close circle of her family and friends. The question of euthanasia must be posed in the light of that kind of human spirit first, because it is that spirit which is authentically attuned to what the Christian means by the goodness of creation.

But what is one to say to a father or mother who knows he or she is suffering a terminal disease and who knows that continuing treatment will eat up the financial resources needed to provide for the children after he or she is gone? Would the parent be justified in seeking to terminate life? Would a compassionate physician be justified in helping? Of course, it is an intolerable piece of social irresponsibility that permits a family to face such a dilemma alone. Extremely costly forms of treatment, if warranted at all, should be borne by the whole community, and a compassionate community does not neglect those who have lost parents and spouses. The Health Service in Britain and comparable programs in a few other countries show that this kind of basic social decency is not at all inconceivable. Nevertheless, in our imperfect world fathers and mothers can face such cruel dilemmas. Surely the burden of proof must continue to be placed against suicide or euthanasia. If a family is bound together by genuine ties of love, it will be worth a great deal of subsequent economic deprivation to know that everything possible was done; and, moreover, the continued existence of the terminally ill patient would be considered an intrinsic good. It should also be emphasized that a considerable subsequent family sacrifice in terms of standard of living would be warranted. In American society, at least, it is not often the case that financial hardship is so great for survivors that a family is broken up, the children cannot be educated, or other drastic things happen. The burden of proof could not be met by establishing only that a family's standard of living would be relatively lessened (though still well above the poverty line), for one cannot balance relatively desirable economic goods against the final yes or no of physical existence itself.

Even in the case of what medical practice terms the "withholding of support," euthanasia should have to bear the burden of proof. Where the possibility of life support remains, the presumption should lie with efforts to preserve life. Even in cases where a human organism has been reduced to vegetable existence, with no apparent possibility of revival of consciousness, the burden of proof should show that the situation really is hopeless. But where the appropriate tests, including electroencephalogram and the lapse of a sufficient period of time, indicate the overwhelming improbability of a recovery of consciousness, the normal presumption for medical efforts to maintain life might well be set aside. The presumption for life does not mean that in every instance persons ought not to be permitted to die.[2]

Similar points could be made about abortion, except that here distinctions must be made corresponding to the developmental stage at which abortion is contemplated. In the earliest stages of pregnancy, fetal life exists as potentiality for the experiencing of the goodness of creation, while in the later stages it may be realistic to refer to the fetus as already experiencing reality. In either case, a moral presumption could well be entered against abortion. But the burden of proof might more easily be met in the earlier stages of pregnancy if there are sound reasons why the pregnancy should not have occurred in the first place. Certainly one would not want to establish a general presumption in favor of bringing as many children into the world as possible, since creation itself implies limitation and the resources needed to provide for new life are not infinite.

Another important illustration of the goodness of creation is presented by sexual life. Sex is a powerful force, and every civilization has greater or lesser difficulties in regulating it. Now and again in Christian history, attempts to regulate sexuality have gone to the extreme of portraying sex itself as evil. This is a pronounced tendency in Augustinian thought (in part perhaps because of Augustine's reaction against his own promiscuous early years). Even some of Paul's writings convey a negative view toward sex ("It is well for a man not to touch a woman," 1 Cor. 7:1b), although Paul also explicitly taught that sex in marriage is no sin and that husband and wife should "not refuse one another except perhaps by agreement for a season" (1 Cor. 7:5a). One of the important vows of most monastic orders was the vow of chastity, and it is difficult to escape the implication that the life of chastity has thereby been regarded as having higher moral status. Some interpretations of the doctrine of original sin have conveyed the impression that sex is somehow responsible for its transmission. The Roman Catholic position on use of artificial contraceptives and a strong residual element of Victorianism in some Protestant cultures suggest that sex, per se, is at least suspect from the moral standpoint.

And yet, despite all this, a clear implication of faith in the goodness of existence is the positive value of sex. It is not a question of sex's being a necessary evil that must regrettably be tolerated since this is the only way the species can be propagated. The burden of proof is not to be placed against sex as such. As an important aspect of our creaturely existence, sex is good. Of course the regulation of proper use of sex is another matter. Here the relationship between sex and covenantal good faith must be considered, and the fact that sex is good does not mean it should not be disciplined in some way. But the point to be made now is that any moral judgment concerning sex which begins with the presumption that sex is essentially evil must bear the burden of proof. It is likely to be a wrong judgment, for it is based on a faulty premise. The same point can be made concerning every asceticism that suggests the normal life of the senses is evil. Quite the contrary: The Christian presumption is that the life of the senses can be affirmed as a God-intended condition or basis for the spiritual life. The spiritual life is not to be opposed to the physical, as though it could only occur through the defeat of our physical nature. Physical nature is not the same thing as spiritual life. It is not the *meaning* of our existence; it cannot be made an end in itself. Nevertheless, it is a good.

The goodness of creation is also to be affirmed in a presumption against the disruption of nature. In recent decades, environmentalists have reminded us that human freedom to dominate nature has distinct limits. It is even possible that humanity, in its arrogance, may succeed only in destroying the conditions necessary for its continued survival. Frederick Elder has pointed to two strands of ancient Hebrew tradition concerning the relationship of humanity to nature.[3] According to the first, humanity is viewed as lord of nature, responsible for filling the earth and subduing. This strand gives rise to a human-centered view of nature, with nature existing only to serve human interests. This strand, according to Elder, has led to a highly exploitative view of nature. According to the second tradition, on the other hand, human beings exist *in* nature and as a part of it. While nature extends certain facilities and opportunities to us, we do not have unlimited dominion over it. This distinction, suggested by Elder, is an illuminating one, although even the first strand of tradition in the Old Testament may not be so much human-centered as it is God-centered. People have dominion, to be sure, but only in the form of a stewardship or responsibility given them by God. We are responsible for the exercise of this stewardship to God. So really in both traditions the presumption should be against any reckless dealing with nature. We need not be opposed to the economic development of the earth, nor do we have to apologize for viewing humanity as a higher level of creation than other aspects of nature. But nature is to be respected. Accordingly, a proper understanding of the goodness of creation should lead us to a strong presumption in favor of conservation. Wasteful and destructive dealings with nature and its resources should always have to bear the burden of proof.

This section cannot be concluded without noting that humanity today has, for the first time, the power to destroy the planet earth as a fit habitation. Quite apart from other things we shall say subsequently about war, it should be noted here that nuclear war poses an awesome potential threat to the future of the world. A strong presumption for the goodness of creation should stand also as a strong presumption against actual preparation for nuclear war. A casual attitude toward nuclear war can only reveal a low regard for the goodness of creation. A highly publicized 1986 pastoral letter on nuclear war, issued by United Methodist bishops, was aptly entitled *In Defense of Creation.* For, as the letter asserted, "the creation itself is under attack."[4] Clearly, the moral burden of proof must be borne by any policies of military defense seriously threatening termination of life on this planet.

To summarize: It is not possible for a Christian to base a judgment on the proposition that God's created physical world really does not, after all, matter very much. It matters very much indeed. It is the material basis of God's covenant with human beings and may have further, deeper purposes we cannot fathom.

2. The Value of Individual Life

It is almost a cliché among many people deeply influenced by the cultural values of Western civilization to speak of the "sacred" or "infinite" worth of the individual. Christian faith is not opposed to this cliché; indeed, it is to a considerable degree the source of it. However, we should remember that personal or individual life is not self-validating. The dignity and worth of individual life cannot be derived from analysis of individual life itself. Human beings are not "the measure of all things." Whatever value people have is strictly transitory unless it is in our relationship to some ultimate source of value outside ourselves.

Christian faith understands human value as being established by our relationship with God—a relationship created and given by God. It is because we have our being from God and sustained by God that we can meaningfully affirm the value of individual human life. Christian scripture and tradition have always made this affirmation, even when insisting on human unworthiness and sinfulness. The essence of this faith is that despite our sinfulness God has chosen to relate to us as parents do to their children. We may be miserable worms (as one old gospel hymn suggests), but if so we are still *God's* miserable worms, and that makes a considerable difference. We are created *imago Dei.* By virtue of God's love of individual human beings, we properly regard one another as having boundless value. What God loves, no one should despise.

Nor can we treat human value as though it were predicated only of humankind as a whole. While the social dimension of human existence requires equal stress (as we shall note in the following section), the Christian faith concerns also the radical worth of the individual person. Each of us must, as Luther said, do our own believing just as we must do our own dying. What Luther meant is that regardless of whatever else we may say about our social nature, justification by faith means that *each* person is the beneficiary of God's gracious love. Nor does this mean simply the value of each *Christian's* life, as though non-Christians are not yet to be treated as the children of God. The parables of Jesus that emphasize God's loving concern for even the least of the lost sinners and Paul's insistence that God's grace is a gift to us notwithstanding our total undeserving both underscore that relationship with God, which is the source of all our value as individual human beings, is prior to our own responsiveness. To be sure, the effect or fulfillment of personal value may be lost on people who have no faith in the source of their own worth as individuals—as we explored in chapter 2. But this does not mean that that value is itself the result of what people do. God's creation and grace, which are the basis of our value, are prior to our response (or our works, as Pauline theology put it). Viewed from this perspective, faith is itself a coming to awareness of God's immeasurable gifts. Faith is a release, on the one hand from frantic efforts to create some transitory illusion of value and, on the other hand, from callous disregard for the value of each of our fellows.

When it is really understood, the presumption for the value of individual human lives runs directly against the grain of much contemporary culture. Actions and policies have often been taken quite for granted that should rather have had to bear the burden of proof because of their callous disregard for human life. This century of total war, of nuclear armament, of genocide, of concentration camps, of racism, and of political repression has often reversed the order of presumptions. The "majority report" of the twentieth century may well have been expressed in Bertrand Russell's arresting words: "Brief and powerless is man's life; on him and all his race the slow, sure doom falls pitiless and dark."[5] But, if so, Christian judgment must reverse this majority report and insist rather that each individual life is of infinite value. It must insist that no life can be disregarded as unimportant. Whenever it is apparently necessary to treat persons as objects to be used or to be removed, the burden of proof must be met that such an exceptional action is clearly necessary for the sake of God's whole human enterprise. Even when persons must be "used," the Christian will try to do so in such a way that the person's worth continues to be affirmed.

Thus the burden of proof falls against any action or policy or social movement that has as its rationale the alleged unimportance or disvalue of any individual lives. Grosser illustrations, which leap to mind, need not detain us. Obviously genocide or chattel slavery or the use of unsuspecting individuals in dangerous medical experiments can be excluded by Christian judgment on the face of it.

Other kinds of problems may pose more difficulty for sensitive Christian consciences in our time. There is, for instance, the problem of capital punishment. While the historical momentum in many countries is clearly running against capital punishment and it has been outlawed in a number of places, there are Christians who still strongly believe in it and who wish to see this momentum reversed—as it has been, in large measure, in the United States during the past decade. These Christians should reflect more deeply on the meaning of the presumption of the value of each life. The Christian moral presumption should be against capital punishment even when it is punishment for the crime of murder. I find it conceivable that under extreme circumstances some form of capital punishment might be necessary as a deterrent. The burden of proof should still be against it. It should not be used unless there is very strong evidence that it is necessary as a way of saving lives and as a way of affirming the sanctity and security of all life in community. (Actual evidence to that effect is lacking in most areas of the world.) Nobody claims that capital punishment is capable of bringing back the life of a murder victim; it is only a question of what should be done with the murderer. Apart from practical questions of deterrence or disablement of a criminal so that the crime cannot be repeated, capital punishment rests on the postulate that the criminal is no longer fit to live. It is this postulate that has to be rejected. Even the perpetrator of the most heinous of crimes has a life that is of value to God. The value of life in general cannot be affirmed if the value of *this* life is denied. One suspects that even in purely practical terms, the net effect of capital punishment may often be to decrease society's respect for life and thereby, ironically, to increase the rate of killing. Suppose, in the case of Adolf Eichmann, the authorities in Israel had found it possible to spare his life in spite of the enormity of the genocide in which he had had a prominent part. Might this not have been a significant witness to the value of life that would have tended more to emphasize than to minimize the enormity of the crime? At any rate, I believe the burden of proof ought to be against capital punishment.[6]

Similarly, it should be against disregard for life in war. The question of whether war itself can ever be justified is involved here, and it is worth noting that the classical just-war criteria emphasized regard for the worth of life as a major consideration in deciding whether war should be commenced at all. Assuming the possible justification of war itself, however, the burden of proof would still need to be placed against any particular taking of life even within the war. Nobody can be written off simply as "the enemy." Even an enemy remains a person who also has his or her life from God. It is reported that the President of the United States decided to use the first atomic bomb on Hiroshima and Nagasaki because this would save countless American lives.[7] Possibly the bombs did have this result, and conceivably the net result was also to save more Japanese lives as well. But one could not as a Christian decide the question on the basis indicated. Life as such was morally at stake, not just American life. During both world wars, the mass media in most of the participating countries betrayed a striking tendency to portray their respective enemies in subhuman terms, thus helping to legitimize the increasingly vicious methods of extermination.

Regard for the value of personal life also entails a strong presumption for personal freedom. Freedom has become an increasingly ambiguous term in the modern world because many people claim the freedom to infringe upon the freedom of others. But freedom to exploit others, to discriminate racially, or otherwise to injure one's fellow human beings is not the freedom of the Christian presumption.

Unfortunately, the association of the term "freedom" with injustice has helped confuse discussion of a truly central human value. For without some kinds of freedom to be and to express one's selfhood, talk of the value of individual life is meaningless. Religious liberty is perhaps the most basic of all forms of freedom, since it involves expression of the individual's relationship to the transcendent ground of all life. Religious freedom implies a basis for personal being that lies beyond social conformity and civil obligation.

It includes respect for freedom of communication and creative expression and freedom from being required to express loyalties and beliefs one does not hold. All forms of what we term "civil liberties" are involved—freedom of the press, freedom of speech, freedom from arbitrary search and arrest—including, in our time, freedom from electronic forms of eavesdropping and freedom of peaceful assembly. A strong presumption in favor of such freedoms must be fixed in law and custom, as indeed it is wherever bills of rights are fully respected.

Freedom is, in fact, a problem in most countries. Dominant majorities often conclude that the freedom of despised minorities to express unpopular views is not morally required.[8] But the burden of proof ought to be borne by those who think this or that form of communication or aesthetic expression cannot be tolerated. Among some Christian groups this burden of proof should be accepted more seriously even in cases of alleged pornography. There may be forms of communication that are, as the courts sometimes put it, so devoid of redeeming social value as to merit no legal protection. And a case can certainly be made that some pornography is exploitative, particularly as regards young and impressionable minds, thereby constituting a limitation of the freedom of others. But the burden of proof should be against censorship even so, and it is difficult to think of any good-faith expression of ideas that should be forcibly suppressed even when the ideas themselves are thoroughly repugnant to most people.

In evaluating the plethora of conflicting social movements and organizations, all bidding for support from unaligned persons, a Christian confronts especially complex problems of judgment. But the presumption for the value of every person presents us with at least one important criterion. Insofar as a group depends for its rationale on the proposition that some categories of persons can be disregarded altogether, the Christian must require that group to bear the burden of proof before supporting it or even cooperating with it. A Christian can vigorously support or oppose a movement, but not to the extent of dismissing the humanity of his or her opponents. Our presumption must be for the worth of *all* people, even those to whom we are vigorously opposed.

3. The Unity of the Human Family in God

If Christian faith entails a strong presumption for individual worth, it also implies that life cannot be lived in isolation. The two presumptions cannot really be separated. That relationship with God which establishes our value as individuals is at the same time the basis for our unity, our fellow humanity. The epistle to the Ephesians expresses this unity of the human family by speaking of the way in which Christ "has broken down the dividing wall of hostility" that previously had separated members of the community of Israel from the rest of humankind (Ephesians 2). Prior to

Christ, the Gentiles were considered to be "alienated from the common-wealth of Israel, and strangers to the covenants of promise, having no hope and without God in the world." The significance of Christ is that he has reconciled humanity to God and thereby reconciled both Gentile and Jew "to God in one body through the cross, thereby bringing the hostility to an end." It is through our unity with God that our unity with one another is established. The divine-human covenant has created a covenant commu-nity. Israel always understood this covenant as the basis of its own national unity; now, in Christ, it is to be understood that the whole of humankind is the covenant community. This theme, treated more or less explicitly in Ephesians, is implied elsewhere in the New Testament. Even in those pas-sages that seem to exclude some of the unity of the human family, it is because of their own rebellion against that unity and its basis in God. In principle the whole of humankind is included.

L. Harold DeWolf has pointed out that love itself needs to be understood as the affirmation of our basic unity in God and that a regrettable tendency of much discussion of love in Christian ethics has been to imply a curious insularity.[9] Even *agape* can imply a kind of atomistic individualism. This characteristic word for love in New Testament Greek has been taken by contemporary theology to mean a total, unselfish form of love which utterly disregards its response. The problem is that such an understanding of love implies that it is entirely a matter of what I do to or for somebody else "out there." DeWolf argues that Christian love cannot be individualized in this way. Love, rather, is a sharing of experience, an expression of our recogni-tion of our underlying kinship in God. In this understanding, love is neither a matter of seeking an object *(eros)* nor of altruistic self-giving *(agape);* rather, it is an expression of mutuality in which the giving and the receiving are united. DeWolf regards the New Testament term *koinonia* (from *koinos,* "common") as a better linguistic clue to the meaning of Christian love, since it suggests its fellowship-creating and fellowship-fulfilling character. The point is well taken. Etymological analysis of terms for love in New Testa-ment Greek is a particularly complex undertaking, and our understanding of love ought not to hinge simply on such analysis. Ancient as well as modern theologians use the same words differently, and it is impossible to establish fixed meanings to words when it is precisely the work of theology to establish more profoundly what certain terms *really* mean. But the decisive test is whether a given understanding of love accords well with the overall meaning of Christian faith. And here DeWolf properly reminds us that Christian love is a sharing in the gift that God has given alike to all of us. We love because God first loved us. Our love is an expression of our God-given unity.

Paul Lehmann and Joseph Haroutunian are among other theologians who have also emphasized the importance of social unity as an implication of Christian faith. Lehmann speaks of the "fellowship-creating reality of

Christ's presence in the world" manifest in the *koinonia* and contrasts this with the "individualistic error" which has crept into many interpretations of the thought of Paul. While acknowledging Jesus' own concern for the individual, Lehmann insists that his messianic identity "is unintelligible apart from the covenant community, the corporate structure of God's activity in the world."[10] Haroutunian likewise notes the importance of the individual and individualism but points out that we do not exist as human individuals: "We do not know our 'nature' except in our transactions with our fellowmen. We do our speaking and thinking, our purposing and acting, in the process of our mutual transactions."[11] To be truly human is to be a "fellowman," not a rugged, selfish individualist.

The effect of such an understanding of Christian love is indeed to make every question of moral judgment a family question. It is no longer possible to treat another human being as though he or she were an alien. Our love for the other is no longer based simply on his or her value, much as we do continue to affirm the value of every child of God. Now it is also based on our own inescapable involvement in his or her life. We cannot, of course, become acquainted personally with more than a tiny fraction of the population of the world. Yet, by faith, we affirm our kinship with all. In any situation of decision, those human beings who are affected by our judgment, whether or not they have previously been total strangers to us, are to be regarded as sisters and brothers in the human family. Each new person we chance to meet is not to be considered alien; even before we know the person's name we know that he or she is one with us. We need not be sentimental about this unity. It is in fact only as we come to recognize this unity as an objective reality that we are saved from undue sentimentality about love. As, in a human family, kinship dominates decisions despite the ebb and flow of emotional feelings, so the Christian's understanding of the objective kinship of all humankind dominates decisions. Love thus is given a steady, objective character. It is not without feeling, but its roots are deeper than feeling.

Such a conception of the unity of humankind would, if generally accepted, create a Copernican revolution in society. No longer would it be possible to treat life as a competitive struggle between alien beings grasping for the prize. No longer would it be possible to treat some part of humanity as a moral universe in itself, excluding all others. The fact that this sense of the unity of the whole human family is not generally accepted and the fact that it is clouded by selfishness in all of us may require compensating negative actions apparently in sharp conflict with unity. This point will be explored more carefully in the next chapter. Nevertheless, the unity of the human family serves as a moral presumption of the first importance. The presumption is always for the most direct expression of human unity. The burden of proof must always be borne by every apparent disruption of the unity we have in God. Every barrier that owes its existence to deliberate human action must bear the burden of proof. Some barriers may, for a time at least, succeed in bearing this burden, but only if it can be established clearly that the barrier is itself necessary for the sake of a profounder fulfillment of God's intended covenant community. It must be granted that certain forms of human exclusion are necessary. These are not to be considered in the same way as being a result of deliberate action, although they may seem so. Every concrete relationship between two or more human beings is, in a sense, exclusive. The choice to spend these hours in interaction with these persons, and not with others, is exclusive. In marriage a covenant exclusiveness is established for life. (Even a totally promiscuous approach to sexual life is exclusive in the sense that most people will still be excluded, although some have attempted to exclude as few as possible!) But such forms of exclusion have their basis not in a denial of the fellow humanity of another but in the factual limitations of our temporal existence. The exclusive character of marriage can be understood as having its roots in the facts of biological existence. As Karl Barth reminds us, our created sexuality is the material basis for the profoundest human expression of covenant relationship. Our decision to marry this one person and only this one person and to make him or her the pledge of covenant faithfulness is not predicated upon the belief that *only* this one person is worthy of such a covenant. *All* persons are worthy of such a covenant (though some may be incapable of its physical fulfillment), but the marriage *form* of covenant is such that having chosen one mate we may not choose another. That form has its basis in our created sexuality, not in a denial of human unity. Indeed, it is precisely in our recognition of the underlying unity of the whole human family that we best understand the foolishness of sentimental interpretations of the exclusiveness of marital love. The notion that for every person there is, somewhere, only one intended life mate is sentimental nonsense. It is based on a love exclusion in *principle,* and it is often enough demonstrated that such a sentimental basis for marriage is incapable of maintaining its stability over time.

What we recognize as the physical basis for a factual exclusiveness in marital covenant is in principle similar to other physical limitations. We cannot choose to interact with every other human being all the time. Our created social nature is such that the full exploration of human mutuality requires the cultivation of friendship, and friendship implies exclusion. Even within the family, certain members hit it off with other members to a unique degree. Still, the exclusiveness of friendship, if it is an expression of the underlying unity of humankind, cannot be such that other relationships become impossible. We should find it possible in principle to cultivate specific relationships with *any* other human beings, particularly if we perceive and can respond to their peculiar need. We do not cultivate old relationships or create new ones as something we are doing for some other person; instead, we recognize and bring to fulfillment a kinship that already exists, since we both already exist in union in God.

Our unity with others is therefore a more basic presumption than exclusion, even though some relationships must be exclusive.

In our own time, the presumption for unity has perhaps been tested most severely in the confrontation with racism. Racism is a worldwide phenomenon, with particularly deep roots in the United States and South Africa. Basic to racism is the view that persons of different racial groups may not interact fully and deeply as fellow human beings. While racists sometimes say we should all be united "spiritually," they deny that this spiritual unity should ever be made concrete in actual relationships in the real world. Racial discrimination, segregation, and apartheid arbitrarily transform certain biological characteristics into a basis of exclusion in human relationship. The biological characteristics chosen are generally quite superficial, and not infrequently even imaginary. Racism amounts therefore to the creation of social barriers against the fulfillment of the unity of the whole human family. Racism is utterly inconsistent in principle with Christian faith.

The drive toward racial integration in the twentieth century is solidly rooted in the presumption for human unity. In recent years, however, those who have most seriously supported this drive have had to face a dilemma. On the one hand, they have understood that integration is in the long run the only possible solution to the moral question of how persons with different racial characteristics[12] ought to relate to one another. Race should therefore pose no barrier at all, even in relation to marriage. But on the other hand, people supporting the drive toward racial integration have confronted strong separatist movements within racially oppressed communities themselves. In part, this separatist drive can be understood as a psychological defense mechanism—an assertion of the equal value of black or brown skin—or as an attempt to be sure that important cultural values within the minority group will not be dissolved in some melting pot. In part, however, the separatist drive has asserted the need for real social separation. The development of minority-group economic and political institutions and caucuses may partly represent temporary tactical expedients, designed to establish a more favorable bargaining position and to sensitize consciousness within both minority and dominant groups. But this development may also mean to some a more or less permanent model of how groups should interact in a pluralistic society. The integrationist, regardless of his or her own racial characteristics, has been placed on the defensive. Insofar as, for example, the movement toward black separatism has represented a self-conscious effort to develop racial pride and self-respect in order to make it possible for black people subsequently to enter into full relationships with white people on the basis of mutual self-respect, the objective could hardly be questioned. The presumption for unity cannot be fulfilled without mutuality of self-respect.

Still, in racial matters, a presumption for integration is implied by belief in the unity of humanity. This means that the burden of proof must be placed against racial separatism or segregation, even if only of a temporary kind. This also means that the burden of proof must be placed against a pluralistic model of racial interaction that contemplates the interaction of racial groups as groups but rejects the interaction of individual persons of different racial and ethnic groups. Personality is a fundamental moral category; race is not. Despite pressures for separation from either the "right" or the "left," the Christian must require those who support separatism to make their case. Any residual doubt should be resolved by supporting integration. Even where one's own support for integration is met by rebuff, one must remember that the objective reality affirmed by faith is of a unity or kinship between oneself and those who resist relationship. In many parts of the world, including America, white people must learn something from the rebuffs. Perhaps only through rebuff can one purify the integrity of one's own understanding of integration, while also learning something of the meaning of the humiliation that black people have had to bear for generations. Nevertheless, the burden of proof must continue to be against racial separatism.[13]

In most cases that burden will not be met successfully. This is particularly true in the American and South African contexts for two reasons: In the first place, the sheer magnitude of existing social and economic relationships precludes real separation on a large scale. Even persons living in the great urban ghettos have constant interaction with many outsiders. In the second place, separatism is unlikely to achieve a restoration of self-respect and dignity. Where relationships have been based upon illusions of superiority and inferiority along racial lines, the illusions have to be routed out in the context of the relationships themselves. A retreat from relationship in order to recover one's sense of dignity is more likely to have exactly the opposite effect.[14]

While racial segregation and separatism are paradigmatic of all challenges to the unity we have in God, other barriers also confront Christians. Many outgrowths of nationalism need to be challenged in the light of the presumption of unity. National chauvinism among the more powerful established nations must, in all its expressions, bear the burden of proof. The restrictive immigration policies of, say, the United States and Australia must be evaluated closely in light of the need for stable labor relations, educational facilities, and other considerations. Nevertheless, the burden of proof ought to be against any specific restriction of immigration. Similarly, national policies forbidding travel to other countries ought to bear the burden of proof. At this point, the Marxist countries have been particularly restrictive. Wherever nationalism builds barriers between peoples, the presumption of Christians must be against the barriers and for the visible unity of the whole human family.

The nationalism of the newer, recently colonial societies can perhaps present the strongest case. In Africa and Asia (and, in a somewhat different sense, Latin America), nationalism really represents two forces that are not in principle contrary to the presumption for unity. The first is the force to overcome exploitation by other countries. Exploitation is itself opposed to unity, and the drive to overcome it is a necessary precondition for the restoration of authentic unity. The second force is the drive to create a unity out of diverse opposing groups (such as competing tribal groups in Africa). Nationalism in that sense can be a unifying phenomenon, just as it was historically in the case of the development of European nation-states out of the feudal divisions that existed in the Middle Ages. But even such nationalism has its dangers. In our era, policies growing out of even the more defensible forms of nationalism must bear the burden of proof where their effect is to maintain barriers.

Fuller consideration of the effect of the presumption of unity requires us to proceed to the final positive presumption.

4. The Equality of Persons in God

The presumption of equality can be related to the preceding ones. Equality is implied in the value individual persons have through their relationship to God. When we say that individuals are valued "infinitely" or "totally" by God and that their life's meaning is entirely based upon this relationship of love, we assert that the essence of human life is beyond gradation. "Infinite" value is value without qualification or limitation. Only limited objects can be differentiated and related to each other unequally. It is proper to speak of human limitations, of course. We are finite creatures whose earthly careers are bounded in time and space. But in value we are beyond earthly limitations because our value is based on the valuing of God, who *is* infinite. Those philosophers who challenge any inherent worth or property in humankind as a ground for the equality of persons are not incorrect.[15] Human value is not a property of persons *qua* persons. In Christian perspective, it is rather a gift of God's love. Apart from faith in a source of human worth transcending human life itself, it is dubious whether either human value or human equality can be demonstrated philosophically. But the faith of the Christian in God's total love of each person is at the same time an acknowledgment of the equality of persons. A person who is *totally* loved by God cannot be loved any less than another who is also totally loved. It is in this ultimate perspective that we are equal.

How does this relate to the sinfulness of human beings, which exists both as a general condition affecting all humanity and as a matter of degree, some people being more sinful than others?

The love of God comes before the judgment of God; or, rather, God's judgment is a function of God's love. The distinctive mark of Christian faith is trust in God's love "while we were yet sinners." Gradations in sinfulness, even if we could identify them ourselves with complete confidence, are irrelevant to the source of human worth. God's love cuts through all the gradations to the core of human being. Were God's love rationed out on the basis of relative degrees of human worthiness, it would be accurate to say that God's love is something we must (and therefore may) earn—that "works" are prior to "grace." But the contrary affirmation, that grace is prior to works, cuts the ground from beneath any human pretensions to superiority.

Equality is also implied in the Christian view of unity. There is an immediate sense in which this is true, for the basis of our unity in God is at the same time the basis of our equality. The love that binds us together is the same love that loves us equally and therefore makes us equals in our relations with one another. But unity can be related to equality in other ways as well. Unity in relationship implies mutuality: In relationship with one another, we both give and receive our essential being. As we have noted, people do not exist as truly human apart from social relationship. In relationship we receive back from others a confirmation and fulfillment of our humanity. But we cannot receive the basis of our superiority from inferiors. Ironically (perhaps this is the ultimate human irony), the deference social inferiors pay to their alleged superiors detracts from—rather than adds to—the latter's essential humanity. How could this be so? The one thing an inferior cannot give to his or her superior is the human acknowledgment of a fellow being who is in every respect a *fellow* being. Hegel noted this fact in his analysis of how the master-slave relationship undermines the self-consciousness people must have to be human. When the master refuses to regard the slave as a fellow human being, deserving of equal recognition, he or she is thereby deprived of recognition by another self-conscious human being.[16] Inequality alienates us, not simply from others but also from our own humanness.

Nowhere is this more evident historically than in the relationship between the sexes. The created sexual nature of men and women provides the possibility for the deepest kind of mutual affirmation and fulfillment, as Karl Barth has argued profoundly. It can, as he noted, serve as a physical symbol of the whole meaning of covenant and of the overcoming of every form of human alienation. Yet it is ironic that the role inferiority of women throughout most of recorded history has tended to deprive both men and women of the deeper fulfillments in sexuality. Unquestionably, some differences of function between women and men have flowed from biological differences. But where these differences have led to inequalities of status and perceived value, the humanness of all has been diminished.

To be sure, not every relationship is a human relationship—one based on the premise of equal consideration. The purely functional or utilitarian relationships that involve entirely objective manipulation are not fully "human," though they can become the basis for human interaction. Slavery is, in principle (though not entirely in fact) based on such manipulative, nonhuman relationship. Truly human mutuality has to occur among the slaves and among the free in such a society; that is, it has to occur where people can regard one another essentially as equals. The Christian claim is that wherever there are people there is that essential humanity, and therefore equality. To put all this differently, whatever it is that detracts from our unity helps undermine equality, and whatever vitiates equality also undermines unity. The unity of unequals is not real unity unless the forms of inequality are mutually recognized as unimportant alongside the more fundamental human equality. There can be no "fraternity" without "equality," no "equality" without "fraternity."

If all persons are ultimately equal, a strong presumption exists for equality of treatment in the concrete relationships and structures of the world. Any inequality in existence is a potential threat to mutual recognition of that equality and unity we have in God—and therefore a threat to the fulfillment of our unity with God. Equality cannot merely exist on the "spiritual" plane; existential equality is an important condition of spiritual recognition of equality. It aids the fulfillment of our true humanity while existential inequality impedes it. The burden of proof must therefore be placed against every factual inequality. On the face of it, it is inequality that requires justification. Equality has an immediate presumption of rightness.

Nevertheless, *absolute* equality in existence is both impossible and inadvisable.

It is *impossible* because even the natural distribution of the conditions of life is uneven. Such things as physical constitution, health, and mental capacity differ widely, even though hereditary equality can itself be affected to some extent by greater equality in the distribution of the goods of life. It appears unthinkable that a day might come when all persons would inherit precisely equal physical and mental capacities.

But absolute equality is also *inadvisable,* because unequal distribution of facilities and rewards appears, to some extent, necessary for the sake of greater social benefits. The case for unequal distribution of facilities is almost self-evident, both in terms of differences of need and differences of function. A person with eye difficulties may need the unequal extra something of eyeglasses in order to enjoy equal vision with those who do not have the same difficulties. Some persons require very expensive medical care and remedial facilities in order to correct, even partially, nature's inequalities. This provides the moral basis for the provision of specially equipped automobiles for the handicapped at public expense by the British government.

But different social tasks or roles likewise require different facilities. Different crafts take different tools. Even intake of food must vary with the strenuousness of functions performed. It is arguable that some particularly unpleasant or nerve-racking forms of work require unequal recreational facilities or a higher degree of freedom from economic worries. In contemporary education, provision is often made for the variable needs of mentally retarded children, on the one hand, and for the particularly gifted, on the other. Both can be defended as ways of equipping the young to make their fullest contributions to society. Justification of an apparent deviation from the presumption of equality would here take the form of a demonstration of needs, which, if not met, would themselves create inequalities.

But it is also arguable that some unequal distribution of social rewards may be advisable as a means of influencing behavior in society. Here the determinant of unequal treatment is not one of need but of merit, as socially defined. In a perceptive essay, Ralf Dahrendorf argues that a reward system of some kind is implicit in the very notion of society:

> Human society always means that people's behavior is being removed from the randomness of chance and regulated by established and inescapable expectations. The obligatory character of these expectations or norms is based on the operation of sanctions, i.e. of rewards or punishments for conformist or deviant behavior. If, however, every society is in this sense a moral community, it follows that there must always be at least that inequality of rank which results from the necessity of sanctioning behavior according to whether it does or does not conform to established norms. . . . The origin of inequality is thus to be found in the existence in all human societies of norms of behavior to which sanctions are attached.[17]

It is certainly the case that all known societies have had reward systems of some sort. Complex modern societies have numerous, sometimes conflicting systems of rewards corresponding to the different subgroups and cultures. Much sociological study is, in one way or another, occupied with the analysis of relationships between social norms, social behavior, and social rewards. Social stratification—the status system of a society—is partly a matter of social reward for behavior advancing social norms; it is also a matter of symbolizing and providing support for leadership roles. Inequality of rank and power thus becomes intertwined with the designation and distribution of rewards. It is important to remember that social rewards are not entirely economic. Any scarce values (that is, any objects of desire that do not exist in sufficient quantities to satisfy demand) require a distribution system, and any distribution system will embody different kinds of social reward in accordance with social norms. Economic values, social prestige, and social power are all scarce values and are all apt to be involved in a reward system.

Needless to say, no social reward system is likely to remain very efficient. The problem is that persons of high status have disproportionate power in determining the allocation of future rewards and the norms upon which such allocations will be made. Merit cannot be rewarded in any simple, objective way because those who do the rewarding will themselves have a major stake in the outcome. They will tend to define merit and reward in such fashion that they continue to merit and receive the best rewards themselves. This is a practical difficulty.

From a Christian moral perspective there is an even more serious problem. When a reward is sought in the form of scarce values (that is, when one seeks wealth, power, or prestige in order to have more of these values than others have), the effect of this desire is spiritual isolation. This is ironic. When one seeks fulfillment through a higher status in life, the "reward" of higher status is precisely the undermining of the only true basis for fulfillment in covenant community with God and other people.[18] This is the Achilles' heel of social reward systems: The reward offered is alienation. The more intensely it is desired and pursued, the greater the alienation. It is primarily internal and subjective. Alienation accompanies the desire for status even when the reward is not pursued successfully. Alienation might not occur among those who receive social rewards without having sought them. But the latter point is unimportant for this analysis because the question is whether social rewards, entailing inequality, ought to be offered with the intention that people should desire them and seek to merit them.

Is society, then, at war with itself? Is the factual precondition of civilized community in conflict with the normative precondition of fellow humanity? Even the fact that all recorded societies have apparently had social reward systems is not sufficient to make this an adequate basis for exception to the presumption of equality. All recorded societies have also been plagued with murder and other social pathologies. It may be that a reward system creating inequalities should be tolerated by Christians only in the same way they tolerate murder: It is only to be accepted when one does not have power to do anything about it.

But even within the context of the presumption for equality, some form of social reward system might be able to bear the moral burden of proof. If it is evident that *without* a social reward system, organized society would collapse or economic productivity would fail to meet basic needs, or if equality can only be attained, for example, by suppressing basic civil liberties and arousing general social bitterness, a case could be made and the reward system, inequalities and all, would be considered a price well worth paying. In his study of justice, John Rawls argues that justice begins with the examination of every question of social policy from the standpoint of the least privileged members of society. Only those policies that can be regarded as being in the interest of these least privileged persons can be regarded as just.[19] Inequalities cannot be justified by benefits accruing to those who already benefit too much. But if a fully rational, less privileged member of society considers the inequality to be in his or her own interest, the price might be worth paying. Rawls's argument is based on criteria of rational self-interest; such a position can be presented even more powerfully with a theological orientation based on faith in God and deep human mutuality.

It should never be forgotten that inequality is costly in moral terms, even when necessary. I shall say more on this point in the next chapter in connection with the problem of the "necessary evil." But here we may note that the method of moral presumption permits us to accept undesirable realities where every alternative is even more undesirable. The burden of proof is against inequality, but that burden will be met if it can be shown that more evil will result by clinging to equality than by accepting some inequality. It should not be forgotten, moreover, that any society (which may mean *all* societies) which depends on inequalities for motivational purposes is, to that extent, probably incapable of the fulfillment of real covenant community. There may be a sense in which it is pointless to sacrifice some tolerable justice and social cohesiveness and purpose for the sake of the kingdom of God on earth, if the kingdom of God on earth is not a factual possibility anyway. I do not wish to press this point too hard, for what is at stake is not either/or but, rather, degrees of equality and inequality, of fulfillment and alienation. The presumption for equality is a useful method of keeping the pressure on inequality and alienation. In the absence of such tension, we settle too easily for morally undesirable policies and practices. In a very real sense, this does mean that society must be at war within itself. And so it shall be, it seems, until the final consummation of history.

In discussing the use of unequal distribution of scarce values as a social incentive, we must bear in mind an important distinction. Elsewhere, in the context of an analysis of income incentives, I have suggested that "absolute" incentives need to be distinguished from "relative" ones.[20] An absolute incentive is one that turns the fundamental conditions of a person's social existence into rewards or punishments. The reward for approved behavior is one's social existence itself. The punishment for disapproved behavior is deprivation of the conditions of social existence. Capital punishment is the prime illustration of the latter; normal security in the community illustrates the former. A relative incentive, on the other hand, is one that offers rewards or threatens punishments which are only relatively desirable or undesirable. A small raise in pay or some small symbolic recognition is a relative incentive.

If inequalities can be justified morally by the Christian, they should generally be of the relative rather than the absolute kind. An absolute incentive is predicated on a distinction between those who have the right to exist as members of the community and those who do not. The fundamental, underlying equality of persons is not recognized, and the united fellow humanity of persons in the community is, in principle, denied. The first claim of all people, which precedes all justification of inequalities of privilege, is the claim on the basic conditions of life. This precedes every-thing else, because nothing else can be justified apart from the social exis-tence that is intended by God. Relative incentives do not in principle deny the premise of equality and fellow humanity. We must remember, however, that there is a point beyond which relativities of inequality begin to act as severe impediments to fellow humanity. A society might abolish poverty altogether (in the absolute, objective sense in which poverty means depriva-tion of the conditions of life and health), but if some were permitted to accumulate wealth and privileges vastly in excess of others, it would be difficult for social relationships to proceed on the basis of mutual recogni-tion and shared experience. This is why even relative incentives should be required to bear the burden of proof: Are they really necessary for the sake of some greater social good? Will they not create such great disparities as to erect formidable barriers to human mutuality?

I do not doubt that relative incentives can, in every conceivable society, meet this burden of proof up to a certain point. But requiring such incentive rewards to bear the burden of proof will make it easier to define that point. In most modern societies, not excluding Marxist ones, excessive privilege is to be found alongside deprivation in the economic and/or political and legal conditions of authentic human life.

Meanwhile, there is every presumption in favor of social incentives based not on selfishness but on social fulfillment itself. It is sometimes mistakenly supposed that recognition of the uniqueness of the contributions of in-dividuals and groups is the same thing as recognition of inequality. But uniqueness and inequality are not the same thing. A unique contribution is, to the extent of its uniqueness, literally incomparable; and incomparable things cannot be related to each other as equal or unequal. By what intrinsic criterion would we attempt to compare the Mona Lisa with Beethoven's Fifth Symphony? We may be more greatly moved by one than by the other, but these are unique expressions of art. Only in an external, secondary sense can they be compared. Recognition of every person's contribution is a recognition of every person's humanity. It is a celebration of the expression of our human worth at the same time it is gratitude for its value to the community. Social recognition does not have to be accorded by means of reward in scarce values; it is not necessarily a matter of what we give to one not being available to give to another. To illustrate this point obliquely, and at the same time to bring the discussion back to Dahrendorf's argument concerning the necessity of society's use of a reward and punishment sys-tem, it can be pointed out that the reward for not violating criminal law is available to everybody. In a reasonably just society nobody needs to go to jail. But similarly, everybody in the community can be commended for their contributions and all can rejoice together in the creative and useful treasures that each person can, in his or her own way, bring to the common store.

Even a social stratification system can in principle function in this way—

where leadership is not sought as a means of separating oneself from one's "inferior" fellows but is the contribution that persons with particular forms of talent can make. Where leadership positions are sought as a means of self-aggrandizement, they are corrupting and unfulfilling. Where leadership is unselfishly offered and received, it can help in the fulfillment of the whole community. The kind of leadership structure that serves in this way is not a threat but a confirmation of the essential equality of persons: "Whoever would be first among you must be slave of all" (Mark 10:44).

Are These Presumptions Specifically Christian?

The attempt in this chapter has been to illustrate the ways in which Christian faith can supply the positive content for our moral presumptions. A question worth raising is whether such presumptions are, in the final analysis, specifically Christian. In an otherwise friendly review of the first edition of this book, Charles Milligan commented that "Christian faith can motivate and energize action, but there is nothing distinctively Christian about asserting the value of the individual or the unity of the human family."[21] Are presumptions of the kind discussed in this chapter "distinctively Christian"?

Expressed only as abstractions, they may not be. As we have seen, abstract values such as "freedom" or "justice" can be argued in a variety of ways, and much depends on the moral tradition supplying their essential meaning and justification. Throughout this chapter we have considered the *theological* grounds for the presumptions, and it seems clear that the actual meaning of the presumptions depends largely on whether or not one accepts the truth and validity of the Christian theological perspective. To that extent, the presumptions clearly are "Christian."

They are, however, also abstractions that attempt to draw insights from the Christian perspective into ethically usable form. Another commentator on the first edition thought I was attempting to express the "content of Christian ethics" in "a few *propositions* about persons, evil, ideology, and the like."[22] But of course this is inaccurate if taken to mean that the whole of Christian ethics can be summarized even in *many* propositions! The presumptions do help us draw insights into more usable form—and that is the perennial task of Christian ethics as a rational discipline.

But that also suggests a sense in which the presumptions are not entirely unique to Christians. For as we attempt to express Christian theological insight in workable ethical form, we also discover that we are making connection with ethical insight drawn from other sources. Should that be a theological surprise? The whole world is, after all, God's world. And every valid ethical insight about that world, formed in whatever tradition, is dealing in some respects with the same human reality.

Christian ethics does not have a stake, finally, in the uniqueness of its insights; it does have a stake in their faithfulness. If other religious and philosophical traditions arrive at exactly the same conclusions about moral values, then so much the better! But, regrettably, few such traditions have the same deep grounding for the goodness of existence, the value of each human life, the unity of humanity, and the equality of persons. These things simply do not mean the same thing to everybody.

6

Negative Moral Presumptions

The positive presumptions we have been considering express the goodness that is at stake when moral judgments are made. Were we living in a world in which existence simply demonstrated the power of such presumptions, there would be little need to speak of exceptions to the presumptions. Some exceptions are little more than logical applications of the presumptions to somewhat complex problems. These, then, are only apparently exceptions. But other exceptions represent real contradictions to the positive presumptions. They arise from obstacles to the fully positive organization of life on the basis of Christian faith. By speaking of presumptions we indicate that we have made judgments and that any exceptions will have to bear the burden of proof. But the question remains: Why should a Christian be willing to speak of moral exceptions at all? Has Christian faith been compromised or abandoned when exceptions to the presumptions implied in Christian faith are admitted?

The weight of this question has been felt by every serious Christian moralist. If deviations from the direct moral implications of Christian faith are capable, in principle, of bearing the burden of proof, then the theological rationale for such deviations is a major problem. Some moralists in the long tradition of Christian perfectionism deny that such a rationale is possible. Others have sometimes assumed that there must be some deviations or exceptions for "practical" reasons without wrestling with the implied meaning of this "practicality" in terms of Christian faith.

As we begin to explore this problem, we do well to remember that there are negative as well as positive implications of Christian faith. A part of Christian understanding is the insight that important limitations are built into the human condition. Part of this pertains to the realities of sin and evil; part to the simple fact that we human beings do not have unlimited intelligence, knowledge, and capabilities. The word "negative" may not be quite right if it suggests only sin and evil. But this word does indicate points at which we must say no to illusions about human nature and the possibilities of realizing *perfect* goodness and justice in this world. This negative aspect of the Christian view of reality in fact suggests further presumptions that must also be taken into account in the formation of judgments; a burden of proof must also be borne by those who totally neglect them. I propose to state these negative implications of Christian faith in the form of two presumptions.

Human Finitude

To be a human being is, first, to be limited. In our short span of life, each of us is capable of experiencing only the tiniest fragment of reality. Our best judgments will never be informed by *all* the relevant facts, nor can we regard our understanding of the meaning of Christian faith itself as infallible. To be sure, the meaning of incarnation is that the infinite God has manifested the divine nature to finite people in concrete form. Christian faith, including the positive presumptions outlined in chapter 5, requires confidence in the dependability of this divine self-disclosure of God in Christ. Unless it can be affirmed that the infinite God is also capable of self-limitation through self-disclosure and that God's essential nature is indeed revealed in Christ, there remains little basis for Christian faith. But a part of the character of this revelation is the paradox that through it we come better to understand how it is that in our creatureliness there is much we cannot understand. As John Dillenberger has put it, following Luther and others,

> both Christian thought and experience imply a concept of a hidden God. It is affirmed, not eliminated, through God's activity. It is not that God is hidden and then discovered. Nor does he simply step out of hiddenness into the sight of man. Revelation, which is always revelation to someone, itself established God as hidden or veiled in imparting himself, and as hidden in the depths of his being. Revelation shows the hidden character of God.[1]

Or, to put this differently, it is revealed that while God's goodness in covenant love for human beings is decisive, no one possesses the mind of God. Now we see only in a glass darkly; under the circumstances of our creaturely existence we may not see "face to face."

This would be true even if we could justly claim moral perfection, a point that is emphasized scripturally through the doubt expressed by Jesus on the cross and by the agony of his wrestling in prayer. Even philosophers who have a high degree of confidence in the human mind (such as Thomas Aquinas) have recognized that our intellects are connected with the actual world only through the physical senses and that the senses are capable of deceiving as well as of informing our conscious experience. This is what, in theological perspective, is meant by being a creature dependent upon a physical body. Kantian epistemology demonstrates unalterably that the mind does not *know* the thing outside the mind *in itself.* One does not have to accept Kant's exact formulation of the categories the mind imposes on external data to conclude with him that we do not have immediate (unmediated) contact with the essence of the objects of our experience. Even the experience we do have is sharply limited in time and space, and our ability to act upon what knowledge and wisdom we can accumulate is limited by time, physical location, and finite power.

These points, which were touched upon in chapter 3, are a reminder not only of the tenuousness of our own moral judgments but of the tenuousness of the moral judgments of others. They suggest that we can approach every problem secure in the understanding that every participant in the situation is *also* finite. The relevance of this to our judgments will be explored further below.

Human Sinfulness

Paul, in the epistle to the Romans, writes that "all have sinned and fall short of the glory of God" (Rom. 3:23). This theme, which looms so prominently in the writings of that first Christian theologian, is really an inescapable part of the biblical drama. We need not be detained here by the details of a doctrine of sin to note what seems essential in this biblical theme for our methodological purposes. There are two crucial questions: Is there any warrant in the Christian view for regarding *any* persons as sinless? And, even if so, is there any way we can be sure who these sinless people are?

The function of the myth of the fall or of the doctrine of original sin is to emphasize the universality of sin. *All* people are sinners. Precisely how this has come to be may be unimportant, as we noted in chapter 2. The key point is that everybody must be presumed to possess this same tendency. Nobody can be presumed ever to be totally sinless.

There is also another way to approach the problem of the universality of sin—through the universality of moral freedom. Insofar as people are free to choose good, the logical corollary is that they are also free to choose evil. By affirming that human beings will always possess this freedom to choose good, we are at the same time asserting that every person in every time and place of moral decision is at least *potentially* capable of sin. So long as people are free, sin is always a possibility. Thus, even if we were to satisfy ourselves that this or that individual or group were in fact now sinless, we could not (as long as we also regard them as free moral beings) be confident of their continuing in that state of perfection.

What then of grace? Is it not also a biblical understanding that grace is capable of redeeming humanity from the grasp of sin? This problem has challenged theology almost from the beginning. Is grace irresistible? Is it at least powerful enough to overcome the power of sin? Have we any warrant to establish human sinfulness as a methodological presumption of Christian moral judgment?

Two things can be said in response. First, as generally developed in the Pauline tradition and in much subsequent theology, grace is understood as having effect despite our continuing struggle with our tendencies toward self-centeredness. The doctrine of sanctification, as we noted in chapter 2, speaks of growth toward holiness or wholeness. But this implies that we continue to be affected by the tendency toward sinfulness. Second, if grace is to have authentically human significance, it must be understood as a reality that affirms human freedom, not one that sets it aside. Paul speaks of grace as setting us free from the "law of sin and death." Grace makes it possible for people to escape the bondage of a self-centered life and of a hopeless prospect toward death. But it also opens up possibilities of genuine choice. Some great Christian theologians, including Augustine, Calvin, and possibly Paul himself, have felt it necessary to picture grace as finally overwhelming every human resistance among the "elect." Yet is this not even more to make human beings slaves to an external power apart from their own responsive action? Would this not be dehumanizing in the fullest sense of the word? To know, through the grace revealed in Jesus Christ, that one is a child of God is, on the one hand, to realize that one is free to rebel against God but, on the other hand, that one need not do so to fulfill the meaning of one's humanity.

The basic proposition remains that all people are sinners, all are somewhat disposed toward self-centeredness. The methodological significance of this point will be developed below. But it should be added here that even the degrees or relativities of human sinfulness may be of small importance. It is one thing to argue that some people are more sinful than others—a point established clearly in the biblical tradition. But it is quite another to assert that we can dependably *know* who are the greater and the lesser sinners. It is one thing to insist that grace is at work to redeem us from our wretched selfishness; it is quite another to claim the power to judge the extent of that work of grace. Some relative judgments have to be made, after much serious struggle. But the more ultimate judgments have to be left to God. Moreover, so far as our own judgments of ourselves are concerned, there is a very strong New Testament tradition of the importance of first confessing our own sinfulness. Those who feel most self-righteous are most likely to be, in fact, the most self-centered.

Of course, too great a preoccupation with the pervasiveness of sin can lead to cynicism. We can make too much of the presumption of sin and too little of the power of the positive presumptions. False complacency can be created either way. We can give in too readily to the inevitability of sin (thus expecting too little of people), or we can ignore sin altogether (thus failing to deal realistically with sin's power to wreak havoc amid God's intended purposes for human life).

The Effect of Negative Presumptions

The most immediate effect of the negative presumptions is to call into question any social policy depending for its justification on the assumption that some persons *are* infallible or morally perfect. To the extent that proposals or movements depend on such assumptions, they must be presumed to be wrong—or at least highly suspect. Since, according to Christian insight, everyone is presumed to be a finite sinner, no one ought to be treated as though he or she were all-wise and perfectly good. Policy proposals or social movements that seem to depend on such a wrong view of human nature should be made to bear the burden of proof.

Extreme viewpoints of both "right" and "left" often need this kind of correction. Marxist movements, for instance, have depended to a considerable extent on their claim to have discovered the science of human social history. They rather too neatly divide humankind between those who know and those who do not know what is to be done to advance the authentic destinies of humanity. They tend to absolutize the goodness of the revolutionary class, the evil of exploiting classes, and the goodness of future humanity whose life will no longer be corrupted or repressed by class exploitation. But how could a Christian rely on a diagnosis of a particular social problem that depended, for its validity, on taking such absolute claims at face value? This is not to question the Marxists' capability of astuteness in judging particular issues. Rather, it is to say that one must expect the overall Marxist assessment to be distorted. One must therefore place the burden of proof against the Marxist assessment *as a whole* while weighing carefully the particular judgment.

An illustration of the failure of a Christian writer to be sufficiently cautious at this point is Harry F. Ward's book *In Place of Profit,*[2] which was published in the 1930s. Taking Soviet claims at face value and accepting almost without reservation the Marxist criticism of non-Communist societies, it completely missed the viciously repressive side of Soviet life in the 1930s and would have ill-prepared the reader for the realities of Stalinism, which were exposed by Nikita Khrushchev in the 1950s and by Mikhail Gorbachev in the 1980s. A Christian might have been more alert to the danger signal posed by the absolute moral pretensions. Again, this does not mean that Soviet life was all bad or that Marxist criticism of the West was devoid of merit. But particular claims, criticisms, and proposals have to be detached from their packaging of pretensions and illusions about human nature.[3]

The intellectual and moral absolutizing of the left has had its counterpart on the right. For more than half a century Americans have tended to go far beyond mere criticism of Marxist communism. Communism has recurrently been pictured by many people as the very incarnation of evil. The Communists' own Manichaean conflict between the powers of oppression and the forces of revolutionary liberation has its Western counterpart in the conflict between "freedom" and the Red menace. As one militant anticommunist, the Rev. Billy James Hargis, explained the dynamics of his own following:

> They wanted to join something. They wanted to belong to some united group. They loved Jesus, but they also had a great fear. When I told them that this fear was Communism, it was like a revelation. They knew I was right, but they had never known before what that fear was. They felt better, stronger, more secure in the knowledge that at last they knew the real enemy that was threatening their homes and their lives. They came to me and I told them.[4]

Another such leader, Dr. Fred Schwarz, attracted quite a following in the early 1960s while describing communism as a cancer—a term hardly calculated to encourage careful distinctions among the truths and errors of Marxism.[5] The fault, at bottom, is the implied doctrine of human nature: an inability to take into account that we are all finite sinners. Movements of disadvantaged groups have often had to combat such self-righteousness. One recalls the response of tycoon George F. Baer during the U.S. coal strike of 1902: "The rights and interests of the laboring man will be protected and cared for, not by the labor agitators, but by the Christian men to whom God in His infinite wisdom has given control of the property interests of the country."[6]

Those words have been echoed wherever workers have sought to organize for collective bargaining, the scenario reenacted in the railroad, steel, coal, and automobile industries and most recently in agriculture. In respect to the last, many good Christian growers in California and Florida argued that migrant field workers should trust the growers to pay the best possible wages and to guarantee the best working and living conditions without joining Cesar Chavez's union. Some Christians who had no immediate stake in the dispute were inclined to take this position at face value. But how could they? To accept without question the growers' views would have required one to have unlimited faith in both their wisdom and their goodness. In fact, however, the growers represented only one side in a conflict of interest, and their views corresponded rather directly to their own self-interest. Should one not have been on guard against their demonstrated inability to take their own sinfulness into account? Some aspects of the views of the growers might well have been true; yet the burden of proof needed to be placed against their views as a whole, for no allowance had been made for the fact that the growers also were finite sinners. It was his encounter with similar attitudes among the Henry Fords of the auto industry that gave rise to many of Reinhold Niebuhr's sharpest insights into human sinfulness and our capacities for self-deception.

As an outgrowth of a realistic Christian appraisal of human finitude and sinfulness, there is much to be said for two compensatory presumptions.

The first might well be a presumption *against one's own self-interest* in any decisions where one's own tendencies toward selfishness might be expected to be expressed. Most of us have a tendency to accept at face value the apparent congruence between universal truth and goodness and our own personal self-interest. One need not be overly cynical in taking this into account. The process is very largely unconscious with most people. Yet this is just what makes it so great a distortion of reality. People tend to place the burden of proof against whatever challenges their self-interest rather than the other way around. Thus, when new taxes are proposed the initial reaction of many people is to be strongly opposed unless it can be shown beyond doubt that the taxes are needed. Legislative appropriations for foreign assistance or poverty programs often have to bear a heavy burden of initial opposition because such expenditures are considered by many people to be wasteful. Or people without school-age children may object strenuously to taxes designed for public school education. An attempt to correct such myopia by placing a compensatory presumption against one-self may be as useful as it is difficult.

The other compensatory presumption could be *for the underdog.* The negative presumptions of universal human finitude and sin create important reasons why a Christian should seek especially to empower the weak. The strong cannot be presumed to be righteous enough to determine the fate of the weak. In a dispute between the powerful and the weak, the presumption must be for the weak in order to compensate for their powerlessness and for the presumed sin of the strong. This does not mean that the strong are necessarily more sinful than the weak, but only that they have more means whereby to express their sinfulness. Indeed, yesterday's oppressed may easily become tomorrow's oppressor. One should be neither surprised nor disillusioned by this. It is rooted in the sinfulness of humankind. But neither should one avoid being particularly sensitive to the interests of both yesterday's and tomorrow's weak ones. The interests of the weak will be defended by those concerned for justice even in the full awareness that those who are defended today may have to be fought tomorrow when they come to power. A striking statement from the Message of the Amsterdam Assembly of the World Council of Churches embodies such a presumption for the powerless: "We have to make of the Church in every place a voice for those who have no voice."[7] So does Walter Rauschenbusch's comment that "those who have been deprived of intelligence, education, and property need such championship as the ministers of Jesus Christ can give them, and any desire to pardon and excuse should be exercised on their behalf."[8] So, likewise, does the expression "preferential option for the poor," made famous by Latin American liberation theology.

Compensatory presumptions of this kind certainly need to be used with intelligence. The two mentioned here can even come into direct conflict.

Suppose one is oneself a member of a weak, repressed group or class. Should one then have a presumption for the underdog position, or should one's presumption be against one's own self-interest (which happens to be that same underdog position)? Perhaps even here a person should be particularly alert to the ways in which his or her own personal self-interest can distort the appraisal of the just interests of one's own group. The problem can be illustrated in relation to the social-change methods of Saul Alinsky.[9] Alinsky's own motives apparently were an outgrowth of his sense of outrage at the injustices inflicted by the strong upon the weak in our society. He often enlisted similarly motivated clergy and others of good will in his campaigns. But his method of approach was based on the assumption that the organization of a community (such as a ghetto neighborhood) can only be effected by appealing to the outraged self-interest of its residents. Such people will presumably be ill-equipped to be at all sensitive to the elements of truth or goodness embodied in their opponents (collectively to be treated as the enemy). A community organized by means of such an appeal to self-interest would not seem to be a particularly promising place to recruit selfless champions of other disadvantaged groups. The approach to this problem represented by Martin Luther King, Jr., might represent a more promising way to overcome the tension.

Having explored some possible applications of the negative presumptions, we must return to a theological problem. The presumption against human infallibility may be easy enough to accept. But placing a similar presumption against the sinlessness of persons and groups may seem more doubtful. Does such a presumption vitiate our faith in the power of grace? Can we presume against the sinlessness of any particular person or group and at the same time acknowledge the power of grace to overcome all human sin?

It is to be remembered that such a presumption of human sinfulness is solidly biblical and in accordance with most human experience. But it is also to be remembered that any social movement or social policy that depends for its appeal on the alleged perfect goodness of its own supporters or members is not making an isolated judgment about those people alone. It is also comparing itself with other people who support contrary viewpoints, judging these other people to be uniquely sinful. The claim has not been made that humankind is universally good, but only that this or that particular group is good. It is one thing to affirm the power of divine grace to overcome the effects of sinfulness; it is quite another to assert that grace has in fact already done so only with respect to this or that limited group of people. Even the church should never make such a claim. The church has no ground for believing that its members are now freed from the sinfulness that infects others. Even Augustine, whose high conception of the church helped pave the way for medieval tendencies to identify the visible church with the kingdom of God, was careful not to say that all persons within that visible church have been transformed by grace. Only God can be taken to know ultimately who has and who has not.

It may be more helpful to regard both sin and grace as being at work within every person and thus to do justice to the destructive, distorting aspects of the one and to the redemptive possibilities of the other. The presumption of the sinfulness of every person is an attempt to take this into account lest we slip into naïveté or self-righteousness.

The Problem of "Necessary Evil"

The problem of moral exceptions or necessary compromises with evil has apparently occupied Christians from the very beginning. Jesus' own consideration of divorce in Matthew includes the view that Moses had permitted the dissolution of marriage only "for your hardness of heart": that is, as a lesser but still necessary evil. Jesus in the same passage permits divorce under the circumstance of unchastity. Paul argues that under present circumstances it would be better for all to be like himself—living a celibate life—but that marriage and the mutual exchange of conjugal rights can be accepted as a "concession" (1 Cor. 7:6). Early Christian thinkers had to wrestle with the hard realities of slavery, war, the exploitation of the poor by the rich, and so on. The underlying problem addressed by these thinkers was how far Christians should go in accommodating themselves to such a world. The earliest writings are strongly, though not exclusively, perfectionist in tone. This is partly because of their expectation of the end of the age and of Christ's own return to earth, although early Christian perfectionism cannot simply be regarded as an *Interimsethik,* a temporary ethic, which such thinkers would not have believed in apart from their eschatological views. Arguments for pacifism, for instance, would have been just as valid in form were there no expectation of Christ's imminent return. With the passage of time, however, and with the growing influence and power of Christianity (and its final arrival at official status), Christian thinkers increasingly developed arguments permitting moral exceptions in response to perceived dangers and necessities.

It is worthy of mention that early Christian grappling with this problem was parallel with and influenced by that of the Stoics. Stoic philosophy, like Christianity, was positive and universal. It viewed humanity and nature as both being governed by rationality and goodness. Such Stoics as Seneca even spoke of a golden age in the past in which humankind lived in unity on the basis of equality: "Men enjoyed Nature in common, and she that begot them supplied them all as guardian and assured them possession of shared resources."[10] The Stoic golden age was, in considerable measure, governed by the positive presumptions discussed in the preceding chapter. But "avarice invaded this happy system, and in its desire to withdraw property to subvert to its own uses it alienated the whole and reduced itself to narrowly delimited instead of undefined resources."[11] In this fall away from the golden age of reason and goodness, according to Stoicism, humankind fell under the necessity of coercive laws, selfish property rights, and even the institution of slavery. Given the fall away from goodness, social policy could no longer be expected to function on the basis of a positive natural law alone. A remedial, relative natural law must now be employed to compensate for the effects of the fall and to maintain a tolerable degree of harmony with the pure law of nature.

This general picture found its parallel in the doctrine of the fall employed in later Christian patristic writings and in many of the patristic discussions of property, slavery, and war. Augustine, for example, did not regard slavery and war as being consistent with the gospel except in the sense that they are a necessary remedy for the effects of the human fall into sin. Augustine's discussion of the just war clearly recognizes that war is a tragic evil, to be avoided if at all possible. But, in the light of the fall, he also considers it a sometime necessity if even greater evils are to be prevented. As a last resort, a Christian ruler can go to war to protect the commonwealth from aggression.[12] Subsequent Christian thinkers, including Thomas Aquinas, Martin Luther, and many others, have also contributed to this general line of thinking. Even most of those who strongly oppose such an approach to moral judgment would probably agree that this has been the majority report of most Christians through the church's two-thousand-year history.

Notwithstanding this, can a Christian legitimately speak of a "necessary evil"?

Before considering the problem directly, we must clarify a semantic point. The term "necessary evil" must not be equated with "necessary sin." To say a given deed is evil in its effects is not the same thing as saying it is sinful. The term "sin" is attitudinal and volitional. It must be reserved for attitudes and acts that intentionally violate the good. It is a turning away from goodness, or being alienated from goodness. Evil, on the other hand, refers to a condition or effect that frustrates the good, whether or not it is prompted by sin. In theological perspective, we can refer to evil as a frustration of God's good intentions. The possibility of a "lesser evil" thus depends on the relative character of such frustrations. It is *conceivably* an act of moral goodness, and therefore no sin, to choose a lesser evil in a situation where choice is in fact limited to actions or inactions that can only result (one way or the other) in *some evil.*

But the question we must now face is whether such situations *do* exist or whether, when the only actions available to us are evil, it is invariably best to do nothing. Is there always some creative, positive option? Notwithstanding the realities of sin, is it indeed desirable to organize our judgments and actions entirely on the basis of positive presumptions?

I know of no more persistent effort to do this than that of Leo Tolstoy. In his spiritual memoirs,[13] Tolstoy reports that his own personal moment of illumination came upon recognizing that pure obedience to the positive ethic of Jesus was not only intended by Jesus but represents the only possible way of incorporating the Christian gospel into actual existence. The Sermon on the Mount, in its declaration that we must not resist evil, should be fully, precisely, and literally obeyed. Resistance to evil implies compromise with evil. The Christian must live entirely on the positive plain of love, trusting that this example, like that of Jesus, will prove contagious. And if it does not, the Christian must be willing to abandon self to suffering, knowing all the while that one's life will not have been wasted—as it would have been had one yielded oneself to the use of evil. In many of his later writings,[14] Tolstoy expresses the view that if we would cease to rely upon armies and police and prisons (and other supposedly necessary evils), we might expect those who are presently evildoers and criminals to turn toward positive goodness, since it is the coercive institutions of society that in fact turn people toward evil.

In response to this, we may begin by noting with many of Tolstoy's literary critics that there is a curious sterility in much of his later writing. Perhaps it was to have been expected. The later Tolstoy was captive to the principle of nonresistance, which he took to be the essence of Christianity. The principle, as held in his mind, had two flaws that help to account for the comparatively lifeless way in which he expressed it. First, it tended to reduce Christian faith to an ethical principle, thus substituting a "works righteousness" for grace. Second, the particular ethical principle employed required him to reduce humanity to abstract goodness: If not repressed by society, people are bound to be good. Thus, the late Tolstoyan novel *Resurrection,* while possessing all the materials for a profound exploration of the capacity of grace to transform human sinfulness and the ambiguities of human existence into the victory over sin and death, in fact turns out to represent propaganda for Tolstoy's principle. Human sinfulness and the ambiguities of human life are there. But they are overcome more by moral tour de force than by love active through freedom. It is freedom itself that has been violated. Profounder moralists have generally understood that unless human beings are in some sense free to sin, human goodness means little. If people are sinful *only* because of the institutions that have conditioned them, how are we to suppose that goodness is not likewise merely a product of conditioning? In order to preserve the Christian ethic in a positive, perfectionist form, Tolstoy has been forced to sacrifice our very humanity.

Tolstoy's position has the indubitable advantage of utter consistency. In contrast with some present-day pacifists, he recognizes that the absolute case for pacifism takes one far beyond simple rejection of war into rejection of all violence and coercion—even that of the local police and certainly that of the revolutionary (no matter how justified the revolutionary cause). He has honestly faced up to the problem that there is no place to draw the line between outright condemnation of violence in war and the limited acceptance of physical coercion by the local police, if violence itself is in principle absolutely wrong. The moment one begins to justify coercive actions taken by the local police to uphold the law, one has begun to imply the existence of criteria under which further uses of violence might possibly be justified. In other words, one has unconsciously exchanged the pure pacifist position for some variation of just-war doctrine. Tolstoy certainly has not done that, although his apparent abandonment of human freedom and his overlooking the realities of sin seem desperate prices to pay for such ethical consistency.

Is it possible to reject all violence and coercion absolutely without at the same time abandoning belief in human freedom and recognition of the realities of sin? Can it not be argued, even from quite different premises, that the best Christian *response* to the sinful human misuse of freedom is always still a direct, positive, loving application of the gospel? Two contemporary Christian thinkers have sought to do so, and both raise significant issues that cannot be avoided by any Christian who wishes to justify any use of coercion and violence.

In his discussion of violence, Jacques Ellul acknowledges the depth of human sinfulness and makes no claims for the possible effectiveness of nonviolence as a technique. He even argues that, apart from the gospel, we are driven to respond violently; it is a part of the law of our fallen, sinful nature. But Ellul refuses to condemn people who respond violently, since they can scarcely help doing so. His argument is on a different level. It is simply that even though people *must,* in a sense, respond to violence and frustration violently, violence is *never* good in its effects. Nor can it be a relative good even in the limited sense of treating it as a lesser evil. It is always better, from the standpoint of what a Christian considers to be good, *not* to do violence! Ellul offers a series of laws of violence which suggest that the use of violence always contributes to a vicious circle of more and more violence. The argument against violence is not a moralistic one. It is not that violence is contrary to some moral principle. It is not that violence is a specific sin we are to avoid in order to guard our moral purity. Rather, Ellul contends that violence simply does no good and that it always contributes to the further career of evil in this world.[15]

Ellul, like Tolstoy, is consistent in his application of this judgment. He does not suppose that violence is one thing on the level of international war and another thing on the level of coercive local institutions within a society. The tendency of his thought, like that of Tolstoy, therefore is also anarchist.[16] Government is founded upon violence. Without violence, government is unthinkable. But violence, in Christian perspective, is always contrary to good. Thus government, inasmuch as it must be founded upon violence, is not really capable of doing good. Ellul does not argue that

government could not be positively good, but he does not think any government could be based on what a Christian would consider to be good in a
world of fallen humanity. Ellul, however, avoids the alternative of sectarian-
ism. Christians, though aware of the necessity and futility of violence, are
not to withdraw from contact with the world. They are not to fear "getting
their hands dirty." They are to identify with the weak and the troubled; they
are to maintain prophetic contact with the rich and powerful. In every one
of their human contacts they are to bear witness to the saving reality of Jesus
Christ, to the authentic freedom from the realms of necessity (such as the
necessity of violence) that infect this world. But they are to remember that
only through the grace of Jesus Christ is it possible for human beings to find
real liberation from the structures of necessity.

Ellul's approach to violence can be extended to other apparent moral
compromises. It can also be argued that all lying, all appeals to baser
motives, and so on, however necessary they may seem to be in a fallen
world, are in fact futile in the light of the Christian understanding of the
good.

It is difficult to refute the claim. In order to do so we cannot point to the
immediately tangible effects of such alleged necessary evil. Despite the
apparently desirable consequences of some action involving a "lesser evil,"
it usually remains arguable that the ultimate *long-run* consequences will
involve the perpetuation and deepening of evil. For instance, if it is argued
that the dropping of atomic bombs on Hiroshima and Nagasaki shortened
World War II and saved millions of lives (itself an unprovable proposition),
the moral calculus must be extended beyond that immediate benefit to the
effects upon the attitudes and expectations of the whole human race. Was
a brutalizing precedent established through those acts of war? Did those
bombs contribute to the willingness of countries to build up nuclear arma-
ments, numbing them to the morally unthinkable consequences of actually
using such devices? Was an evil genie of barbarism set loose and given a
newer, firmer grip on the human consciousness by the fact that in this time
and place people actually did such deeds? In short, did something happen
on the cultural level, the level of human values, that quite transcended in
seriousness and ultimate peril the supposed gain of even a few million lives?

Moral absolutism of this kind can lay claim to the indefinite future,
regarding present sacrifices made through the neglect of "realism" as tragic
requirements if humankind is ever to become aware of God's loving intentions. The important, all-consuming cause of Christian witness must be the
proclamation of the value, unity, and equality of the whole human family,
created and redeemed by God, in as direct and pure a fashion as possible.
Refutation of this position is nearly impossible because it rests upon
grounds that lie beyond tangible evidence—and also, of course, because
positive moral absolutism has never been practiced on a large enough scale

or for a sufficiently long period of time to test the question of lasting consequences.

The other contemporary thinker who has proposed a powerful and fairly consistent basis for rejecting a doctrine of necessary evil is John Howard Yoder.[17] In Yoder's view, Christ represents a third way between the false alternatives of using evil for good ends or acquiescing to evil. Christ's way combines political relevance with refusal to use or countenance methods involving evil. The two usual alternatives are false "if Jesus is confessed as Messiah." For if Jesus is Lord, then Christian ethics cannot abandon his approach to political action without at the same time abandoning faith in the meaning of history as this is revealed in Christ.

In an interesting exegesis of the famous hymn on Christ's humility in Philippians ("Have this mind among yourselves, which is yours in Christ Jesus, who, though he was in the form of God, did not count equality with God a thing to be grasped," Phil. 2:5–6), Yoder argues that Jesus himself did not seek to invade God's province by attempting to manage the course of history. Jesus' renunciation of any claim to "equality with God" was an "acceptance of impotence." That is, "Christ renounced the claim to govern history."[18] Like Christ, we are not to seek to be "effective" by assuming responsibility for the course of events. We are to call into question the whole logic of "the 'strategic' attitude toward ethical decisions" with "its acceptance of effectiveness itself as a goal." We must instead face the deeper question of "whether it is our business at all to guide our action by the course we wish history to take."[19]

But, according to Yoder, this does not mean that we have to sacrifice being relevant. Jesus himself "gave up every handle on history,"[20] but he thereby became more, not less, relevant:

> *Because* Jesus' particular way of rejecting the sword and at the same time condemning those who wielded it *was* politically relevant, both the Sanhedrin and the Procurator had to deny him the right to live, in the name of both their forms of political responsibility. His alternative was so relevant, so much a threat, that Pilate could afford to free, in exchange for Jesus, the ordinary Guevara-type insurrectionist Barabbas. Jesus' way is not less but more relevant to the question of how society moves than is the struggle for possession of the levers of command; to this Pilate and Caiaphas testify by their judgment on him.[21]

Still, the question would have to be faced whether Caiaphas and Pilate had the last word: Did Jesus, for all his relevance, simply lose out? If we follow that example, will we similarly be "relevant" but lose thereby any prospect of really affecting history?

It would be possible to answer this question by pointing toward the many good consequences that have flowed from the life of Jesus and his followers. But Yoder himself does not claim a full historical vindication for Jesus.

There is far too much evil and injustice in the world for us to be able to say that Jesus' way has been clearly and decisively effective. At the same time, the empirical results of misguided Christian efforts to govern history along the Constantinian pattern show that "effectiveness" can often mean sabotage of the real meaning of history. But the Christian's relationship to the course of historical events ought not to be pitched on this plane at all. When we link our lives to Jesus, the Lord of history, we can take it on faith that our obedience to his way will in the end be used for God's own purposes in the fulfillment of the kingdom. Ultimately, this is the meaning of the resurrection: God has placed a final seal of approval and guarantee of final triumph upon the life and the faithfulness of Jesus, and Jesus has become the Lord of history. Using the imagery of the "war of the Lamb" of the book of Revelation, Yoder puts it this way:

> The cross is not a recipe for resurrection. Suffering is not a tool to make people come around, nor a good in itself. But the kind of faithfulness that is willing to accept evident defeat rather than complicity with evil is, by virtue of its conformity with what happens to God when he works among men, aligned with the ultimate triumph of the Lamb.
>
> This vision of ultimate good being determined by faithfulness and not by results is the point where we modern men get off. We confuse the kind of "triumph of the good," whose sole guarantee is the resurrection and the promise of the eternal glory of the Lamb, with an immediately accessible triumph which can be manipulated, just past the next social action campaign, by getting hold of society as a whole at the top.[22]

To be a Christian, then, is to affirm one's faith in this eschatological perspective. It is to renounce evil and at the same time to live obediently and lovingly, knowing that one's life will be fully relevant to the only history that counts.

But would Yoder not make allowances for the possibility of God's setting aside the whole normative frame of reference outlined by *The Politics of Jesus*? In a discussion of Karl Barth's attitude toward war and other "necessary evils," Yoder argues that we have no reliable guide other than Christ to serve as an indication of what God has commanded. Accordingly, he rejects Barth's idea of a *Grenzfall*, or extreme or exceptional case in which it is possible that God might command actions which involve doing evil:

> Barth has not constructed in the *Grenzfall* a reliable method of theological ethics in which it would be possible to found either logically or with relation to the revelation of God in Christ the advocacy of certain deviant ways of acting, such as killing when killing is otherwise forbidden. He has simply found a name for the fact that in certain contexts he is convinced of the necessity of not acting according to the way God seems to have spoken in Christ.[23]

In summary, Yoder's position is a powerful one; it is not easily to be dismissed by any faithful Christian. Acceptance of that position would not necessarily destroy the value of using moral presumption as an approach to uncertainties of judgment, but it would undermine the proposition that a part of moral uncertainty is doubt concerning cases where evil is or is not to be used in order that good may be done. That aspect of the problem of Christian ethics would be settled in absolute, not relative, terms.

What are we to say to this kind of moral absolutism? I believe there are two reasons for not accepting it too readily—at least in the forms proposed by Tolstoy, Ellul, or Yoder.

The first is that the position tends to understate the importance of objective economic, social, legal, and political *conditions* in the fulfillment of God's loving intentions for humankind. All these thinkers are, of course, specifically concerned about such conditions. All are distressed by poverty and resolutely opposed to every form of legal and social tyranny that humankind is capable of exercising or institutionalizing. But the point is that, notwithstanding this concern, each of these thinkers believes the attempt to deal with dehumanizing conditions must be subordinated to the exigencies of a positive Christian witness in *every* case where there is an apparent conflict. In *no* case can conditions be so bad, so frustrating of God's loving intention, as to justify negative actions. *Nothing* on this earth is worth defending by the sword: not food or drink for the hungry, not freedom for the enslaved, not the right to vote, to speak, to write, to associate. "The Christians who preach violence in the name of the poor," writes Ellul, "are disciples of Eros and no longer know the Agape of Christ."[24] Translation: Such Christians are concerned only about their attachment to objects; they no longer are attuned to the life of the spirit which is other than the world of things. They have placed their treasure on earth where moth and rust consume. Tolstoy, in his admonitions to military officers, flatly asserts that "it is not true that you are concerned with the maintenance of the existing order: You are concerned only with your own advantage."[25] Even if this were not so, Tolstoy urged his officer readers to view every institution or order that can only be preserved through killing as being unworthy of preservation.

But does not this view come into tension with a Christian doctrine of creation? What are God's intentions through creation? Without ascribing intrinsic significance to the things that may be vulnerable to attack on the human plane, is it not so that objective conditions *serve* intrinsic ends and that intrinsic ends can never be actualized in the real world apart from their fulfillment in and through objective conditions? To argue otherwise is to turn the gospel into a neo-Docetic spiritualism. Of course human beings do not live by bread or freedom or justice alone. But is it not mere sentimentality to argue that the conditions of existence do not partake of the ultimacy of the ends they serve?

Ironically, the absolutist argument can even be turned on its head. If the conditions of bodily life are relatively unimportant, what is so important about killing? Negative actions (even killing) can thus be relativized along with absolutist inactions (such as permitting others to kill or enslave). The reader will note that I am very seriously opposed to killing. But the point is that those who are willing to sacrifice all concern for the conditions of human existence when necessary to guard what they consider to be perfect obedience to the loving command of God may have undermined the basis of their own case by casting doubt on the whole realm of worldly conditions and bodily well-being. In the specific case of Yoder, it must be said that his eschatology has too greatly dominated his doctrine of creation. God's final triumph and the lordship of Christ would not be too helpful to those people whose lives have been utterly ruined or tragically unfulfilled because of Yoder's unwillingness ever to approve the wielding of the sword for the sake of social justice. Can we so easily disclaim responsibility for the factual course of history? Is there no point at which the Christian is driven to be the instrument of God's factual victory over specific injustices? Is there no time or place for the Christian to exchange the abstract perfection of the ideal for the concrete possibility of human fulfillment?

Still, the "conditions worth fighting for" must be understood in a relative light. The foregoing arguments should not be taken as neglecting the more ultimate claims of loving relationship. Here, a second objection to the moral perfectionism of Tolstoy or Ellul or Yoder must be entered: They are too skeptical of the possibilities of positive Christian witness in the face of negative actions. They too greatly doubt the Christian's ability to do negative things in a redemptive way.

Admittedly, this is hazardous ground to traverse. How many people, really, can "kill lovingly"? Probably not many. But can it be done at all in those situations of last resort? Luther's doctrine of "strange love" is based on the possibility; it is the love which is strange because it is in negative form, but which still is love because however negative the action is, it is dominated by a positive end. Luther himself would countenance no self-defense for the sake of self. But negative action for the sake of the preservation of others is, he felt, possibly a loving responsibility. It seems to me that it is indeed a possibility, but only when appropriate limiting criteria are met, when negative action is dominated by concern for objectively good ends, and when persistent creative effort is made to interpret even negative action in the light of good will toward those against whom the action must perforce be directed. Can the police do this? There is much affirmative evidence to be drawn from many different societies, despite many evidences of police abuses. Can soldiers? This is more difficult in a wartime situation, but expressions of human concern for the enemy have not been unheard of. The vast impersonal mechanisms of modern war pose more difficult arenas in which to symbolize sensitivity for human good. This may tell us, among other things, that it is nearly impossible to reconcile today's coldly logical capacities of immense destruction with the Christian conscience.

But before adopting the absolutist position it is well to recall specifically that the whole taxation system in contemporary society rests to a considerable extent on the ultimate prospect of coercion. To abolish this or put it on a voluntary basis would quickly undermine the universal opportunity of free public school education, along with other social welfare benefits of immense scope. It would literally be a life-or-death question for multitudes of people, and for many more it would be a question of whether any meaningful degree of human fulfillment is possible. I question whether the figures we have considered in this chapter have weighed sufficiently the concrete life and possibility of fulfillment of those who would be most vulnerable to any abandonment by Christians of responsibility for the government of human events. It is not enough simply to commend the vulnerable multitudes of human society to God's provident care in some future time. God expects more of us than that.[26]

Nevertheless, such writers have reminded us that negative actions *always* pose problems for the Christian conscience and must never be treated as commonplace virtue. Karl Barth, who was not a pacifist, may have expressed the point well in his own statement on the question of war: "All affirmative answers to the question are wrong if they do not start with the assumption that the inflexible negative of pacifism has almost infinite arguments in its favour and is almost overpoweringly strong."[27] In this quotation, the word "almost" is very important, for it marks off Barth's unwillingness to accept the absolute perfectionism of the pacifists. Yet the other words are also important, for they point out the positive direction of normal Christian presumption and place the burden of proof powerfully against the negative.

The weight of arguments against *any* negative actions is sufficiently strong to require that they bear a heavy burden of proof—and this is all I wish to claim. The negative presumptions should require us to be open to the possible use of negative means, but we should always be reluctant to do so. We should *not* do so until it has been established beyond reasonable doubt among persons of good will that more in the long run, as well as in the short run, will be gained in terms of faithfulness to God's loving intentions. We need, moreover, to acknowledge that *any* theoretical justification of moral exceptions can readily become the basis of arrogant rationalization. Having admitted that an exception *might* have to be accepted, we will always be tempted to regard every attractive moral shortcut as that acceptable exception. The fact that just-war doctrine has been perverted so easily into rationalizations of military policies is largely responsible for its bad name among many sensitive Christians. This should remind us again that Christians themselves partake of the sinful nature against which the moral intelligence must ever be on guard. Structuring moral decision by use of moral presumptions is the best way to handle this need for self-critical sensitivity without abandoning responsibility.

7

Polar Moral Presumptions

In the last two chapters we have examined both positive and negative presumptions based upon Christian faith. They point to tensions and conflicts that are inescapable in arriving at moral judgments. Many of our more serious decisions are actually quite complex. It is not as if any one of the positive or negative presumptions could by itself structure our decision-making, although each may have much insight to contribute. Often we find ourselves having to choose between two goods or between various shadings of evil. The use of moral presumptions helps us to engage our minds more clearly than simple reliance upon intuition, but it is a way of handling risk, not of avoiding it.

The Complementary Claims of Polar Values

In this chapter we must examine a further complexity in judgments involving competing goods. I shall argue here that there are some apparently competing values that must not be treated as if they were mutually exclusive. These are polar opposites, values that actually belong to each other even though they are apparently contradictory. Moral judgments involving polar values must somehow include the good represented by each of the opposite poles. Neither pole can continue to exist without some inclusion of its apparent opposite. Some physical analogies help illustrate the point. A world without either women or men is imaginable, though farfetched. But "male" or "female" would each be meaningless without its complementary term. Similarly, mass and energy, as physical properties, are necessary to each other. One thinks also of light and darkness, north and south, and other opposites. In a truly polar relationship, the opposites are not really in competition with each other. Each is needed even to define the other.

It must be emphasized in a study of moral judgment that some good things can only be had when their polar opposites are also preserved. Many ideological debates or disputes over public policy treat opposites as if they were mutually exclusive when, in fact, the conflicting values actually depend on each other. A presumption in favor of *some* maintenance of the balance requires us to place the burden of proof against a policy proposal or ideological appeal that seems to neglect one side altogether. A polar moral presumption cannot tell us exactly *what* relationship should exist between the two poles, but it can require that neither side be used to exclude the other. For instance—in relationships we shall soon examine more closely—freedom should not be set over against responsibility as though one had to choose only one, nor should the individual be opposed to the community. In both these cases, one value cannot be meaningful in the total absence of its apparent opposite.

The literature of ethics, ancient and modern, frequently appeals to this insight, although popular ethical discussion often neglects it. Aristotle's principle of the golden mean is an important example. By this, Aristotle did not mean a simple mathematical averaging of conflicting claims. He was rather concerned to protect the legitimate values of each. In Aristotle's world, as in ours, conflicting and mutually exclusive claims were registered between those who saw human fulfillment in terms of gross sensual indulgence and those who advocated asceticism. In his judgment, both were wrong because both neglected the truth contained in the opposite ethical attitude. Aristotle identified the golden mean as that judgment or action lying "between excess and deficiency." Too much sensual indulgence is excess, too little is deficiency. One cannot easily state what the right balance is, but it is clear that total excess and total deficiency are to be avoided. We can therefore say that a polar presumption exists against the complete exclusion of some sensual fulfillment and of some sensual control.

Of course, some kinds of opposites are not related in this way. Sometimes all of one side is no excess and none of the other is no deficiency. In the conflict between justice and injustice, we do not seek a proper balancing so that we shall not have too much justice or too little injustice. We can *never* have too much justice or too little injustice when these terms are properly understood and applied. Nor, in the conflict between honesty and dishonesty, is there any reason for presuming there must be some dishonesty. There can never be an excess of justice or honesty, since these values are aspects of the good in itself—although, to be sure, justice and honesty also need to be expressed with practical wisdom. Injustice and dishonesty are never to be sought as values in themselves, although in the real world they must sometimes be tolerated in one form in order to avoid them in other, more serious forms.

L. Harold DeWolf has appealed to certain dialectical values such as "devotion to the community and affirmation of the individual" and "loving service to the neighbor and realization of the highest values in the self."[1] Such pairings truly represent mutually supportive values. Neither side can be neglected without diminishing its opposite as well. Edward LeRoy Long, Jr., while not employing the dialectical principle, appeals to a similar inclusiveness in his rejection of "polemical exclusion." By this he means the use of one approach or "motif" of Christian ethics to the total exclusion of others. Thus we may use a prescriptive (deontological) approach to the exclusion of relational or deliberative (teleological) motifs. But ethics requires the use of all three dimensions. Long urges a "comprehensive complementarity" in which we do not neglect the insights of any.[2] It may be difficult to say how, exactly, ethics should balance itself so that the truth of each of these motifs (and others pertaining to the implementation of ethical decisions) is preserved comprehensively. It is easier to notice when any motif is totally excluded.

One of the dangers in analyzing moral judgments in dialectical terms is that in the nice balancing of opposites we may completely dilute the force of clear moral judgment. The on-the-one-hand this but on-the-other-hand that, which is typical of much dialectical thinking, can easily keep us aloof from engaging the real issues. Such aloofness is more likely when we attempt to use a polar presumption to locate the precise directions of judgment rather than as a corrective of one-sidedness. The stating of polar presumptions is most useful, not in identifying precise judgments but in identifying the boundaries within which precise judgments must lie. We know there must be some freedom and some responsibility. This judgment has great force where freedom has been crushed or responsibility is openly mocked. But the polar presumption cannot by itself tell us in a given situation how to relate the two; it can only say that neither should be excluded. Where either seems excluded, a burden of proof must be met.

An important instance of this can lie in the attempt to balance overemphasis in moral discourse or in the culture at large. Utilizing the approach of "burden of proof," one may deliberately wish to compensate for what seem to be one-sided emphases. In a celebrated passage on the golden mean, Aristotle seems to have this kind of corrective presumption in mind when he writes that "he who aims at the intermediate must first depart from what is most contrary to it. . . . We must incline sometimes towards the excess, sometimes towards the deficiencies; for so shall we must easily hit the mean and what is right."[3]

A corrective emphasis of this kind, for the sake of the neglected good, requires us to place a burden of proof against fanaticism. Fanaticism is not generally wrong in the values it espouses but rather in the one-sidedness with which it espouses them. Those who seek to correct this one-sidedness may be made to appear weak or indecisive, but in reality their judgments are likely to be closer to the mark.

Five Polar Presumptions

Are there, then, specifically Christian polar presumptions paralleling the positive and negative presumptions of the preceding chapters?

There is, in one sense, a certain polar relationship between those positive and negative presumptions themselves, at least so far as a Christian view of human possibilities is concerned. The positive presumptions indicate the positive directions of God's intended goodness, while the negative presumptions mark off the limitations within human nature. I shall discuss the implications of this point more fully. Most of the polar presumptions now to be outlined can also be understood and accepted quite apart from Christian faith. Nevertheless, Christian faith both supports each and provides it with an ultimate context of meaning. Without pretending that the list is exhaustive of the possibilities, I wish to suggest five such polar presumptions.

1. Individual/Social Nature of Human Beings

There has been a striking tendency in the public policy debates of the past two centuries to play off the individual against the social aspects of human nature. Western societies such as the United States tend sometimes to overemphasize individualism. Against this tendency, revolutionary movements and fascism have often overemphasized this or that form of collectivism. The former is illustrated characteristically by economist George J. Stigler:

> The supreme goal of the Western World is the development of the individual; the creation for the individual of a maximum area of personal freedom, and with this a corresponding area of personal responsibility. Our very concept of the humane society is one in which individual man is permitted and incited to make the utmost of himself. The self-reliant, responsible, creative citizen—the "cult of individualism" for every man, if you will—is the very foundation of democracy, of freedom of speech, of every institution that recognizes the dignity of man. I view this goal as an ultimate ethical value.[4]

While this does not go so far as to state that individualism is the *only* ultimate ethical value, it clearly has neglected the social side of human nature.

The other extreme is suggested by some variations of bolshevism and (perhaps most unforgettably) by the fascism of Mussolini's statement that "the fascist conception of life stresses the importance of the State and accepts the individual only in so far as his interests coincide with those of the State, which stands for the conscience and the universal will of man as a historic entity."[5] Much military discipline presupposes the same moral one-sidedness: the individual is nothing; the group or the cause is everything. Sometimes this kind of one-sidedness is even characteristic of rhetoric within the church: the church or the kingdom of God (as a cause) is everything; the individual is nothing—despite the fact that concern for the individual belongs to the very definition of the meaning of the church and the kingdom of God.

But it is not possible for a Christian to think of human life in either purely individual or purely social terms. Karl Barth confronted the need for maintaining both.

> Might not humanity be a corporate personality of which individuals are only insignificant manifestations or fragmentary parts? Or might not the whole notion of humanity be a fiction, and the reality consist only of a collection of individuals each essentially unrelated to the others and each responsible only for himself? Romans 5:12–21 points in neither of these directions. If we base our thinking on this passage, we can have nothing to do with either collectivism on the one hand or individualism on the other.[6]

What we need to do, he continues, is to see "the man in humanity and humanity in the man." The point is that we cannot be either individual or social alone, but both at once. The destruction of our individuality undermines genuine human society; the undermining of our social nature for the sake of individualism destroys not only society but our individuality as well. A really human society is made up of creative individuals. A real individual is a person fulfilling his or her personhood in community.

The effect of this presumption is to require any proposal or social movement or ideology that rests upon either absolute individualism or absolute collectivism to bear the burden of proof. If, for instance, a proposal (such as that of Milton Friedman[7]) to return all the national parks and state schools to private ownership seems to rest principally upon a one-sided individualism, we may well place the burden of proof against it, requiring it to show that it takes the social nature of human beings seriously. It may be that good and sufficient reasons can be found to place the national parks under private ownership (although this seems inconceivable to me), but if the main reason advanced for such a move is a kind of ideological individualism, we must place the burden of proof against it. Ideological individualism cannot stand alone as an ethical principle without some reference to the complementary pole of social relatedness. Or if, in the name of some conception of corporate good, it should be decided that medical experimentation known to be harmful to the subjects might proceed because of supposed benefits to the whole of society, we must place the burden of proof against it in the name of the value of the individuals involved. The old practice of experimenting upon "volunteers" from prison inmate populations is a case in point. Why were prison inmates singled out as potential volunteers? Presumably a judgment was made at some level that such persons are of less value to society and hence are more expendable. Their individual value somehow has less weight when measured against potential good for society as a whole. There may, of course, be good ethical arguments for giving people an opportunity to volunteer for particularly hazardous experiments or missions, but important questions have to be raised when certain classes of individuals are singled out for such experiments or missions because their lives are regarded as having less worth. Indeed, the burden of proof might well be placed against all social policies requiring the sacrificing of certain individuals for the sake of the greater public good. From time to time every society has to do this in some way or other, but our ethical evaluation would seem to hinge on whether the actions are fully voluntary and not predicated on invidious judgments of the expendability of some classes of persons.

2. Freedom/Responsibility

This is a similar presumption, since freedom is personal or individual in its roots and responsibility is social in its context. In a theological perspective we speak of God's gift of freedom and of human responsibility before God for the exercise of that freedom. Somehow these two must be kept in tension. To be real, God's gift of freedom to every person must be radically individual and uncontrolled. Even the idea of submitting one's will to God's will, if it is authentic, is an expression of our freedom and not an abdication of that freedom to some power altogether external to ourselves. And yet, freedom itself cannot be exercised in a vacuum. Apart from a context of responsibility—something outside ourselves that is worth responding to— freedom is meaningless. This point is of great importance in the ethics of H. Richard Niebuhr, who emphasizes the responsive character of all ethical action. In our moral life, we exercise our freedom by responding to our relationships with God and fellow beings. "All action, we now say, including what we rather indeterminately call moral action, is response to action upon us." The important question to bear in mind is, "To whom or what am I responsible and in what community of interaction am I myself?"[8] But, on the other hand, the self that responds does not do so only reflexively. It is not a self unless it responds freely, and that freedom cannot be abrogated in the name of responsibility without undermining the meaning of responsibility.

Some of the hardest moral dilemmas in jurisprudence concern the rights of the accused to freedom before conviction versus the need to protect the public. Further dilemmas occur in such areas of social policy as the regulation of pornography and the distribution and use of harmful drugs. We cannot enter into careful consideration of the best resolution of such dilemmas here, but most such dilemmas illustrate the operation of a polar presumption, for it is morally wrong to treat the issues as though *only* freedom or *only* social responsibility were at stake. Both are engaged together. A resolution that disregards freedom altogether will tend to be wrong from the standpoint of social responsibility, and a solution that neglects social responsibility will, in the long run, work to the detriment of freedom. In my own judgment, the law should be as permissive as possible about pornography. For the sake of freedom, the burden of proof should be against coercive restriction of movies, literature, and the like. At the same time, it seems clear that pornography can debase community values and human sensitivities in ways that ultimately undermine respect for freedom itself. Thus, while placing the burden of proof against legal coercion in this field, we may at the same time place a burden of proof against irresponsible exercise of that freedom. The distinction must in this way be made between legal freedom and moral freedom, between legal restraint and moral restraint. Certainly even legal freedom cannot be absolute in such areas, but the presumption can be in its favor.[9]

The polar character of the relationship between freedom and responsibility can be demonstrated rather sharply by pursuing literally the implications of the standard Jeffersonian quotation that that government is best which governs least. The reductio ad absurdum of this was supplied by Henry David Thoreau, who added that "that government is best which governs not at all."[10] Few people really believe that freedom can extend to the point of absolute legal anarchism—though Robert Nozick and the libertarians come very close.[11] We may be willing to place a burden of proof against all coercion, but implicitly most of us would also place a contrary burden of proof against complete anarchism as a method of guaranteeing freedom. We understand that there must be some context of responsibility before the community or we shall lose our freedom. The polar presumption will not, by itself, define for us the correct relationship between these two poles, but it will help us avoid neglecting either side altogether.

3. Subsidiarity/Universality

This presumption refers to the level of social organization at which problems should be addressed. The term "subsidiarity," as we noted in chapter 4, is an outgrowth of Roman Catholic consideration of this question. According to the doctrine of subsidiarity, as developed in various papal encyclicals, social problems should be dealt with at the most immediate (or local) level consistent with their solution. Any problem that can be solved by the family ought not to be referred to the state; any problem that can be solved by a local community ought not to be taken over by regional or national government. In the name of subsidiarity, twentieth-century popes have resisted state dominance in the field of education and affirmed the moral rights of private ownership. The principle itself suggests a tension, for the higher collectivity must certainly be invoked when necessary.[12]

But the principle also needs to be seen in relationship to the reverse principle that problems can be dealt with most responsibly on the widest possible scale. Since solutions to problems, however immediate they may be, tend to have ramifications far beyond the immediate situation, a case can be made in the name of responsibility for the involvement of the wider community in arriving at solutions. Can education in America best be dealt with locally? Perhaps so; but then how is the wider community to protect itself from the results of poor educational systems in many localities? And how can resources then be redistributed from wealthier to poorer communities and states?

Maximum claims have sometimes been made for neighborhood control of schools and community life, with only the loosest thinking about how the various neighborhoods should relate to one another.[13] One can understand why. There has been a quite understandable reaction against the inexorable development of immense, impersonal institutions of government, industry, education, and even religion. Local people have lost a sense of participation in the vast, impersonal institutional forces that seem to control their destinies; nor are problems being solved effectively, because those who control the solutions are remote from local realities.

Perhaps in the interaction between the vast corporate institutions and the local movements we can see an irreducible polar tension at work. Most important problems have both universal and local dimensions. All of us exist both locally and universally. We do not want to trade our local identity and powers of self-determination for a fragmentary and often illusory slice of participation in the politics of society as a whole. But at the same time we do not want to cede the opportunity to affect the destiny of human history on the larger scale. The point is sometimes lost on the neoconservatives in their enthusiasm for "mediating structures" in democratic society. While correctly citing the need for social structures standing between the individual and the vast, impersonal political, economic, and religious institutions of our time, these writers often overlook the importance of accessibility of power in institutions (particularly political institutions) of vast scale. If democratic government does not have power to affect the crucial social and economic realities by which one's life is determined, what good does it do to have mediating institutions relating one to that government?[14]

A tension of historic importance exists between movements espousing nationalism and self-determination of peoples and the inexorable movement of the world toward institutions of interdependency. Taken literally, self-determination has the incompleteness of a polar term, for total independence and self-determination are never possible, either practically or morally. Practically, the world has become far too interdependent for any society to go it alone. Theologically and morally, the world is ultimately one community—however little it may behave like one. The maximum claims of nationalism have become a dangerous anachronism in a world where the behavior of each nation affects all others. Nevertheless, criticism of a one-sided quest for self-determination can itself become one-sided. The slogans

"self-determination" and "self-development" may not be so much in opposition to true universalism (as represented, for instance, by the concept of
world law) as they are in opposition to imperialistic controls by more
powerful nations and multinational business corporations. Imperialism is
not genuine universalism; rather, it is a perverted form of localism. It
expresses the domination of one local group by another. Still, even ideal
universal forms of social organization, such as those encouraged by world
federalism and "world peace through world law," need the corrections of
subsidiarity, for world-scale institutions cannot hope to manage most local
problems. We cannot here define a proper relationship between universality
and subsidiarity. We can only say that something is missing when either is
neglected. The burden of proof must be borne where either has been totally
disregarded.

4. Conservation/Innovation

It is a part of the timeless folklore of humanity that some people are more
prone to change while others seek to maintain the status quo. It is not
unusual for older people to be more conservative, more resistant to change,
more protective of established values; nor is it unusual for younger people
to be more inclined to seek change and impatient with things as they are.
This may be true in part because, up to a point, the older people become,
the more apt they are to acquire personal stakes in existing social reward
systems. Nevertheless, neither change nor conservatism could become, by
itself, a defensible presumption for all people. It may be a good thing that
some people tend to place the burden of proof against change while others
tend to place it in favor of change. The truth is that in any imaginable social
situation there are likely to be *some* values worth preserving in the ongoing
continuity of human experience, and it is equally true that in most social
situations some change is morally imperative. If God is at work in a society's history, there are values present to be preserved. If sinful human beings
are also there, motivated as they are by selfish interests, there are bound to
be unjust relationships and institutions that need to be reformed or
uprooted.

We should place the burden of proof, therefore, against the notion that
everything about any situation needs to be changed. But we should also
reject the presumption that *nothing* should be changed. In the light of
human finitude and sin and in view of the static and dynamic elements of
ongoing history, basic values will be neglected if either change or change-
lessness is made into an absolute. Thus, Walter Rauschenbusch's forthright
statement that "if a man wants to be a Christian, he must stand over against
things as they are and condemn them in the name of that higher conception
of life which Jesus revealed"[15] needs to be corrected by Rauschenbusch's
own appreciation for *some* present embodiments of the good—such as some

features of family life, some achievements of political democracy.[16] Total commitment to change promises nothing for future achievements, and thus change itself, when absolutized, becomes meaningless. But on the other hand, William James's conservatism, as expressed in his 1891 essay on "The Moral Philosopher and the Moral Life," needs correction in the opposite direction. James wrote that

> the presumption in cases of conflict must always be in favor of the conventionally recognized good. The philosopher must be a conservative, and in the construction of his casuistic scale must put the things most in accordance with the custom of the community on top.[17]

This passage can be corrected by some of the themes of James's own pragmatic method, which suggests a perpetually developing appreciation of the meaning of the good and hence some real openness to change. But both these quotations, one from a theologian and the other from a philosopher of the Progressive Era, should remind us how easily we can be trapped into rhetorical abandonment of either existing values or of needed changes.

This rhetorical problem is almost inevitable in every dynamic period of history, for in such periods self-conscious forces for change or in resistance to change are most intense. But the burden of proof should be placed against both change for the sake of change alone and sameness for the sake of sameness alone.

It is worth remembering at this point that the term "radical" is not properly placed in polar opposition to "conservatism." To be a radical, to have a radical point of view, is to approach problems at the root. The true radical will therefore understand (at the root) that some proposed changes are a threat to basic values which need to be preserved. But he or she will also be the first to support needed revolutionary changes in deeply entrenched injustices. To illustrate the point in relation to the women's liberation movement: A true radical may well perceive gross injustices in many of the roles to which women have been relegated under the guise of protection of the family and of honoring motherhood. The radical may find language itself a subtle reinforcement of oppression, as male metaphors are utilized to convey images of strength, creativity, and independence, while female metaphors suggest passiveness and dependency. Thus, the radical may be led to demand sweeping social and cultural changes. At the same time, the radical may be concerned over the loss of primal institutions of marriage and family, which historically have offered protection and nurturing for the most intimate relationships and commitments of love between persons of opposite sex and between parents and children. Through the inclination to defend such institutions, the radical may properly be called conservative. Radicalism, in this way, is deeper than either conservatism or change in themselves. We are always called to be radical in our perceptions.

5. Optimism/Pessimism

Optimism and pessimism are not forms of moral principle or judgment, but they do represent opposing types of attitude toward situations that need to be kept in balance. They represent answers to the following questions: Should the Christian make judgments and act on them in the expectation that what she or he believes to be good is also a real possibility? If the answer has to be negative, then the positive presumptions of chapter 5 are essentially meaningless. But the answer cannot be fully affirmative as long as human sinfulness and finitude exist. Christian realism must be both hopeful and skeptical. It should be neither deluded and naïvely optimistic nor cynically pessimistic. Cynicism flourishes in the belief that the good is always powerless in the actual world. Without some hope, moral endeavor itself becomes pointless. On the other hand, unreal expectations breed disillusionment—and ultimately cynicism—when they are dashed to pieces on the rocks of reality.

The theologians of hope have stressed the grounds in Christian faith for a long-term attitude of optimism, despite all present frustrations of the good. They remind us, as does the broad mainstream of Christian tradition, that the Christian eschatological perspective is always ultimately optimistic. In the *long* run, at least beyond human history, God's loving will can in faith be expected to prevail. But the tension between optimism and pessimism cannot be left simply as a conflict between total pessimism about the present world darkness and optimism about God's ultimate redemption of life beyond history. Pessimism and cynicism will continue to distort our moral perspectives unless something of that long-run eschatological hope can also infect the short-run concrete present reality. It may even be impossible to sustain much hope for life beyond history in the absence of some evidence of God's redeeming power within the events of history. Our rhetoric sometimes belies our deeper attitudes at this point. Throughout Christian history there have been those who seem to have abandoned all prospect for the experiencing of goodness in this world. But even among the sectarians who advocated and practiced withdrawal from what they took to be a hopelessly evil world, there has usually been some effort to organize the social life of the faithful in such a way as to embody God's intended goodness—a little beachhead of God's kingdom in the fallen world. Most Christians have gone beyond such a little shred of optimism in the expectation that it may be possible to be quite effective servants of good if they work at it vigorously enough.

Sometimes Christians have gone too far in the other direction. One recalls the early twentieth-century Student Volunteer Movement and its goal (and presumed expectation) of making the whole world Christian "in our generation." Some of the less cautious representatives of the social gospel movement of the same period spoke of "building the kingdom of God on earth" as if that were a manageable human possibility within a calculable period of time. The "Constantinian Christianity" against which Eastern European Christian theologians have reacted with such force—the Christianity of triumphal Christendom—represented many centuries of Christian determination to organize a thoroughly Christian civilization without sufficient self-criticism or awareness of how subtly selfishness can infect lofty ambitions for the success of the gospel.

Use of optimism/pessimism as a polar presumption thus requires us to hope, but not too much. The burden of proof stands against either total optimism or total pessimism concerning future events. We act on the presumption that there are real, but not unlimited, possibilities in every human situation.

The American civil rights movement was almost paradigmatic of this balance, not least because its leaders were so largely prompted by a hopeful Christian realism. But after the political victories of the movement in the 1960s, American society witnessed a period of conservative reaction in the so-called "white backlash," and a corresponding sense of frustration and impotence developed among many black people. Resistance to racial desegregation, previously most evident in the South, now tended to center in northern urban areas. Black people in the ghettos were finding it difficult to escape poverty. Many felt themselves locked into vicious circles of low income, inadequate education, poor housing, and political vulnerability. Urban riots, crime, violence, and drug addiction represented, in different ways, predictable responses to hopeless frustration. Not infrequently black intellectuals found themselves seriously questioning whether, in the final analysis, the civil rights movement had accomplished anything at all. Its major gains seemed to have been on paper. In the real world, blackness seemed still to represent second-class citizenship and dehumanization. Martin Luther King, Jr., remained a symbol of goodness and nobility, but after his assassination he became for many a symbol of naïveté and tragedy. In retrospect, it is apparent that neither the most euphoric claims concerning the accomplishments of the civil rights movement nor the reactive pessimism were altogether reasonable. Clearly the movement had not fully ushered in a new day of freedom from racism, but equally clearly the legal gains had been quite real—with major political gains following in the 1970s and 1980s. My purpose in citing this historical illustration, however, is not to assess the civil rights movement but rather to say something about the climate of Christian moral judgment regarding race relations during its aftermath. The polar optimism/pessimism can lead one, in periods of that kind, to keep faith with the hopes nourished by previous accomplishments while also maintaining realism about the incompleteness of those accomplishments. If *everything* attempted by the movement had failed, the logical conclusion (actually drawn by some) was that further expenditures of energy would be equally useless.

But this requires us to face again the question raised at the beginning of this chapter: Does the use of polar presumptions tend to lead us into moral complacency? Does it cut the nerve by relativizing both present situations of evil and future possibilities of good?

One answer to this is that it takes both evil and good seriously wherever it finds them—either in the present or in the future. Those who despise or disregard the goodness at work in every present situation are not likely to contribute much to its future possibilities. Those who do not see the evil possibilities in their future visions have probably diagnosed present evils incorrectly. The attitude of complacency, on the other hand, may be evidence that one has broken down the polarity of optimism/pessimism: Either things are so bad that nothing I do will make any difference or things are so good that they will continue to be good and to improve regardless of what I do. Maintenance of this polarity is absolutely crucial to the avoidance of complacency.

But this also means that we cannot, in our moral judgments, be judicial bystanders, observing the ongoing flow of life in Olympian detachment. Christian moral judgment is action-oriented. In the final analysis it is a strategic perspective—a planning of action to contribute to God's intended good.

More Complex Groupings of Competing Values

The list of polar presumptions could obviously be extended, for many values that appear to be competing are actually necessary to each other. Nor, for that matter, is this kind of analysis necessarily limited to polarities. In a thoughtful response to this chapter, as it appeared in *A Christian Method of Moral Judgment,* Diane M. Yeager remarked:

> I find this an exceedingly helpful structural analysis, and I think it can be usefully broadened beyond the limits to which Wogaman subjects it. The same requirement to balance goods applies even when goods are not in these mutually defining polar pairs, and the groupings of conflicting goods can easily include three, seven, or greater numbers of legitimate values.[18]

Her point is certainly well taken. The presumption, then, must be that we may not totally disregard any good thing for the sake of any other good things, for we are likely to discover that there are linkages between and among them. Ultimately, of course, this returns us to our earlier discussion of the problem of establishing priorities among apparently competing values—with a further reminder that no formal structure of ethical analysis can spare us the task of serious struggle with competing claims and with their theological grounding.

8

Presumptions
of Human Authority

Thus far we have considered the problem of judgment and decision-making as if it were simply a matter of each person's solitary responsibility. In a sense it is an individual matter. We cannot entirely delegate either our minds or our wills to others without undermining our intellectual or moral integrity.

In the third chapter we noted the breakdown of various traditional sources of external authority on the basis of which Christians of the past have often relied for feelings of moral certainty. In part, this breakdown reflects a growing awareness that we no longer have adequate reasons for accepting such external authorities without question. We can no longer believe with our minds that such authorities as scripture, church, and tradition are *necessarily* right and applicable to the decisions we face. Since our minds are no longer wholly convinced, it would be an abdication of moral responsibility for us to turn our moral will over to such external authorities without further question, without being wholly convinced that our judgments reflect our faith.

The Inescapability of Social Influence

Having stated the problem of moral judgment in such an individualistic way, we are forced to remember that we are not simply individuals. We are also social by nature. A purely individualistic approach to moral decision-making is in conflict with the individual/social polar presumption and with the insight that even within our individuality there is a profoundly social dimension. That "self" of which we are aware in our self-understanding is itself substantially a product of our interaction with others. Moral judgment is personal in its essence, but it is also social. Our most private-seeming perceptions and judgments are all infected by the perceptions and judgments of others. In the beginning, our earliest childhood moral judgments overwhelmingly reflect the values and perceptions of parents or other nurturing adults. The residual power of these earliest influences often persists throughout life, unconsciously shaping our moral perspectives. As we grow up, however, other influences also come into play, including the effects of peer groups and all forms of leadership that affect us.

Contemporary social psychology has demonstrated just how significant these influences can be. The evidence is particularly compelling in the insights of reference group theory.[1] Basic to this body of knowledge is the factual observation that people tend to derive values and perceptions from the groups with which they identify themselves. The reason for this is in large measure that the relationships we have with others in our group experiences are important to us. We conform to the values and share the perceptions of the group largely so that we will be accepted by it. The sharing of perceptions and values is intimately linked to one of the most fundamental needs of our humanness: to be accepted and valued by others in shared experience. Through this acceptance of our selfhood by others (what Charles Hampden-Turner and others have termed "self-confirmation"[2]), we gain identity and meaning. We may, of course, belong simultaneously to more than one reference group; we may identify with groups by which we are not recognized; the "group" may be historical (it is possible to identify with persons and groups long dead, adopting through imagination values and perceptions having the conjectured approval of such persons and groups); the form of reference identification may even be negative, in the sense of a rejection of values and perceptions associated with groups we reject or that we are rejected by. The social realities summarized by the theory of reference groups is obviously very complex.

Social psychologists have demonstrated the enormous power of group association, including the great psychological difficulty of dissent on important matters where we find ourselves opposed to the unanimous judgment of our reference groups.[3] Some social experiments have even shown, disturbingly, that many subjects will go so far as to inflict serious suffering on others in order to conform to what they believe the group or an authority figure (such as a social scientist conducting the research) expects them to do—a fact we should not find surprising in light of the vast evils inflicted by officials in Nazi Germany and elsewhere in obedience to the orders of those in authority.

Should we conclude that we are controlled by groups and other forms of authority despite everything that has been said about personal moral judgment? To concede this altogether is to abandon the morality in moral judgment. The degree of group influence, while great, is still variable. In none of the social psychological experiments have all subjects exhibited the same measure of control. A few, while manifesting some psychic pain at their own deviation, have nevertheless had the inner resources to dissent from the absurd or the immoral. Their behavior can also be accounted for by reference group theory, but it may suggest the influence in their cases of an absent or transcendent reference. If the polarity of individual/social is based on reality, we may suppose that even in the cases of those most easily swayed toward immediate social conformity, some shred of a subjective "I" is interacting with the overpowering "they" of the group. Few people, if any, can stand aloof from all social conformity. But for most of us there is at least the possibility of choosing the reference groups and individuals by whom we will allow ourselves to be influenced in our moral judgments. And there is reason to suppose that we, as a part of the overall social fabric, will also influence the moral perceptions of others.

It is important to speak thus of our judgments being "influenced" by other people but not being *determined* by them. Absolute conformity to the judgments of others is not consistent with Christian faith, for it necessarily absolutizes other people whom we know to be both finite and sinners. But there may well be reason consciously to accept—even to seek out—the judgments of others in order to be influenced by them. When we approach the judgments of others in this spirit, we are involved in a different kind of presumption from those dealt with in previous chapters; now we treat the judgment of particular individuals or groups as *probably* moral or true, and we then require other judgments to bear the burden of proof. This is what happens when we give "great weight" to the opinions of particular people. It is not that those opinions will *necessarily* be followed, but only that for various reasons those opinions will be followed unless it can be proved to us that they should be set aside. As indicated in chapter 4, this is what usually happens in executive decision-making, where a generalist must consult those with specialized expertise. The judgment of the specialists may not be followed, but it probably will be unless a convincing case is mounted to oppose it.

When we choose to follow particular human authorities, we give them the benefit of the doubt. The earliest of life's moral authorities, parents or parent substitutes, often exert this kind of continuing influence for many years, whenever we come upon problems that have been anticipated by the values they have passed on to us. Sometimes this influence persists throughout a whole lifetime. We may well be open to new insight (we certainly *should* be), but we are still likely to measure each new viewpoint against those early moral influences and to require the new viewpoints to bear the burden of proof. It may be that the influence of the "elders" of society is at a historic low ebb, in light of the vast sweep of social and technological change in this century and the inability of older and younger generations to experience things in the same way. Sweeping changes mean that the generations of elders have not developed traditions of judgment about many commonplace new realities, and young people of the past few decades have had to go it alone to a much greater degree than previous generations.[4]

Still, there is no way to avoid the influence of human authorities of various kinds, which means that the choice of authorities and the manner in which we permit ourselves to be influenced by them are serious moral questions.

The Selection of Moral Authorities

We must therefore address the interesting question of how we should go about choosing those individual and group authorities by which we wish to be influenced in our moral judgments. Which authorities are most likely to reflect Christian insight into moral questions? Under what circumstances should different kinds of authorities be permitted to influence our judgments?

For these to be meaningful ethical questions, we must be able to give reasons for choosing to be influenced by some rather than by others. But a somewhat intricate distinction needs to be made. Our reasons for choosing one authority over another are not the same as the reasons the authorities themselves offer in support of the judgments they have made. When we allow ourselves to be influenced by another person or group *as an authority,* this means that to some extent we choose to follow their lead even when we do not fully understand their own reasons. When we treat specific human authorities as probably or presumptively right, this means that we choose to listen to them more than to others and, in cases of lingering doubt, to continue to follow these human authorities rather than others. We will follow even apart from the intrinsic persuasiveness of their presentation of a case in favor of their judgment.[5] We follow their lead partly because we have reason to believe they will be right even when we do not fully understand them.

Every rationalistic or individualistic age naturally shrinks from accepting such leadership on the grounds that we should not commit ourselves to any judgment we cannot personally comprehend. But how can we possibly comprehend for ourselves the relevant facts of all the situations in which we must make judgments? Even when our understanding is very great, do we not need to compensate in some measure for the needed corrective others can give? Pure rationalism is not humble enough concerning the limitations of our capacity to know, and pure individualism overlooks the depth of our dependency on the influence of others in all areas of life. It is certainly true that all of us, even the most rational and independent, will in fact be influenced by the judgments of others whose judgments we have, for whatever reason, come to trust. Still, as we have said, such influence is morally responsible only when we can give solid reasons for our trusting and only when our trusting functions as a presumption—open to modification if it becomes evident that the trusted human authority is probably wrong.

I wish to consider five forms of human authority that can be treated as sources of dependable presumptions for Christian moral judgment.

1. The Biblical Witness

While, as we have seen, the Bible's moral authority has been diminished substantially for large numbers of people, it continues to exert very great influence upon Christians. If it is no longer possible for thinking people to accept biblical literalism, this does not mean that the Bible has become irrelevant to Christian judgment of moral issues and problems. In part, this is because the Bible is the primary locus of Christian theological insight. I shall make further comments about Christian tradition in general, but clearly the Bible is the quintessential starting point. It is the most contemporaneous record of the formative events of the Christian narrative, particularly those associated with Jesus Christ but also including the history of Israel and the gathering of the Christian church. But its central significance is not simply based on questions of relative historical accuracy. It represents the faith of the community of faith in its deepest form. I shall also refer to the community of faith as authority. But in respect to the Bible it is true that the canonization of scripture by the church is one of its most important exercises of moral teaching. That these writings and not some others are chosen to represent the heart of Christian theological teaching is to invest these writings with whatever teaching authority the church possesses. In that sense, it is true that the Bible is ultimately an expression of the authority of the church. And yet, the church acknowledges itself to be accountable to the Bible, and in that sense the church can also be seen as an expression of the authority of the Bible.

In neither case, however, is authority to be understood as arbitrary. One does not believe what one reads in the Bible just because the church says to, any more than one participates in the church because the Bible says to. The considerations dealt with in chapter 3 have, one might suppose, irretrievably banished that conception of biblical or ecclesial authority among thinking people. But there is a deeper sense in which the authority of the Bible lies in its intrinsic capacity to interpret reality profoundly and persuasively. That is the ground on which its real theological contribution lies.

So when we speak of the Bible as a source of authority for Christian moral judgment, it is most profoundly on the level of the shaping of perspectives and values. The fact that we have returned again and again to biblical perspectives in dealing with basic Christian presumptions in this volume is a reflection of that level of biblical authority. Inevitably we have been selective. I do not think this merely means choosing those biblical passages we find most useful in buttressing viewpoints derived from nonbiblical sources. Rather, it is selection of the points at which biblical words are most illuminating of the problem at hand.[6]

But what about the authority of specific teachings of the Bible on specific moral issues? Clearly, as we have seen, there are many contemporary issues that the Bible does not address at all. And many of the issues addressed by the Bible are no longer issues—or at least the cultural context is now so different that the biblical word is less than helpful. Nevertheless, in addition to the overall weight of the "deep" message of the Bible—which is crucial and formative for Christian moral judgment by grounding our theological perspective and presumptions—it still seems to me that the specific teaching of the Bible on a specific moral point should be accorded some presumptive weight by Christians. It should be taken seriously enough that a burden of proof should be borne by contrary viewpoints. Obviously that burden can be borne easily in many cases—such as the commandment against women speaking in church or the requirement that apostates be stoned to death. But the biblical writings are an expression of how the faith tradition was applied to the circumstances at hand by those who articulated most clearly and contemporaneously the basic meaning of the tradition. Their view of how that faith should be applied to particular problems should be taken seriously into account, insofar as the problems were the same or nearly the same as those faced by later generations. Such a presumption must, however, be very far from absolute, lest the central message, the deep theological perspective, itself be compromised.

2. The Community of Faith

On matters of moral judgment an obvious case can be made for relying upon that reference group which most clearly expresses our deepest personal values. Christians can scarcely ignore the church as a source of presumptive authority, and strong and sometimes persuasive claims have often been made for the church as *the* authority on moral issues. In chapter 3 I was critical of certain aspects of Paul Lehmann's "contextual ethic," but there is much to be said for his insight into the way in which Christian *koinonia* shapes and influences, but does not violate, the moral judgment of the Christian. It is in the *koinonia* that Christians arrive singly and together at those moral judgments which best express the meaning of what God is doing in human history "to make and keep human life human."[7] While Lehmann's method of moral judgment is basically intuitive (and therefore subject to the criticism that it offers little actual guidance), it does at least implicitly subject intuition to the test of consensus within the company of the faithful. This is certainly better than purely individual intuition. Moral judgments arising as a group consensus among those sharing the same basic faith are likely (1) to be purified of individual idiosyncrasy and self-interest and (2) to represent a cumulative reflection of the best insights of the entire group. To be sure, even the church can also debase the lofty purity of the individual, but if it is really the church it is a community of faith based on and accountable to authentic Christian values.

The consensus of the community on moral questions is registered in every imaginable kind of Christian church. Sometimes the process is highly authoritarian, sometimes very democratic. The old-style and purist Society of Friends waits for the "sense of the meeting" to develop—a visibly democratic process, possibly limited to some extent by the inner dynamics of group life in which some participants tend to be more equal than others. The end result of this consensual formation has been highly influential in the judgments of individual Quakers, particularly since a consensus could not be registered in most cases until all were truly agreed. Other Protestant bodies also have means of developing moral consensus both denominationally and ecumenically, often through formal declarations at national, regional, and local levels. The student of denominational and ecumenical pronouncements on moral questions is struck by the capacity of those who participate in formulating them to put aside local biases and self-interest when challenged to work together in formulating a distinctively Christian judgment on an issue. Assuming, as we must, that Christians often experience internal conflict between their faith perspectives and their self-interests and idolatries, we might expect this to happen with some frequency. The collective judgment, formally determined, is certainly a better index to the deeper Christian consensus than a casual opinion poll of the same Christians is likely to be. This is why the statement that church pronouncements do not represent the thinking of grass-roots Christians is often superficial. Round up the dissident Christians and give them the solemn responsibility of formulating a truly Christian response to a controversial social issue, and the effect of this new responsibility upon their judgment is likely to be noticeable.[8] For such reasons, the authority of church bodies may, with good reason, be given a presumptive status by Christians.

In most Protestant churches a somewhat less democratic form of moral authority is frequently expressed through the pastor's sermon. This is typically an individualistic and one-way form of influence. Dialogue is generally not encouraged by the way in which this is institutionalized in the life of the church; when it is, the pastor's views in the dialogue are clearly weighted more heavily than those of laypersons. I believe there ought to be more dialogue and more opportunity for laypersons to register their own convictions on moral issues in an effort to influence the community of faith. Nevertheless, when it is not corrupted too much by the pastor's self-interest or fear of adverse congregational reaction, there are sound moral reasons why Christians should allow themselves to be influenced to a considerable extent by this form of communication. The pastor has, in effect, been designated by the community to reflect deeply on the meaning of Christian faith and to speak clearly and honestly to them about its implications for everyone's lives. They are likely to know the pastor's personal limitations, intellectually and otherwise, and to take these into account. But the process by which the pastor was originally designated and trained for this form of leadership and the freedom and responsibility that have been institutionalized into the role are all likely to be conducive to more insightful moral leadership than might be expected from a random sampling of individual Christians. It is not irrational, therefore, to anticipate that Christians will receive from the pulpit a form of moral leadership that is worthy of respect. It will be all the more worthy of respect if it is known that the pastor has gathered into his or her own judgment the best insights available from the moral perceptions of others in the congregation. But again, the pastor's moral authority can be no more than presumptive in the sense we have been using that word.

Within Christianity as a whole, the maximum claims for the moral authority of the church have been advanced by Roman Catholicism. These claims have gone far beyond the presumptive authority of which we speak, to the point of insisting that the church, through its properly designated channels of authority, is worthy of the unqualified obedience of believing Christians. Few Protestants or Eastern Orthodox communicants accept the maximum claims of Tridentine Catholicism, and increasing numbers of Catholics either reinterpret the substance of these claims or reject them altogether. Nevertheless, it may be important for ecumenical Christianity to continue to explore the insights of Catholicism on the question of the magisterial authority of the church and to struggle toward a new ecumenical consensus that retains the valid insights concerning the authority of the church.

Honest dialogue may require both a yes and a no to this Roman Catholic tradition of authority. Few Christians who are not otherwise committed to Roman Catholicism can say yes to the maximum claims advanced by the first Vatican Council, which defined the dogma of papal infallibility. It is worthy of mention that even that council did not accept the most sweeping claims of papal authority on the part of some leaders of the church. The English Catholic W. G. Ward, for instance, wrote that "all direct doctrinal instructions of all encyclicals, of all letters to individual bishops and allocutions, published by the Popes, are *ex cathedra* pronouncements and *ipso facto* infallible."[9] Others spoke of the Pope as "the Man with whom God is forever, the Man who carries the thought of God," whose inspired directions "we must unswervingly follow" or as a man who, when he thinks, "it is God who is thinking in him."[10]

Such excessive rhetoric, which comes close to deifying the Pope, is patently arbitrary. But even the most restrained dogma, which limits the Pope's infallibility to very rare and very carefully circumscribed dogmas of faith and morals, could not readily be accepted by any Christian who considers the Pope to be a human being alongside other mortals. The Second Vatican Council, in the Dogmatic Constitution on the Church *(Lumen Gentium)* greatly broadened—and, some might say, weakened— the exclusively papal locus of infallibility. This authority was more clearly marked off as a gift to the whole church. Still, it treats infallibility as an exercise of the whole college of bishops, acting with the Pope:

The infallibility promised to the Church resides also in the body of bishops when that body exercises supreme teaching authority with the successor of Peter. To the resultant definitions the assent of the Church can never be wanting, on account of the activity of that same Holy Spirit, whereby the whole flock of Christ is preserved and progresses in unity of faith.[11]

The basis thus remains for the claim that the human authority of bishops and Pope (or Pope alone, acting properly for the whole church) is necessarily an expression of the Holy Spirit and therefore to be obeyed without question by the faithful. This is a claim that few Protestant or Orthodox Christians would wish to make, even for the church taken as a whole.

In recent years, the dogma of infallibility has been subjected to continuing scrutiny by Catholic thinkers. Some have sought new interpretations, seeking to preserve the serious intent of the dogma while avoiding superhuman claims for a human authority. Others have so sought to circumscribe the definition of an exercise of infallibility that it could remain only a theoretical problem.[12] The problem must be pursued ecumenically for both negative and positive reasons. Negatively, even a rarely exercised infallible authority continues to distort all Christian perceptions of the real authority of the church and can potentially be used in the future much more than it has in the past. Positively, however, the claims of authority registered by the Roman Catholic Church may convey a dimension of truth that all Christian ethics needs to hear.

From an ecumenical standpoint, the most promising interpretations developing within Roman Catholicism are frankly critical of the term "infallible" as being too ambiguous and misleading to be useful. Edward Schillebeeckx, for instance, speaks of "ideological and sociological difficulties that seem almost insoluble" surrounding the term "infallibility,"[13] and Hans Küng gained wide support (and opposition) for his proposal that the term be abandoned in favor of the more accurate designation of the "indefectibility" or constancy of the church's being in the truth.[14] The church can, in his judgment, be "in the truth" even while voicing erroneous propositions—a point suggesting the existence of different levels of truth and the church's basic faithfulness to the deeper levels.

Charles E. Curran discusses the teaching authority of the church with recognition both of the centrality of this responsibility and of the risks of error that the church must run in accepting it. The church, he writes, "must raise its voice on particular issues facing the world and society today with the understanding that it does not speak with an absolute certitude but proposes what it thinks to be the best possible Christian approach with the realization that it might be wrong."[15] It must recognize that the more concrete and particular its judgments are, the greater will be the risk of error. It therefore fulfills its responsibility as moral teacher on two levels: the basic level of criteria and principles used by Christians in decision-making and the level of actual solutions to concrete problems. A good deal of the teaching responsibility of the church lies in helping people to think more clearly for themselves, rather than handing over answers to be accepted passively. Curran accurately anticipates that such a view of the magisterial role of the church would not be an obstacle to church union, however inadequately he may have anticipated his own difficulties with the Vatican.[16] I do not believe this undermines the role of designated leaders (such as Pope, bishops, priests) in articulating the ecclesial consensus that develops around moral issues under the guidance of the Holy Spirit within the church. But it does require a more modest expression of the consensus by those whose office it is to do so, and it suggests that the consensus on moral questions should be accepted somewhat more tentatively (than the word "infallibility" implies) by other Christians. Of course, authority is not real unless it is accepted as valid. At the deeper levels of life within the community of faith, appeals based on authority cannot be effective unless they express to a real extent what is already written in the consciousness of those to whom the appeals are made.

The necessary degree of tentativeness in the stating and accepting of church moral teaching can best be expressed by treating such teaching as having presumptive standing. As members of the community, the faithful are obliged to take the church's efforts at moral guidance seriously. This means that they will in some sense place the burden of proof against contrary viewpoints. The more profoundly democratic a community of faith is, the more successful it is likely to be in securing this kind of presumptive support for its formal moral leadership. But whether the church is explicitly democratic or not, continued membership within it implies a commonality of moral perception that ought to find expression in this kind of presumption.

3. Tradition

A presumption in favor of the moral teachings of inherited tradition is in fact an extension of the regard given to the teachings of the community of faith. Tradition is the cumulative deposit of the moral experience of that community through time. One must be cautious in treating this form of authority with too much respect, lest the result simply be conservative or even reactionary. Nevertheless, if we can assume basic identity with the faith and values of previous generations in our religious community, we should give considerable weight to the collective judgment of these generations of forebears on the problems we face today. A presumption in favor of such a judgment will be all the greater, of course, if it reflects a consensus of moral teaching in more than one previous era and if previous generations have been known to face problems and alternative solutions comparable to our own.

The relationship between past and present in the moral experience of a community of faith was stated particularly well by Alexander Miller:

> We may have to live life without general principles, but we do have the resources of a cumulative inheritance. The community to whose *ethos* or *mores* we are concerned to conform, which has its life from Christ and its charter from the Scriptures, is a living community of faith, in whose corporate experience most of the problems we confront have been up for decision either in the precise form in which we meet them, or in forms not unrelated to our contemporary dilemma. Communities not only generate mores, they form habits. And just as any wholesome family inculcates habits of restraint and consideration which condition conduct, so the ongoing life of the Christian *koinonia* fosters a life of such a style and shape that it predetermines conduct in many a representative situation.

Miller acknowledges that these habits may be bad as well as good, but when this is the case "the best resource for their correction is within the tradition of the Church itself, in the recollection of its primal origin and its original charter."[17]

The burden of proof against a presumption of tradition can more easily be met if it can be shown that the tradition was peculiar to a particular historical context with its own sociocultural uniqueness. If, for instance, we are to regard Paul's condemnation of long hairstyles among men as a kind of tradition, it can be shown quite easily that this was nothing more than a reflection of the peculiar taste of a particular period, having no claim upon Christian conscience in any way. Regrettably, some traditions have been able to gain considerable prestige over long periods of time, which nevertheless have been exposed as thoroughly inconsistent with the basic Christian presumptions. One must remember here the long and tragic Christian experience with slavery and with the persecution of heretics. If time alone were the determinant, we would still be forced to hold presumptions in favor of the institution of slavery and coercive measures against heretics because in both cases more generations of Christians accepted these barbarisms than have been in revolt against them. Nevertheless, in both cases liberating historical experiences and more careful theological analysis have shown us that many previous generations of Christians were flatly wrong.[18]

Christian traditions concerning marriage and family may provide us with a more positive illustration. Granted, practices among Christians have varied widely through the centuries, including promiscuity, ascetic chastity, homosexuality, polygamy, and various forms of monogamous marriage, and these and other variants of marriage and family organization have all been endorsed seriously at certain times by particular groups of Christians. It remains true that the mainstream of Christian experience and teaching has continued through the centuries to affirm the moral wisdom of covenant faithfulness in monogamous marriage (while also affirming that not all are called to marriage at all). This fact is particularly impressive in light of the wide variations of historical context respecting other aspects of social, economic, and political life. Christians of many eras, on the basis of their values of love and their concern for sexual fulfillment and the nurturing of the young, have concluded from their collective experience and experimentation that the inviolate covenant of monogamous marriage is the most humanizing form of sexual and family life. Our own era, with widespread breakdown of monogamous marriage and with much experimentation with other "lifestyles," is clearly putting this tradition to the test. The Christian ought surely to be open to the *possibility* that new institutionalizations of sexual and familial relationship will be equal to or even better than the old in protecting and enhancing human fulfillments. (I will discuss this further in the next chapter.) But this long tradition should at the same time create a certain presumption. A burden of proof should be met before Christians abandon the institutions of marriage covenant and family, in light of the vast amount of Christian moral experience that previously has confirmed them.

Most of the truly difficult decisions facing Christians in our era are troublesome precisely because they are so new. The church of the ages—the historical extension of the community of faith—has had little opportunity to acquire experience in dealing with many new problems. This is not so much the case with problems of familial and political relationship, for such problems are often perennial. But new technologies, new environmental hazards, new sociological insights are another matter. What kinds of urban planning provide the most humanizing possibilities? How much wilderness needs to be preserved? What are the moral consequences of cloning? of genetic engineering? of organ transplants? of surrogate motherhood? Should we pursue the technological capability to determine the sex of our offspring? What is the optimum population size for planet earth, and by what means can we best attain it? How much of the economy should be private sector and how much public? In an increasingly worldwide economy, how can inflation and recession and injustice be prevented?

What is at stake in answering such questions may remain fairly clear to the Christian who understands his or her own basic moral presumptions. But tradition does not provide us with very many clues as to *how* the basic moral presumptions of Christians are involved in these problems. It may be a mistake to try to stretch tradition beyond its base in the actual experience of previous generations of people.

This cautionary note needs especially to be heeded by the scholars and teachers within the community of faith who are too ready to impose a largely irrelevant past onto a largely uncertain present. Otherwise, however, the biblical and historical scholars of the church provide the main linkages we have between Christians of other generations and those of the present.

Their weight in the dialogue on moral questions within the community of faith ought therefore to be very great.

4. Technical and Factual Expertise

Sincere Christians are most apt to be wrong in their moral judgments, not because of wrong basic values but because of inadequate grasp of the factual situation and difficulties in relating facts to values. Who of us has not shuddered at some of the moral pronouncements that church bodies have sometimes solemnly offered forth in the name of God to guide the thinking of the faithful, totally innocent in their technical and factual errors? Such erroneous judgment did not begin with the Galileo case, nor is it likely to end soon. Clearly the human authority presumption for the community of faith and tradition needs to be supplemented by a presumption in favor of factual and technical expertise. Some would argue, in fact, that many problems ought simply to be turned over to the experts.

Putting aside for the moment the question of how we know who the experts *are,* we need to examine this possibility. Paul Ramsey, expressing his disgust with the results of an ecumenical study conference on church and society, was particularly critical of the tendency by church bodies to make judgments that are too specific on political and social questions. He remarked that "concerning a great many choices it has to be said that only a deliberately or inflexibly imprudent decision would be wrong. . . . The principle of prudence (among a Christian's teachings) definitely refers the matter in question to the magistrate or to the political process for decision."[19] In Ramsey's judgment, therefore, we are best advised to refer such decisions in their entirety to those having greatest factual contact with the problems.

Should we at least acknowledge a presumption of human authority here, placing the burden of proof against those who challenge the competence and wisdom of the persons whose office it is to engage the facts directly?

To some extent we must certainly do so, but an important caution must be raised. Much depends upon the values as well as the competence of those to whom we thus delegate our moral judgment-making. I shall have more to say concerning the specific problem of presumptions in the political realm, but note here in Ramsey's words the importance he attaches to the principle of prudence. I know of no principle of prudence that can be invoked by Christians to delegate their judgments on moral questions to those whose basic values are different from their own. Prudent judgments wisely relate means to ends. They necessarily involve technical grasp concerning the means to be employed. But just as necessarily they involve value-impregnated choices of ends to be sought. How can we presume the moral rightness of those experts or authorities whose "prudence" is in the service of ends that are not commensurate with Christian faith? "Prudence" is not some ethic all its own upon which all "prudent" people can agree—though Christians may, for their own reasons, unite with non-Christians in regarding a particular course of action as prudent because they also agree about some particular ends.

But prudence in service of the wrong ends should carry no weight with Christians. Much debate over economic policy bears scrutiny at this point. A given nation, such as the United States, may adopt policies "prudently" ensuring a more competitive international position. A coalition of banks may "prudently" insist on terms of repayment from Third World nations that can only be met by drastic reductions of living standards among already impoverished people. Political leaders may "prudently" adopt tax policies whose net effect is to increase the share of national income received by the wealthiest five percent of the population. A government may "prudently" cut back on health and welfare programs in order to finance vast increases in military expenditures. Obviously, much depends on whether one agrees with the value judgments informing such exercises of "prudence."

During the Vietnam War much appeal was made to the U.S. President's access to superior sources of factual information. But even that may invite scrutiny. In a perceptive analysis of that period, David Halberstam demonstrated how captive the whole administration was to assumptions about Vietnam and communism that were not altogether accurate. Moreover, as doubts began to grow among top advisers and decision-makers, many were inhibited by their own career aspirations (which embodied their really operative moral values) from admitting previous errors and challenging any present policy commitments. On some matters, ironically, the President was the "very last to know."[20]

As a further illustration of the problem, research on decisions to undertake surgery demonstrates that such decisions are made much more frequently in countries where surgeons are compensated on a fee-for-service basis than in countries where surgeons are paid by salary,[21] which suggests that material values other than the health of the patient and the admitted expertise of the surgeon greatly affect the judgments made.

Still, methodological respect must be paid to expertise. Having established what are the most dependable sources of factual and technical knowledge, we do well to give them the benefit of the doubt on factual and technical questions. In doing so, we must be rigorously careful not to permit such expertise to determine broader questions of judgment and policy unless we have other reasons to suppose that the factual experts are *also* persons who share our basic moral presumptions and who have the ability to connect their factual and normative perspectives. Many high public officials might have a difficult time meeting the test, for how many are fully committed to the value and equality of all human beings and to the fundamental unity of the whole human family in God? In treating the judgments of public figures, we do well to take carefully into account the interests sustaining them in power.

Great ecumenical conferences, such as those of the World Council of Churches, and the highest moral teaching authorities of the Roman Catholic Church, such as the Pope and Council, generally have sought to make use of experts whose technical competence is beyond question but who also manifest personal commitment to the church's basic values. This is not an easy selection to make, but I cannot agree with Ramsey in treating this as virtually impossible when he writes that

> the notion that laymen who are experts, for example, in the political and economic sciences can enable the church to speak a relevant Christian word to today's world and at the same time to point out the particular policy to be followed is simply an illusion. It takes an expert to pick an expert. Or rather the experts disagree; and if there is any reason at all and not just an accident why one set of experts and not another comes to council, the decisions concerning which ones are to be picked to inform church councils will inevitably be made by some *curia* or persons in control of setting up such councils in terms of the particular interests, positions, or trends of thought the experts are already reputed for.[22]

Here, in other words, we are invited to leave expertise to the experts (rendering, we might say, unto Caesar what is Caesar's) and to eschew all efforts to give specific point and illustration to the moral teaching of the church.

But when the church abandons specificity in moral teaching it really abandons the field of moral teaching altogether. Even the teaching of generalities and principles and attempting to affect the ethos will be pointless unless the meaning of the generalities and principles can gain concrete rootage. Why restrict the church, the community of faith, to the generalities? I do not think it is because commentators like Ramsey have wanted to save the principalities and powers of this world from the church's criticism. It is more likely because they fear that the church's mistakes on specific matters will obscure the force of its witness to the fundamentals of its faith. Surely that risk is present. But how, in this life, can we avoid the risk of being mistaken? Does not the church run a greater risk in conveying the impression that moral life should be left to pious generalities, detached from the real world of tough-minded magistrates and expert elites, and that the latter should be permitted to run things to suit their own self-interested conceptions of prudence?

All the same, picking our experts to provide factual authority can be difficult. Surely it is not simply a matter of expecting only the experts to pick experts—for then even the executive or legislator would never be able to determine which experts could be trusted presumptively. The lay world always knows its experts best by the visible results of their work. Has the plumber in the past, generally speaking, been able to stop the leaks? Have impressive numbers of cancer patients been cured by acupuncture? by cobalt treatments? by surgery? by Christian Science practitioners? Have engineers and architects with particular kinds of credentials managed to build skyscrapers and bridges that did not collapse in high winds or spring rains? Do social scientists, international relations experts, economists, and other authorities in the policy-relevant academic fields have good predictive records that are translatable into effective policies?

Accreditation standards developed in the various guilds and professional societies represent, more or less, the forms of mutual recognition by persons whose specialized results can also be perceived by those who are not specialists. If I have had successful results from two or three electricians I am more likely to trust a completely unknown person who is in some fashion, personal or impersonal, recommended by these electricians as a fellow electrician of like competence. This may seem fairly obvious, but it must be recalled lest we treat expert elites as a twentieth-century equivalent of the mystery cults, in which knowledge was accessible only through initiation.

The critical use of expert presumption requires that more be said, however, about how to minimize the risks. In a useful analysis of this problem, Daniel D. McCracken proposed a series of questions to be taken into account by decision-makers who are not specialized experts when evaluating the advice of those who are:

1. Is the proposed expert actually well informed in the precise subject area?
2. Does the expert have a hidden agenda: i.e., motivations for giving the technical testimony that make his technical testimony unreliable?
3. Is the expert seeing the issue in a too-narrow technical light?
4. Has the expert gone out of his field completely?
5. Is the decision-maker looking for information or ammunition?[23]

Such critical questions ought not to lead us away from use of technical experts as sources of human authority, but they do tell us something of the difference between real expertise and merely apparent expertise. In relation to the first of his questions, for instance, McCracken warns us that many experts continue to give advice long after they have lost touch with the details of their own field. And number two suggests that the expert may have a conflict of interest in offering technical advice if one kind of advice will be more personally profitable than another. And we should not assume that technical competence confers wisdom on broader aspects of a question. The military expert may well know all about logistics and firepower without knowing anything about the nuances of international diplomacy and the psychological and cultural factors at work in a conflict situation.

The benefit of the doubt, within the comparatively narrow bounds of relevant technical information, can be granted to the experts—and a corresponding burden of proof must be borne by those whose credentials cannot be recognized as clearly. And even the best technical expertise must not be presumed right in determining, overall, what is the best *Christian* judgment.

Inevitably, within the Christian community, we find ourselves leaning on others in areas that lie outside our own competence and interest. Most of us probably have informal and possibly unconscious ways of doing this. For decisions on how to vote in the school board election we may particularly trust one person's judgment, even though that person's views on international relations may seem totally unreliable. Where we lean heavily on the overall judgment of any other person we ought, of course, to be clear that their value presuppositions are as dependable as their facts.

In this connection it can also be noted that the known *unreliability* of the expertise or values of certain persons can create a negative presumption: If "they" are for it, we must presume it to be wrong. Translated, what this means is that if other persons or groups are known to be against our own fundamental values, we should presume that any social policies they favor will probably be opposed to what we stand for. Pacifists may automatically oppose suggestions coming from the Pentagon. American liberals will vote against members of Congress earning too high an approval rating by the Americans for Constitutional Action, just as conservatives will react against those approved by Americans for Democratic Action. I suppose this kind of prejudice is inevitable and, to some extent, a prudent part of decision-making. But we ought never to forget that just as every person must be presumed to be part sinner, so everyone must be expected to be on the side of the angels at least some of the time. Mussolini's alleged improvement of Italian rail service and Napoleon's sale of Louisiana to the United States need not have faced a burden of proof from Christians, although the net effect of the careers of both leaders may have been decidedly on the negative side.

5. The Covenants of Civil Society

To a striking degree, people permit their actual judgments to be formed for them by law and civil authorities. I know no other way to account for the great body of evidence from 1945 on of the popular readiness in the United States (at least) to alternate between anticommunist paranoia and euphoria over summit conferences and evidences of detente. On such matters, it has not been so much a question of public readiness for new moves as it has been presidential leadership that has determined the course of action. Plainly, on matters of utmost substance, large numbers of people are prepared to have their judgments dominated by the political leadership. A passage from the wisdom of Confucius illustrates the universality of the attitude:

> Tzu-chang asked about government. The Master said, "The requisites of government are that there be sufficiency of food, sufficiency of military equipment, and the confidence of the people in their ruler." Tzu-chang said, "If it cannot be helped, and one of these must be dispensed with, which of the three should be foregone first?" "The military equipment," said the Master. Tzu-chang again asked, "If it cannot be helped, and one of the remaining two must be dispensed with, which of them should be foregone?" The Master answered, "Part with the food. From of old, death has been the lot of all men; but a people that has no faith in their rulers is lost indeed."[24]

While not as explicit, Romans 13 and 1 Peter 2:13 express similarly high esteem for governmental authority.

To be sure, not all Christians have gone along with this. We have already cited Jacques Ellul's deep suspicion of government in chapter 6. Michael Novak comments that "it would be much more healthy if Americans assumed, now that television has made government propaganda so powerful, that their government is always lying or, at the very least, coloring the truth."[25] And after making his celebrated comment that "power tends to corrupt and absolute power corrupts absolutely," Lord Acton went on to assert that "great men are almost always bad, even when they exercise influence and not authority; still more when you superadd the tendency or the certainty of corruption by authority. There is no worse heresy than that the office sanctifies the holder of it."[26] Similar things would be and have been said by many advocates of civil disobedience. How indeed could followers of the Galilean subordinate their moral reason to the authority of Leviathan?

Certainly a Christian cannot regard the expertise or moral values of political leaders as binding—even presumptively—apart from rigorous examination of the bona fides of the leaders themselves and the context of their leadership. Nevertheless, there is still some place for a presumption in favor of accepting the state's legal actions. We must distinguish here between the Christian's responsibilities as citizen and as subject. As citizen, the Christian shares in ultimate responsibility for the state's actions. On the other hand, as subject the Christian is responsible to the outcome of the process in which he or she has participated as citizen. As citizen, again, we owe no presumption to government in our judgments concerning the rightness of given proposals or actual policies. But as subjects we should presume the rightness of *obedience* to law. This is because the very existence of the political covenant is at stake in the willingness of people to be subject to law. Christians, as subjects, cannot presume the moral rightness (or wrongness) of any law or authority just because it is a law or authority, but we ought to presume that it would be moral for us to obey it all the same.

Even in our role as subject, we owe no *absolute* obedience to the authority of the state. When the state's action is grossly opposed to basic Christian presumptions, it may become our duty to disobey. In the literature of Christian civil disobedience, it is a commonplace observation that one should be willing to accept the full legal consequences of conscientious violation of the law. I am not willing to make even this into an absolute. The success of the Underground Railway in conducting escaped slaves to freedom in Canada depended for its success upon the ability of those who disobeyed the law to get away with it.[27] The American Sanctuary movement of the 1980s could hardly have been successful in its efforts to give security to Central American political refugees if every move had been advertised, and similar points could be made even more clearly about the responsibilities of Germans harboring Jews during the Third Reich.

Still, a *presumption* should exist, first against civil disobedience itself and then against seeking to avoid the consequences of the action if civil disobedience should prove necessary. Acceptance of the consequences, in the manner of M. K. Gandhi and Martin Luther King, Jr., confirms respect for the civil covenant even when one must disobey it. Civil disobedience can then even be understood as a possible Christian responsibility on behalf of the state. As Christian political thought has well understood from the time of Augustine, the state's injustices are themselves the most likely cause of its own disintegration. By recalling the state to equal respect for all its citizens and devotion to the unity in love of the whole community—first by active criticism as a citizen and then, if necessary, by civil disobedience—the Christian can be seen as acting for, not against, the best interests of the civil society.

The Relativity of Human Authorities

The discussion of presumptions of human authority could continue here with endless specificity, for the fabric of human influence in society is almost infinitely complex. In a summary comment, we must return to the point that no human authority should be treated as absolute and that those human authorities which are to be regarded as presumptively right must always be tested in relation to the basic moral presumptions derived from our faith. We must not avoid being influenced by others, for we are finite beings and we are social by nature. But we are also creatures of faith with personal freedom, critical judgment, and the capacity to transcend social influences. Presumption, applied to the choice of human sources of authority, can help us bridge the distance between our personal decision-making and social influences.

9

Ideological Presumptions

Ideological thinking is both unfashionable and unavoidable. Ideology, in a useful definition supplied by Julius Gould, is "a pattern of beliefs and concepts (both factual and normative) which purport to explain complex social phenomena with a view to directing and simplifying sociopolitical choices facing individuals and groups."[1] In a complex way, ideology combines values and beliefs about the empirical world. The tendency of ideological consciousness is to treat particular forms of social organization as ideal, whether these are past, present, or only potential.[2]

Much Christian thinking (particularly beginning with Karl Barth) has been critical of this kind of thinking for reasons that have already been outlined in chapter 3. God is understood to transcend such human-centered thinking. God is revealed in the event of Jesus Christ, not through ideological thinking. The idealisms of nineteenth-century theology and even of the Social Gospel movement came to be regarded as idolatrous or as a form of salvation by works. Humanity, in Christ, came to be seen as liberated from a "sacralized" culture (e.g., Gogarten, Bonhoeffer).

This theological tendency has been reinforced greatly by revulsion against the use of Christianity to justify political and economic interests of privileged classes in Western society. In the United States, Reinhold Niebuhr led the way in merciless exposure of the economic, racial, and national interests masked by Christian ideological thinking. In recent years such ideological criticism has been represented powerfully by the various forms of liberation theology. The latter have shown how captive Christianity has been to dominant racial and economic interests and to the power of men over women. In many ways the defining agenda of liberation theology has been to recover the gospel from its captivity to such vested social interests. And while, through its utopian vision, liberation theology has done its share of ideological thinking, it is only fair to say that the dominant thrust of those currents of thought has been more the liberation itself than the projecting of alternative social conceptions. In a typical liberation theology motif, static conceptions of social organization are subordinated to the "praxis" whereby liberation movements continue to learn new things about themselves and about future possibilities through their engagement in the struggle.[3] To the extent that liberation theology has been influenced by Marxism, the criticism of Christian "ideological taint" is all the more pronounced. A fundamental stock-in-trade of Marxist analysis has been the exposure of all religion as justification of class oppression and psychological consolation for those who have been dehumanized by that oppression. Not surprisingly, some of the most astute theological reflection on the idolatries and distortions of previous Christian commitments to ideology have come from Eastern European Christian thinkers who have interacted with Marxists. In particular, they have scored the inherited pretensions of "Christendom," with its false triumphalism and churchly privileges masking decadence and oppression.[4]

Such criticisms need to be taken seriously. And yet the problem of overall perspective remains. Is it possible to translate fundamental Christian beliefs and values into ideological forms without idolatry and without those forms becoming pretexts for new social oppression? And behind that there lies the question of our overall attitude toward the forms and structures of human civilization as a whole.

The Christian and Civilization

The question is unavoidable if we truly believe that Christians are called upon to take responsibility for historical decision-making. For when we accept moral responsibility for actual events we can scarcely evade the broader responsibility for the context in which those events occur. And that leads, inevitably, to responsibility for how that context will be shaped by the things we do or leave undone.

Of course, Christians haven't always handled that responsibility very well. Sometimes we have yielded to romantic visions of a "Christian civilization" that conceal the darker side of real history. Consider, for instance, the incredible claim of Christopher Dawson:

> A Christian civilization is certainly not a perfect civilization, but it is a civilization that accepts the Christian way of life as normal and frames its institutions as the organs of a Christian order. Such a civilization actually existed for a thousand years, more or less. It was a living and growing organism—a great *tree of culture* which bore rich fruit in its season.[5]

Granting some element of truth in that picture, does it do justice to the oppression of heretics and Jews, the self-righteousness of the Crusades, the hierarchical rigidity of society, the sexist subordination of women, the oppression of peasants, or the general sluggishness of economic and cultural life? The principal objection to such stated and implied admiration for Christian civilization is that it underestimates the corruption occurring to the living center of faith when it becomes the basis for conscious efforts to manage civilization. It is, at bottom, a question of power. The views of a Dawson must be placed in a more pessimistic perspective when we see what happened to people who refused to organize their lives on the basis of Christian symbols and goals in such a "Christian civilization." The reverse side of their suffering was the external prosperity enjoyed by those who accepted Christianity because it was more comfortable to do so. To the non-Christian and to the Christian dissenter, Christian civilization is idolatry and arrogance. It is a world of alienating power.

But then, in the reaction against the pretensions and oppressions of "Christian civilization," have we come any closer to the truth? A dominant view today, which strangely shapes the perceptions of many Christian sectarians, Barthians, pacifists, and revolutionaries alike, is that the attempt to give a Christian shape to Roman civilization was precisely the time when the early church bit the apple and fell from grace. The church, thinking it had converted Constantine and through him the rest of Roman civilization, woke up centuries later to discover that the church had itself been converted—away from the gospel—to an official civil religion based upon power interests and idolatries.

Part of the problem is the fact that every civilization elaborates a system of rewards and punishments (incentives and disincentives) to govern behavior. It is one thing for Christians to bear witness to the intrinsic good of God's intended kingdom and hope that, by one's words and examples, others will be encouraged to live by these same positive values. But it is quite another thing when we begin to discover that in the actual shape of society there are a thousand points at which the structure of things depends on more selfish rewards and punishments.

This formed the heart of Søren Kierkegaard's "attack upon Christendom." Christendom had made the affirmation of Christianity the most profitable form of behavior. The clarity of the gospel had therefore become hopelessly compromised by the numbers of Christians who weren't really Christians at all. Christendom certainly rewarded being a Christian—and the reward was not confined to the intrinsic values promised in the gospel. Those who have thought seriously about the implications of the gospel have always had to recognize this. Walter Rauschenbusch certainly implied something about use of selfish incentives for good ends in his famous definition of a "Christianized" social order. Whereas the present social order tends to "make good men do bad things," Rauschenbusch held that the Christianized social order will be one that "makes bad men do good things."[6] External incentives are implied by the word "make," and it is as interesting to note that good people can be "made" to do bad things as it is to observe that a better social order will "make" bad people do what they otherwise would prefer *not* to do.

To seek a "Christian" society or civilization is not to avoid external forms of motivation, it is simply to redirect them in the service of what are considered to be "Christian" ends. But by tempting people through use of external rewards we may undermine what must, for the Christian, be the only real incentives.

Accordingly, as we project our ideologies and utopias, we confront what could be called the dilemma of Christian civilization: Any supposedly Christian civilization will create social, economic, and cultural rewards for being "Christian"—and thus, paradoxically, where Christianity prospers most and thus brings greatest prosperity to its adherents and leaders, one can least know whether people are Christian out of pure faith and devotion or for the sake of those personal advantages.

But can we really avoid this dilemma through sectarian withdrawal into some new (or old) form of moral absolutism and a disavowal of responsibility for the course and character of civilization? We must remind ourselves that the dilemma of civilization is not limited to those who seek objectives for the whole of society or to those who belong to social establishments of various kinds. Even the most radical, revolutionary, or sectarian movement—including those most disdainful of the creature comforts and vanities of "the establishment"—rewards the faithful with psychic compensations and ego enhancements not intrinsic to the movement's objectives as such. How can one *know* that the revolutionary leader is motivated more by the cause than by the gratifications involved in leadership? How can we be sure that the leader of the sectarian movement or the pacifist is not activated by the prestige gained within the movement? In the case of the writers of radical or sectarian or pacifist literature, it is even possible in some cases that the gratifications and vanities of publication may be more important than the cause. These are hard words, and this is, of course, a sword by which we can all be slain. But that is exactly the point. All of society, including the "new community" to be created by faithful Christians, is subject to the dilemma of civilization because every community, new or old, has quite worldly rewards and punishments to distribute. The New Testament church is in no sense an exception, as the book of Acts and most of the epistles make clear.

These words are not written in cynicism, because God's power of grace—the power of resurrection—is also at work. But it is pure sectarian nonsense to hold that this power of grace is at work in some altogether novel, categorically different way in the management of the new community and in the movement of Christians than it is in the life of society at large.[7] The church is surely called to be a fellowship of those whose devotion to God is clearer, more radiant. When it is true to its calling, it understands, as no other community can understand, that God's gift of grace transforms all of life. But that does not mean that the church will be able to do something with its own life that is utterly different from what Christians can do in society—both because there are recurrent possibilities of evil in the management of the church and because there are recurrent possibilities of good in the management of society.

The problem posed by the critics of "Christian civilization"—how to maintain the relevance of the gospel to society without losing the gospel—can better be treated through use of presumptions, applied now on the level of our broader visions, dreams, and ideologies. The problem really is *not* whether or not Christian faith can tolerate attempts to direct the course of social history. Such attempts are almost inevitable. Nor is it whether or not Christian faith should countenance the use of extrinsic forms of motivation. That truly *is* inevitable, even when we seek to avoid it within the life of the church itself. Rather, it is in the faithfulness with which we do this planning. The question must always be, Which ideological conceptions really do manifest faithfulness to God, and how can we serve those conceptions more effectively? Which ideologies are most Christian and how can we best learn from the experience of Christians who have supported the wrong kinds of models of civilization? Those models which, to the best of our faithful cooperative thinking, do exemplify obedience to God's kingdom must then receive presumptive weight in guiding our concrete judgments and decisions.

Two Tests of "Christian" Civilization

The four positive and two negative presumptions dealt with in chapters 5 and 6 can be taken to represent decisive elements in Christian thinking about civilization. The positive presumptions reflect the purposes while the negative (and polar) presumptions define limits in our ideological thinking. In a moment I wish to illustrate how these presumptions can enter into our thinking about these matters and how ideologies and utopian constructs can themselves establish the more inclusive presumptions to guide our judgments.

But in our consideration of Christians and civilization to this point, we have observed the two basic flaws in allegedly "Christian" civilization (or "Christendom") that have most concerned its modern critics. The first of these was the pretension, bordering on idolatry, with which Christian symbols and institutions were thrust upon non-Christians. This has always been a sin against the nonbeliever, but it is all the more evident during the present highly pluralistic age. The second was the use of sub-Christian incentives, including violence, to control people and to shape their future. In any discussion of the possibility of a more Christian civilization, therefore, we might as well begin by saying that the relative avoidance of such things is an important test of such a civilization.

Christians play interesting games with the term "pluralism." Increasingly we are all for it. But we also assume that to make a more "Christian" society somehow must entail further sinning against pluralism. Why should this be so? If a Christian really believes that society *ought* to be pluralistic, then he or she either regards pluralism as a necessary social implication from Christian faith (or at least compatible with it), or the pluralism is held in spite of one's Christianity. Can we not stipulate that a truly Christian society is fully hospitable to the freedom of non-Christian points of view? Christians ought not to seek to create a civilization in any sense that would prematurely vitiate the claims made by non-Christian, un-Christian, and anti-Christian views. We ought not to seek a new triumphalism, enforcing Christian ascendancy over all other perspectives. Indeed, the capacity to accommodate the social interests and creativities of every non-Christian person or group must stand as a criterion of a truly Christian civilization. The old Christendom was based on exclusive (and sometimes idolatrous) claims for Christian symbols and practices. But it is quite another thing to seek to ground culture in a Christian perspective which *in principle* welcomes the contributions of all the pluralisms of the modern world while retaining *in principle* theological grounds for criticizing them on their merits.

The positive principle of Christian theology is at once affirmative of the goodness of being, of the ultimate value in God of existence, and of the potential of finding an authentic witness to God in any or all other faiths. In one sense it may appear narrow by seeking to lead persons into basing their lives and social structures in Christian faith. Nevertheless, it recognizes that any such grounding which prematurely violates the witness of any other faith is contrary to Christian faith itself. The reason for this is partly in the Christian recognition of God's capacity to speak a creative new word (or a needed word of judgment) through those who seem most alienated from the community of faith. A Christian approach to social pluralism has its theological roots in the belief that there is no human being whose life exists outside the boundaries of God's sovereign activity. Any "Christian civilization" which disregards this is more likely to be offensive to the gospel than supportive of it; that point has been made in countless ways by the critics of Christendom. The presumption ought to be *against,* not for, the restriction of non-Christian viewpoints and activities in a Christian society. The old "thesis-antithesis" view of religious liberty, happily in decline these days, should be reversed. Rather than accepting religious liberty only when it can be shown conclusively that the true faith and practice cannot be enforced upon everybody, we ought to insist upon religious liberty unless it has to be limited for absolutely overriding social considerations.

Similar response could be made to the question of whether the civilization-building and maintaining vocation necessarily entails an unacceptable component of use of sub-Christian incentives, including violence. We have already sought to establish that it is an illusion to suppose one can avoid the problem by avoiding the responsibility. Nevertheless, an important test of a Christian approach to civilization would be whether such forms of non-Christian incentive are always made to bear the burden of proof. The internal governance of sectarian communities may provide us with some helpful models for the wider society, although even in such communities there may sometimes be too much use of coercive practices (such as shunning) in social control. The burden of proof, in a Christian society, should always be against violence and coercion and the organization of economic and social incentives in such a way that social effectiveness depends on people doing what needs to be done for the wrong reasons. Human sinfulness doubtless means that some use of wrong incentives will prove necessary within every group, but as we make judgments affecting the shape of civilization it should be with a presumption against it. We should also go further in reminding ourselves that the fact that wrong incentives can exert such power often means that large numbers of people are given insufficient opportunity to experience human fulfillment. Use of external incentives should be limited, where possible, to those things which lead people toward, not away from, real human fulfillment.

The question of whether a civilization substantially meeting such tests should be called "Christian" is then probably a semantic issue of no great importance. Certainly no civilization will be a perfect manifestation of the gospel, but any can be much more so or much less so. Christians and their churches have a vocation to shape their judgments in accord with the more perfect and away from the less.

Ideological Formulations

It is beyond the scope of this book to take up the wide variety of possible Christian ideological formulations definitively. Throughout, we have had to use such materials only illustratively. The meaning of our discussion of Christian ideological formulation should now be tested, however, with reference to more concrete examples of possible ideological thinking. I wish to consider here, though only briefly and suggestively, the ideological problems posed by family, political, and economic life. In each of these broad areas, we confront immense difficulties if we are forced (or feel forced) to make judgments as Christians without the benefit of an overall normative conception—an "ideal model"—of what social life involves and how it should be structured if God's will were truly to be done on earth.

Marriage and Family Life

Moral decision-making in the context of the most basic of human relationships has probably always had its difficulties, but earlier generations may have been able to approach those difficulties with more settled moral assumptions. Marriage was understood to be a monogamous lifelong commitment between a woman and a man. Sexual intercourse was to be restricted to marriage. Children were to be welcomed into the family and cared for, educated, and disciplined until the age of emancipation. While premarital and extramarital sexual relationships, divorce, spouse abuse, and child abuse were by no means unheard of, they were essentially contrary to the moral code. In earlier generations, male dominance was generally taken for granted and symbolized, in the typical wedding ceremony, by the bride's promise to "obey" the groom.

If these institutions and assumptions were relatively stable in previous generations, they clearly are no longer. Increasingly, Christians are having to think through decisions related to human sexual relationship, marriage, and family life as though such decisions were isolated events. The very difficulty of such moral decision-making demonstrates rather dramatically how crucial it is to have ideological presumptions on the basis of which to guide our thinking. What guidance can Christian ethics offer?

We have already noted, in relation to the presumption for the goodness of created existence, that Christians cannot view the gift of sexuality as essentially evil. The other positive presumptions clearly rule out sexist assumptions about male superiority, while also emphasizing the importance of mutual respect and caring. The presumption concerning sin suggests the importance of marriage and family institutions in protecting intimate human relationships from abuse. Do these presumptions and other theological entry points support any particular ideological model concerning marriage and family life?

The development of dependable contraceptive techniques and the widespread practice of abortion have apparently removed those natural law supports for monogamous marriage that were based primarily on the risk of childbearing. If free sex is unlikely to result in pregnancy, the risk of pregnancy is no longer a persuasive reason for restricting sexual intercourse to the marital relationship. It remains that free sex, if detached from a caring relationship, tends to be cheapened. But does that matter? Is there anything about sex that marks it off as different from other human activities? Physically the most intimate form of human interacting, sexual intercourse is also a point of very great vulnerability. To express oneself physically in that way and then be treated with disregard or contempt is deeply humiliating.

I am not sure I would argue, on the basis of physical fact alone, that any particular form of sexual expression is necessarily humiliating. It is quite possible that some people have, in fact, received considerable human fulfillment and enhancement of self-esteem on the basis of short, never-to-be-repeated sexual encounters.

And yet, is there not profound moral insight in the linking of covenantal faithfulness—seen in theological terms as an expression of grace—with the intimacies of human sexual intercourse? The line in the traditional Christian wedding ritual about the marriage of husband and wife as reflecting the relationship between Christ and his church may seem a trifle obscure—and it certainly must not be taken as an analogy in which husband stands for Christ and wife for the church! But if it is understood that Christ is, for the church, the enduring channel of absolutely dependable grace, in spite of the church's imperfection, then the symbolism has great interpretative power. To be in a marital relationship in which one is fully known, in all one's imperfections and vulnerabilities, and still to be loved with absolute dependability, is deeply humanizing. God's grace clearly is not limited to the marital relationship, and there are enduring marriages that are very far from being gracious. Still, is there not powerful theological support for this kind of institutionalizing of the most intimate human relationships with a dependable mutual covenant? To be able to believe that the love of this other is something I can count on in spite of everything else that might happen is a human embodiment of that grace we know through Christ.

When children are added to the picture the point is even clearer, for their lives are even more vulnerable, even more in need of that dependable caring, through thick and thin, in spite of everything. It is very difficult for children who lack this kind of dependable nurturing love to be able to grow morally themselves. To love, we must first be loved. To grow, we must feel that we are deeply accepted in spite of our imperfections. Only then can we venture to live fully and to learn from our inevitable further mistakes.

In light of the human vulnerabilities in sexual relationships and childhood, it should not be surprising that every known society has found ways—both legal and cultural—of stabilizing these relationships through dependable institutions. Questions inevitably follow at the margins where the ideal form of institution may be in dispute and where even the most ideal forms of marriage and family institution do not appear to work well in particular instances.

Some might continue to argue, for instance, that since polygamy seems to work reasonably well in some cultures, it should not be challenged. But while polygamy can be a very stable family structure—and not necessarily injurious to children—it does convey the unmistakable message of the inferiority of women to men and of poor people to rich people, since it is usually a matter of one man to two or more women, and the arrangements are generally limited to those men who can afford to support more than one wife. It is hard to visualize relationships of deep mutual respect and caring in polygamous institutions, even though affection and stability can certainly be present. Still, the relative stability and humanness of polygamous families in cultures allowing them should be reason enough not to seek to disrupt existing family units, as some Christian church groups have occasionally sought to do.

Others might point out, with much empirical evidence in support, that there are large numbers of deeply troubled monogamous family units. Sometimes it clearly seems best for all the persons involved for the families to be dissolved. If the intimacies and commitments of monogamous marriage and family life can be deeply humanizing, that very intimacy and commitment can be deeply destructive where some family members are incorrigibly exploitative and abusive of others. On balance, the humanizing tendencies may greatly outweigh the exploitative and abusive—as I believe they do. But moral judgment must still encompass the problem situations.

Moreover, one cannot forget—in any society—the substantial numbers of people who never marry. What provision, if any, needs to be made for their sexual outlet? And what, specifically, should be our moral assessment of the phenomenon of homosexuality?

These further questions—and one could add many more to the list—are not sufficient reason to abandon an ideological presumption in favor of the monogamous family based on mutual lifelong commitment by the spouses. But such questions do remind us that this kind of ideological view should exist as a moral presumption and not as a universal prescription.

Seen in that light, such a presumption provides a framework for considering moral exceptions. In the case of divorce, for instance, the presumption would be strongly against it. Law and custom should discourage it. But provision should also be made for those exceptional circumstances where a marriage has become more destructive than humanizing. Would it not be helpful for the church to work at defining the criteria under which it considers divorce to be advisable, as it has done in the case of just-war criteria?

The presumption must be against premarital and extramarital sexual relationships. What would count here as exceptions to be approved? If such a question is asked only in a moralistic spirit, the point may easily be forgotten that the only reason for the presumption, in the first place, is that it protects our humanness. The general supposition of sexual relationships outside the marriage covenant is that the partners are, for whatever reason, unwilling to make that commitment analogous to grace. Is it necessarily destructive to engage in sexual acts outside of such a commitment? Perhaps not *necessarily*. But in the case of premarital sex the question may always be raised as to why the partners are unwilling to make that deeper commitment to each other and what their unwillingness to do so says about the quality of their love. In the case of extramarital sex the same question can be raised, plus the question of what this will mean in its effect on the covenant that has presumably been violated. The complexities and ambiguities of human existence may occasionally pose situations where the deeper, more humanizing expression of love is provided by sexual activity in a nonmarital setting, but the burden of proof should remain against it. Much experimentation on such matters occurs in Western societies today, some of it reminiscent of Bertrand Russell's proposal in the 1920s for "trial marriages." The effects of the experimentation will lead either to greater looseness respecting sexual activity or to reaffirmation of the committed, monogamous pattern of married life—and I rather expect to see more of the latter than the former.

What about homosexuality, a subject that has been particularly troubling to church groups in recent years? There appears to be some evidence that a certain small percentage of the population is, for physiological reasons, sexually ambiguous—with ambiguous sexual organs or with organs not corresponding to glandular makeup. Where, for clearly physiological reasons, persons are sexually attracted to persons of the same gender (or who are at least defined by society as being of the same gender), a case could surely be made that such persons should not be discouraged from pursuing what is for them an altogether "natural" outlet.[8] Insofar as homosexuality can be shown to be an effect of distorted relationships in childhood—such as with one or the other of one's parents—that sexual orientation may be an expression of psychological pathologies needing to be worked through.

In any event, the expression of homosexuality, if not considered to be in itself an expression of pathology, will still be most humanizing if grounded in stable, loving, and faithful relationship.

These few illustrations suggest how monogamous marriage and family life can serve as an ideological presumption. While human sexuality is both socially and psychologically complex, the attempt to gain clarity about our presumptions in this way may be helpful in sorting out different kinds of moral judgments.

Political Presumptions

In the most general sense, political ideology is concerned with the organization of social decision-making at the level of the state. In principle, it entails the activity of everybody within the limits of the state, and in this sense the state can itself best be described as society acting as a whole. Most political theorists would add to this that the state functions through law and that it is invested with the ultimate powers of coercion.[9] The political order potentially affects all aspects of human existence. Not surprisingly, the power to determine the policies of the political order is vigorously contested.[10] Political ideologies are mainly concerned with the determination of how that power should be allocated and exercised.

Some political ideologies are, on the face of it, in conflict with Christian faith. The difficulties with traditional monarchy were noted as early as the Old Testament in the dire predictions by Samuel, the last of the premonarchical Hebrew judges, who warned of tyrannies and injustices and pointed out that the people would be treated like slaves if they should create a monarchy for themselves (1 Sam. 8:10–18). Even under the most benevolent of monarchies, there is a sense in which that is still true. Even under the best monarchs the paternalism inherent in that kind of political system cannot accord proper respect to the God-given possibilities in all human beings. Moreover, such a system overlooks the human limits and sinfulness of every monarch, even the best of them. Traditional monarchy violates Christian understandings of mutuality by creating nearly insuperable class and caste barriers to normal human interaction. Hereditary monarchies and aristocracies tend to heighten this problem, of course.

Fascism is even more alien to Christian understanding, even though it often appears disguised in the clothing of populist egalitarianism.[11] Monarchy can at least be respectful of individual rights; fascism swallows up the personhood of its subjects into the absoluteness of the state. As Mussolini stated it, "Fascism conceives of the State as an absolute, in comparison with which all individuals or groups are relative, only to be conceived of in their relation to the State."[12] The glorification of power in fascism frequently reflects deep social anxieties and the fear of disorder, but it is profoundly idolatrous in its theological implications. The value of the individual as a child of God is transformed into mere utility to the state. Human freedom is real only insofar as its expression coincides with the will of the state or insofar as it is irrelevant to the state. Life becomes *public* in the most awful sense. In the polarity individual/social, the individual is lost and therefore the social character is perverted. Fascism also tends to be a chauvinistic creed, to disdain peace, to glorify aggressive warfare against "weak" and "inferior" peoples. In its most virulent Nazi form it was racist. In a word, fascist ideologies run counter to virtually all of the positive, negative, and polar presumptions discussed in this book.

Political anarchism has attracted numerous followers in various forms over the past two centuries. Essentially, it is the view that political power is itself the root expression of evil and should be abolished altogether. Typically, anarchism presupposes a highly optimistic theory of human nature. As we saw in chapter 6, Tolstoyan anarchism regards coercive governmental institutions as the source of evil; once the coercive structures have been abolished, human goodness and creativity will be free to blossom forth spontaneously. But by far the most important form of political anarchism is classical Marxist communism, which views the "withering away of the state" as a scientifically predictable outcome of a successful socialist revolution. In the Marxist form, political power is understood to be an expression of class exploitation and class conflict. In the classless society that will follow the revolution, there will be no need for the coercive state, only for politically neutral institutions of economic administration. Although the point is not often enough understood, Marxian anarchism also rests upon the assumption of the nearly flawless goodness of human nature when it is not alienated by exploitation. Communism, in its political ideology, is often mistaken for a fascist-type totalitarianism primarily because its conception of the state during the period of revolutionary struggle and consolidation makes similar demands upon people and involves similar disregard for individual human rights. Ultimately, however, it is anarchist.

The problem with anarchism in its various forms lies in its understanding of human nature. Its conception is contrary to Christian insight into the sinful aspect of human nature, but it also appears to deny even human freedom to sin in the ultimate society. As many commentators have noted, these ultimate expectations also lead to a blind spot concerning methods to be employed by the party and state during the interval leading up to the classless or anarchist society.[13]

These political ideologies come in countless forms and variations. Our purpose is not to catalog them but to illustrate how ideological tendencies can in themselves be contrary to Christian faith. Logically, what this means is that a Christian cannot organize his or her political thinking on the basis of such ideologies and will tend to place the burden of proof against particular policies that are an outgrowth of one of these ways of thinking. Christians often have to live and work in situations dominated by such ideological tendencies. But their own point of view, as Christians, must be in serious tension with them.

Christian political thinking can relate much more positively to some forms of democratic ideology. Let it be noted with care that when speaking of democratic ideology as being a suitable framework for Christian thinking, I have in mind the political tradition and not laissez-faire economics. Moreover, we are discussing ideal models and not the current institutional practices of any particular country, such as the United States. With these qualifications, we can cite four interlocking principles of democratic ideology: the concept of popular sovereignty, equality before the law, majority rule, and guaranteed civil rights and liberties. Each of these, if properly understood, accords well with Christian faith.

The idea of popular sovereignty has ancient non-Christian roots, principally in Stoicism and in Greek experience with the city-state. The Stoic political philosophers held that the ultimate location of political power is in the people of the civil community, not in their rulers. The basic concept had significance in medieval political thought and emerged in the modern world through such philosophers as Hobbes, Locke, and Rousseau, each of whom expressed it uniquely.

Some Christian social philosophers, such as Jacques Maritain, have been reluctant to speak of popular sovereignty—not because of antidemocratic attitudes but because they consider any human claim of sovereignty to be pretension. Only God is ultimately sovereign.[14] From a theological standpoint this is a point well taken. But it only raises in different form the question of the human channels through which God's political sovereignty can best be exercised. Christians clearly do hold political power to be responsible to a transcendent frame of reference. But the question is, What human beings have this responsibility?

Very strong theological reasons exist for considering the old classical idea of popular sovereignty to be more compatible with Christian faith than any alternative. Only popular sovereignty recognizes, in political terms, the ultimate responsibility that every person has before God. Every other conception of political sovereignty implies that some self-designating persons stand between all others and God. The term "self-designating" must be used here, since those who participate in designating the ruler have a share in sovereignty. The maximum case for "divine right of kings," such as that of James I of England ("The state of monarchy is the supremest thing upon earth: for kings are not only God's lieutenants upon earth, and sit upon God's throne, but even by God himself they are called Gods"[15]), emphasizes that the king's powers are directly from God and that the king is responsible only to God for their exercise. Similar claims have been made for theocracies, oligarchies, and revolutionary elites. But all such political ideologies presuppose theologically unacceptable distinctions between those persons who have this a priori political relationship to God (or to "truth") and those who do not.

Popular sovereignty, on the other hand, means that all are called to have this relationship of accountability to God—and therefore also to one another. The idea was well formulated by the World Council of Churches' definition of a "responsible society" as one "where those who hold political authority or economic power are responsible for its exercise to God and the people whose welfare is affected by it."[16] Here responsibility to God is joined with responsibility to the people, and it is implicitly recognized that no ruling elite can consider itself solely responsible to God or its own conception of justice or truth or human well-being.

The other three principles of democratic ideology can be described as corollaries of popular sovereignty. Equality before the law is clearly implied by the conception of each person as "king." Since political authority is ultimately derived, on the human level, from the whole body politic, all stand equally in relationship to the law. Equality before the law must also be seen as a necessary political application of the presumption of equality, discussed in theological terms in chapter 5. Majority rule also follows from this: If all are equal but unanimity of judgment on policy questions is not attainable, then the larger number of equal people should enjoy the presumption over the smaller number. This does not mean that the larger number is necessarily right, but only that there is a greater probability of rightness attached to the views of the majority than to those of any given minority.

Some have concluded that democratic ideology stops here. But if it does, nothing is to prevent a majority from running roughshod over a minority.

The guarantee of civil rights and liberties for all, whether in a majority or a minority, is also presumed by democratic ideology. There are some things that a majority can never do as an expression of democratic rule. It can never violate the right of minority persons to exist, to be free to dissent from policies established by the majority, and to be free to express themselves in the marketplace of ideas.

Overall, the case for political democracy is impressive enough to make this ideological model the presumptive point of reference. But such a claim is not undisputed. In the political ferment of recent decades, democratic ideology has sometimes been treated as a façade for other (generally economic) interests and has often been dismissed as powerless to serve the interests of real justice. Without question, democratic ideology sometimes has been used as a smokescreen for selfish power interests. And without question, it has often been impotent in the face of such interests.

But as an ideological presumption, democracy is part of the *definition* of justice. Not every country calling itself "democratic" (and which does not?) truly is. The democratic ideology stands in judgment over political practices falling short of that ideal, wherever they may be. As we use this ideological presumption in guiding our judgments in the political order, we insist that deviations from it bear the burden of proof. Conceivably, here and there, now and then, it is necessary for an elite of some kind to govern without formal accountability to the whole citizenry. And conceivably, from time to time, it is necessary to suspend civil rights and liberties in order to cope with a critical emergency (such as that faced by Abraham Lincoln at the outset of the U.S. Civil War). But the burden of proof should weigh heavily against such violations of the democratic norm.

Similarly, revolutionary movements, which are not in themselves democratically organized, must bear the burden of proof that their present methods are necessary for the sake of a future democratic possibility. It can never be assumed that the possibility will automatically be fulfilled unless there is already a deep commitment to it.

In the United States, much judicial attention has been given to the meaning and limitations to be placed upon items in the Bill of Rights. Are freedom of speech and press and religion to be considered absolutes, and, if so, how far do they extend? If they are not absolutes, what can justify limitations placed upon them? In the main, the courts have given the rights great presumptive weight without treating them quite as absolutes. Late-twentieth-century life presents us with puzzling dilemmas, including exploitative religious groups, pornographic excesses degrading to public values, criminals taking advantage of every possible legal loophole, governmental harassment of opposition political groups in the name of law enforcement, and journalists' claim of a moral responsibility to protect their sources from court subpoenas. It is often easy to forget that the protection of the rights of all requires protection of the rights of the unpopular or the questionable. A serious presumption in favor of civil rights and liberties helps us guard against the tendency to disregard the rights of those groups or individuals for whom we lack sympathy. On the other hand, these rights and other aspects of democracy should be held as presumptions, not as absolutes.

Economic Presumptions

Economic ideologies are concerned with the systems of production and the distribution of scarce values. In the main, economic life involves material needs and wants, although some scarce values (such as theatrical entertainment and copyrights) are not exactly material. On the other hand, some material things such as air and sunlight are usually plentiful enough not to be described as "scarce" values in the economic sense. (Although, to be sure, there may be real costs in purifying the air or traveling to climes where we can better enjoy the sun!)

Much social controversy over the past two hundred years has involved the mutually exclusive claims of competing economic ideologies, of which there have been a bewildering number. One recalls the traditionalist defenses of slavery and feudalism, mercantilism, the emergence of private enterprise and free-market capitalism, and the various reformist and revolutionary kinds of socialism, including nineteenth-century utopias, syndicalism, the single tax movement, Fabianism, and Marxism. Such economic ideologies embody an organizing conception of the facts of economic life and a more or less clear attitude toward the moral values these ideologies purport to protect or advance. Strong vestiges of traditionalist economic organization remain in the modern world, with feudalism and even slavery still existing here and there. When put in ideological form, such traditionalist economic systems tend to be paternalistic and to place great emphasis on fixed and inherited social stations. Invariably they are offensive to conceptions of equality. Their models of mutuality are paternalistic, involving the mutual "loyalties" of authority and subject. Often they are highly restrictive of the freedom and opportunity of the subject classes. While some of the language of the New Testament can be used to defend some of this, these are the points in New Testament teaching that seem most bound to the technological and cultural situation of an age now past. Traditionalist economic ideology, the defense of the ancien régime, is now everywhere very much on the defensive.

The great watershed in twentieth-century economic ideology still lies between laissez-faire capitalism and socialism. Few people are either all for one or all for the other. But these two ideological frameworks represent the assumptions people tend to accept and on the basis of which actual decisions are made.

According to laissez-faire ideology, the economic role of government should be restricted to the protection of property and the adoption of regulations guaranteeing fair competition.[17] Economic enterprise fundamentally is and should remain private. Individuals should be free to invent, produce, invest, buy, and sell in a free market without interference. Competition among those who produce and sell will assure maximum efficiency in both production and distribution because buyers will select the best products and services at the lowest prices. People will be motivated to work hard and to produce creatively because they will themselves benefit from this productivity. In a free-enterprise economic system, as Adam Smith remarked, each person's vigorous pursuit of his own self-interest will, "by an invisible hand," redound to the greater good for all—because only by producing and selling goods and services needed and wanted by others under favorable terms will each person be able to serve his or her own self-interest. Under free-enterprise capitalism everybody who is willing to work will find it possible to earn a livelihood, and humankind will be assured of continuing material progress and prosperity. So the ideology holds.

In its Western ideological form, laissez-faire capitalism has been supported by what is loosely termed the "Protestant ethic," an individualistic work ethic emphasizing work (in relation to one's calling) and thrift (in relation to "stewardship"). It was summarized by John Wesley's "Gain all you can. Save all you can. Give all you can." But in its economic ideological form, "give all you can" is to be replaced by "accumulate all you can"—it being understood that accumulation is not idle wealth but the development of capital enterprise for the production of still further wealth. Not that giving is not to be encouraged. The Protestant ethic undergirded a strong drive toward philanthropy. Indeed, by their acquisition of wealth, some people were held to have demonstrated their greater capacity to determine which institutions of culture and charity are most deserving of philanthropy. But the hallmark of the Protestant ethic is its emphasis upon work and its judgment that, economically speaking, we tend to get what we deserve, whether wealth or poverty.[18]

In assessing the influence of this laissez-faire ideology we should be reminded again that the influence persists despite the fact that no present-day economy is a pure example of its logic.[19] To be consequential, an ideology need only shape the consciousness and with it the judgments of people who believe in it. American business and labor interests may both compromise away the purity of laissez-faire capitalism when their concrete interests are at stake, but both have often enough demonstrated mental captivity to the ideology itself.

But does laissez-faire capitalism provide an adequate ideological presumption to guide Christian economic thinking? Its economic advantages center around its incentives to economic inventiveness and productivity, its maintaining of a system of checks and balances through competition, its use of market forces for regulation of prices and wages, its efficiency in channeling productive forces in response to actual demand rather than abstract planning, and its consequent encouragement of efficiencies in production and marketing of goods and services. Its practical disadvantages center around its vulnerability to periods of inflation and recession, with consequent unemployment and poverty, and its overemphasis on production for personal consumption and underemphasis on production for the community as a whole.[20]

But we may be even more interested, from a theological standpoint, in the values conveyed by laissez-faire capitalism and the Protestant ethic. Whatever one may say about its efficiencies, concerning which the evidence is mixed, the ideology comes close to glorifying greed and the naked pursuit of self-interest. Far from decrying competitive attitudes and social inequalities as regrettable necessities if we are to have enough productive drive and efficiency to meet human need, the laissez-faire ideology treats these as positive goods. It is difficult to avoid the conclusion that this enhancement of acquisitiveness—which can justly be termed "principled selfishness"—is theologically idolatrous as well as socially divisive. Taken as a whole, the result seems clearly unsuitable as an ideological presumption for Christians. Where it has seriously influenced the moral thinking of people, this ideology has made them apologetic about measures to meet human need directly and complacent about gross excesses of self-seeking.

The other main contemporary economic ideology is socialism in its now numerous variations. Joseph A. Schumpeter's definition of socialism is satisfactory up to a point. He speaks of it as "that organization of society in which the means of production are controlled, and the decisions on how and what to produce and on who is to get what, are made by public authority instead of by privately owned and privately managed firms."[21] As an ideology, socialism also provides both practical and ethical rationales. The main point is that economic power is formally responsible to the whole of society, through the state, and not simply to those who hold it as private wealth. Accordingly, economic decisions are much more likely to be made in such a way as directly to benefit everybody and not simply those who own the instruments of production. Marx's theory of industrial crisis makes this point in moral terms, if not in the scientific sense he imagined. According to Marx, capitalistic economic decisions will always be made for the benefit of investors, even if the decisions that have to be made lead straight into public economic disaster. Under socialism, decisions can at least be based on social, not private, objectives. There is no need for the scandal of unused plant capacity and stockpiles of products and food rotting because of the lack of private purchasing power. There are not the same obstacles to full production and full employment, since nobody has to make a private profit for production to occur. Inequalities may exist in fact, but unlike capitalism there are no inequalities in principle. The incentives for planned obsolescence and for advertising that exaggerates materialism are removed.

In the abstract, the case for socialism seems indisputable. In actuality, there are also problems, of which Christians must take note. The most important is the problem of power. Who is to control economic power when it is a state monopoly? Private economic power centers are largely irresponsible, but at least there is some accountability to the market (diluted as that accountability may be by private monopoly conditions and saturation advertising). Where political and economic power are united, however, the latter will be no more responsible than the former. Socialism combined with any political system other than democracy will be no more responsible than the political system—a point that most of the Marxist socialist countries have demonstrated all too well. Even combined with democracy, socialism could tend toward the corruption of the political institutions by placing too much power in the hands of officeholders—power that could be used to perpetuate officials in office while generally contributing to corruption. Socialism, while meeting rather well the test of the positive moral presumptions, needs to be checked carefully in relation to the negative ones. Does it offer enough hedge against the human tendency to seize and use power selfishly?

The other main problem with socialism is that it may weaken individual initiative and diminish the responsiveness of the free market. While these points are sometimes offered as definitive objections to socialism, they may simply be points where socialism is undeveloped. In principle (that is, in the ideology), there is no reason why the market mechanism cannot be used or why individual initiative cannot be stimulated in a socialist economy. Even within the American civil service there have been instances of great initiative and creativity (such as in programs of the National Institutes of Health, the Public Health Service, and the U.S. Forest Service). Meanwhile, most of the socialist countries, including the Marxist ones, employ a market system of sorts without doing violence to their ideological purity—and economic reform movements in several of the socialist countries contemplate more radical departures in that direction.

From this brief discussion there may emerge the rudiments of an economic ideology that is more or less compatible with Christian faith. Its economic institutions would be responsible to government, whether directly "owned" and managed by government or not, and government would be responsible to the people. In the development of both governmental and economic institutions, care would be taken to keep too much power from becoming concentrated in a few hands. Economic initiative would be encouraged and rewarded, although a truly "humanized" society would be one in which the grateful recognition of service rendered would be sufficient reward. The presumption in the distribution of economic benefits would be for equality, although absolute equality would hardly be expected. Use of incentives creating inequalities would be kept to the minimum required by the general condition of human sinfulness and the needs of production.

Such ideological rudiments might conceivably be developed either under democratic socialism or welfare-state (or "social market") capitalism. In a system of welfare capitalism, business and industry are permitted to function more or less without restraint, but they are taxed heavily enough by government to finance generous welfare provisions for the whole society. Whether this continues to place too much emphasis on selfishness as an economic motive and whether it concentrates too much power in private hands are the key questions in the debate between this and out-and-out democratic socialism. Welfare capitalism acknowledges the responsibility of all economic endeavor to the whole community, but it continues to permit great inequality and large concentrations of potentially irresponsible economic power.

I have argued elsewhere that classical Marxist socialism is not a suitable ideology for Christian economic thinking, because of its neglect of democratic accountability, and that laissez-faire capitalism is also to be excluded because of its principled selfishness and materialism, as well as its practical defects.[22] In recent years, both capitalism and socialism have been challenged by the wastefulness and ecological irresponsibility of much modern technology. Polluted rivers and smoggy air can exist under either form of ideological sponsorship, and government presumably needs to require higher standards under either system. Laissez-faire capitalism probably has the greater blind spot on this point, however. It is a good deal easier for a private corporation to dump its refuse onto the public and regard it as a good bargain than for a publicly controlled enterprise to do so. The steady, predictable resistance to environmental control measures by private industries in the United States illustrates the point. But concern for ecology belongs in a Christian economic ideology as one of the givens, and it cannot be said that either socialism or social-welfare capitalism has made this a prominent enough concern.

The Use of Theology as Presumption

These ideological illustrations cannot be treated here in the detail they deserve. That is an important continuing task for Christian ethics and, indeed, for every responsible Christian. I have intended by their use to suggest how the basic presumptions of Christians can be translated into broader conceptions of what society ought to be. Such ideal models of social organization cannot usually be judged by their immediate practicality, although we should question the adequacy of any model that is impractical on its face. Ideological thinking helps us organize our moral judgments even when confronted by the elusiveness of our noblest conceptions of the good.

By accepting the presumptive validity of our ideal models of society, we can at least recognize a compromise when it is forced upon us. We can at least require deviations or exceptions to bear the burden of proof.

We must remind ourselves yet once again that no ideology is to be regarded as an ultimate in itself. All such ideal models gain their value from their adequacy in reflecting God's loving purposes for human existence. Since none of us is God, we cannot expect to have perfect models in our heads, much less in the actual world.

10

Being, Deciding, and Doing

There is a certain danger implicit in discussion of moral judgment. It is that we unconsciously assume an Olympian detachment from acting on the basis of our judgments. Analysis of our ideals and consideration of what ought to be done can easily become a spectator sport. We can easily assume that intellectual comprehension of issues properly discharges the office of Christian moral judgment. We can become like the ivory tower intellectuals of whom the Marxist philosopher Laszek Kolakowski once wrote, "Thus, the intellectual wants to reserve for himself the right of moral judgment of social reality without any responsibility for the course of social events."[1] Even among Christian ethicists and theologians the word "practical" sometimes carries a tone of condescension, despite the fact that if Christian faith is not permitted to organize our practical experience it is nothing at all. We can drift into the style of life attributed (perhaps unfairly) to the American socialist leader Norman Thomas:

> Norman Thomas was not regarded as dangerous. He preached Christian ethics in government in a perfectly respectable way. At no time did he appear to offer the possibility of putting these ideals into practice. Therefore, he was never hated the way Roosevelt was hated. He was never identified with an organization that seemed about to do anything practical. Here was the kind of Socialist that a decent Socialist was supposed to be—for whom romantic college professors could vote. He symbolized a conflicting ideal without creating a practical working institution which interfered with any of the ideals that Socialism contradicted.[2]

Christians have a responsibility to be not only wise judges but committed activists. We are *engaged* in life. Our engagement is shaped by our comprehension of what life, ultimately, is all about. But the engagement is not supplanted by the comprehension. Liberation theology has helped recover this sense of engagement by emphasizing that Christian life is a life of praxis.

The term is, to many, a bit too esoteric and, perhaps, a bit too suggestive of its Marxist roots. But the idea is exactly right: We learn by reflecting upon our doing, just as our doing is a reflection of our learning. Life is a constant rhythm of thought and action. One without the other leads to fundamental distortion of real life.

There is a similar danger when the entire focus of Christian ethics is upon Christian character and virtue. Clearly no comprehensive picture of Christian moral life is complete without that focus. But to *be* good without seeking to *do* good is truly a contradiction in terms. And to seek to do good without careful thought as to what that good is and how it can best be accomplished leads to frustration and, possibly, to cynicism.

So Christian ethics commits us to respond gratefully to the God who invites us to new life, embodying goodness in our own character and seeking goodness wherever we may in the world. In this volume we have offered suggestions about how Christian faith can guide our thought about the moral decisions and dilemmas we encounter. Let the final word be that we must also act!

Notes

Chapter 1: The Theological Basis of Christian Ethics

1. James M. Gustafson, *Can Ethics Be Christian?* (Chicago: University of Chicago Press, 1975).

2. For an introduction to the vast history of Christian moral teaching, see Waldo Beach and H. Richard Niebuhr, eds., *Christian Ethics: Sources of the Living Tradition* (New York: Ronald Press, 1955); George W. Forell, ed., *Christian Social Teachings* (Garden City, N.Y.: Doubleday & Co., 1966); or Ernst Troeltsch's monumental two-volume study, *The Social Teaching of the Christian Churches* (Chicago: University of Chicago Press, 1931 [1911]).

3. William K. Frankena, "Is Morality Logically Dependent on Religion?" in Gene Outka and John P. Reeder, Jr., eds., *Religion and Morality* (Garden City, N.Y.: Doubleday & Co., 1973), pp. 313–314.

4. R. M. Hare, "The Simple Believer," in ibid., p. 424.

5. I am indebted to the British economist Joan Robinson for this literary gem, though she used it in a different context in her *An Essay on Marxian Economics* (London: Macmillan & Co., 1942, 1974), p. 22.

6. Kai Nielsen, "Some Remarks on the Independence of Morality from Religion," in Ian T. Ramsey, ed., *Christian Ethics and Contemporary Philosophy* (London: SCM Press, 1966), pp. 140ff.

7. G. E. Moore, *Principia Ethica* (Cambridge University Press, 1902).

8. Alfred Jules Ayer, *Language, Truth, and Logic* (New York: Dover Publications, 1952 [1935]), p. 108.

9. Paul Tillich, *The Courage to Be* (New Haven: Yale University Press, 1952).

10. I have argued, in my *Faith and Fragmentation: Christianity for a New Age* (Philadelphia: Fortress Press, 1985), that a religious faith ultimately must stand or fall on the basis of its success in drawing human experience into a believable focus. Religion, thus, is not altogether subjective or arbitrary—although it must be admitted that subjective and arbitrary forms of religion can enjoy substantial success for long periods of time among people who have abandoned the possibility of living with integrity.

11. See especially B. F. Skinner, *Beyond Freedom and Dignity* (New York: Alfred A. Knopf, 1971).

12. The celebrated "Wesleyan quadrilateral," which conceives of scripture, tradition, experience, and reason as inescapable sources in a rounded theological position, may therefore be affirmed even though its use has hardly been restricted to the Wesleyan context.

13. See, for example, Thomas J. J. Altizer, *The Gospel of Christian Atheism* (Philadelphia: Westminster Press, 1966), and William Hamilton, *The New Essence of Christianity* (New York: Association Press, 1961). These writings can be compared with the franker abandonment of theological language altogether in the attempt to construct a humanistic ethics without any presupposition of God, in Paul Kurtz, ed., *Moral Problems in Contemporary Society: Essays in Humanistic Ethics* (Englewood Cliffs, N.J.: Prentice-Hall, 1969). "Value," to Kurtz, "is relative to man and to what human beings find to be worthwhile in experience." According to this humanistic interpretation, "human existence is probably a random occurrence existing between two oblivions . . . death is inevitable . . . there is a tragic aspect to our lives, and . . . all moral values are our own creations" (p. 4).

14. Kurtz, ibid., p. 3.

15. Albert Einstein et al., *Living Philosophies* (New York: Simon & Schuster, 1931), p. 6.

16. James M. Gustafson, *Ethics from a Theocentric Perspective* (Chicago: University of Chicago Press, 1981), p. 271.

17. I am indebted to Dean Walter G. Muelder for this felicitous phrase.

18. This tendency is present in the looser versions of liberation theology and in the older social gospel movement, although major figures in both movements have had a deeper conception of the transcendent dimension of the divine-human encounter.

19. Dietrich Bonhoeffer, *Ethics,* tr. Neville Horton Smith and ed. Eberhard Bethge (New York: Macmillan Co., 1955), pp. 134, 137.

20. Karl Barth, *Church Dogmatics,* ed. G. W. Bromiley and T. F. Torrance, III/1 (Edinburgh: T. & T. Clark, 1958), §41, 2 and 3.

21. Ibid., p. 97.

Chapter 2: Christian Character and the Virtuous Life

1. See especially Immanuel Kant, *Critique of Practical Reason,* tr. Lewis White Beck (Chicago: University of Chicago Press, 1949 [1788]).

2. B. F. Skinner's *Beyond Freedom and Dignity* (New York: Alfred A. Knopf, 1971) is an especially articulate version of such behaviorism.

3. See, e.g., James M. Gustafson, *Christ and the Moral Life* (New York: Harper & Row, 1968); Stanley Hauerwas, *Character and the Christian Life: A Study in Theological Ethics* (San Antonio: Trinity University Press, 1975); James W. McClendon, Jr., *Ethics: Systematic Theology* (Nashville: Abingdon Press, 1986).

4. Bruce C. Birch and Larry L. Rasmussen, *Bible and Ethics in the Christian Life* (Minneapolis: Augsburg Publishing House, 1976).

5. I accept the implication here that a certain dualism is inescapable in the moral life, between the free and transcendent subject—the one who thinks, decides, and acts—and all the influences and predispositions interacting with that subject. See

chapter 7 for further discussion of polarities in human life and moral decision.

6. While Kantian thought has particularly emphasized the centrality of integrity in the moral life, it also appears fundamentally in the "authenticity" of existentialist analysis and the "truthfulness" of those who ground ethics in the theology of story—with great variations of understanding of the basis of that integrity, of course.

7. Karl Barth's conception of the *imago Dei* stands in interesting contrast to both the Thomistic tendency to identify the image of God with our rationality and the Lutheran tendency to identify it with the goodness that has, since the fall, been effaced by sin. According to Barth, it is rather our created capacity to be in covenant fellowship with God—to be addressed by God as "thou" and held responsible as an "I." That capacity, Barth notes, was hardly destroyed by the fall since the "history of God's fellowship and intercourse with man . . . really begins with the fall." See Barth, *Church Dogmatics,* III/1 (Edinburgh: T. & T. Clark, 1958 [1945]), p. 200.

8. Paul L. Lehmann, *Ethics in a Christian Context* (New York: Harper & Row, 1963), p. 117.

9. See particularly Reinhold Niebuhr, *The Nature and Destiny of Man,* vol. 1 (New York: Charles Scribner's Sons, 1941).

10. T. S. Eliot, "Murder in the Cathedral," in T. S. Eliot, *The Complete Poems and Plays 1909–1950* (New York: Harcourt Brace Jovanovich, 1952), p. 196.

11. Dietrich Bonhoeffer, *The Cost of Discipleship* (rev. ed. New York: Macmillan Co., 1963 [1937]), pp. 45–60.

12. I make no apologies for use, here, of that often-abused word. For is it not implicit at the very heart of Christian ethics that all Christians are invited to become saints? Are we not summoned to be totally absorbed in God's loving purposes? Obviously, the word "saint" needs to be rescued from superficial pietism and conventional moralism, for the saint understands the depth of human struggle and the grandeur of the grace by which one is invited to live. The saint does not live by illusions, or without continuing moral temptation and struggle; but still he or she finds it possible to devote life to God's intended good.

13. See, e.g., Stanley Hauerwas, *Truthfulness and Tragedy: Further Investigations in Christian Ethics* (Notre Dame, Ind.: University of Notre Dame Press, 1977), and James W. McClendon, Jr., *Ethics: Systematic Theology.*

14. In the history of Christian thought, the point is especially emphasized by John Wesley. See John Wesley, *Christian Perfection as Believed and Taught by John Wesley,* ed. Thomas S. Kepler (Cleveland: World Publishing Co., 1954).

15. See, e.g., Anders Nygren, *Agape and Eros: A Study of the Christian Idea of Love,* tr. A. C. Hebert, 3 vols. (New York: Macmillan Co., 1932–38); L. Harold DeWolf, *Responsible Freedom: Guidelines to Christian Action* (New York: Harper & Row, 1971); Joseph Haroutunian, *God with Us: A Theology of Transpersonal Life* (Philadelphia: Westminster Press, 1965); Gene Outka, *Agape: An Ethical Analysis* (New Haven: Yale University Press, 1972).

16. See especially Jean Piaget and others, *The Moral Judgment of the Child,* tr. Marjorie Gabain (New York: Free Press, 1965), and Lawrence Kohlberg, *The Philosophy of Moral Development: Moral Stages and the Idea of Justice* (San Francisco: Harper & Row, 1981).

17. See esp. James W. Fowler, *Stages of Faith: The Psychology of Human Development and the Quest for Meaning* (San Francisco: Harper & Row, 1981).

18. Kohlberg, *Philosophy of Moral Development.*

19. In his essay "From *Is* to *Ought:* How to Commit the Naturalistic Fallacy and Get Away with It in the Study of Moral Development," a revised edition of which is published in *Philosophy of Moral Development,* pp. 101–189, Kohlberg explores the relationship between psychological developmental theory and ethical theory and argues that ultimately they are "the same theory extended in different directions" (p. 104). His most recent writing thus does not seek to dispense with moral argumentation and, to that extent, does not "commit the naturalistic fallacy."

20. Carol Gilligan, *In a Different Voice: Psychological Theory and Women's Development* (Cambridge, Mass: Harvard University Press, 1982).

Chapter 3: Moral Commitment and Ethical Uncertainty

1. This way of stating the problem is, of course, quite Kantian. The distinction between moral will and moral intelligence and judgment lies at the heart of all of Immanuel Kant's writings on ethics. The following passage is characteristic: "The supreme principle of all moral judgment lies in the understanding: that of the moral incentive to action lies in the heart. This motive is moral feeling. We must guard against confusing the principle of the judgment with the principle of the motive. The first is the norm; the second the incentive. The motive cannot take the place of the rule. Where the motive is wanting, the error is practical; but when the judgment fails the error is theoretical" (Immanuel Kant, *Lectures on Ethics,* tr. Louis Infield, pp. 36–37; New York: Harper & Row, 1963 [ca. 1780]). This distinction is, however, also assumed by most thinkers in the history of ethics, even though some have attempted to reduce morality entirely to the will, as though we could be sure that an intelligent person would always be a person of good will. The basic approach to Christian moral judgment outlined in the present volume will differ from Kant's in important respects.

2. These three approaches are distinguished from one another and elaborated in H. Richard Niebuhr, *The Responsible Self: An Essay in Christian Moral Philosophy* (New York: Harper & Row, 1963), and Edward LeRoy Long, Jr., *A Survey of Christian Ethics* (New York: Oxford University Press, 1967) and *A Survey of Recent Christian Ethics* (New York: Oxford University Press, 1982).

3. I have explored this point more fully in my *Faith and Fragmentation: Christianity for a New Age* (Philadelphia: Fortress Press, 1985).

4. This point was made particularly forcefully in Paul A. Carter, *The Decline and Revival of the Social Gospel: Social and Political Liberalism in American Protestant Churches, 1920–1940* (Ithaca, N.Y.: Cornell University Press, 1956), pp. 44, 92–95.

5. Pius XI, encyclical *Casti Connubii,* paragraph 54.

6. Paul Tillich, *The Protestant Era,* tr. James Luther Adams (Chicago: University of Chicago Press, 1948), p. xii.

7. See Reinhold Niebuhr, *The Nature and Destiny of Man,* vol. 2 (New York: Charles Scribner's Sons, 1943), pp. 213ff.

8. H. Richard Niebuhr, *Radical Monotheism and Western Culture* (New York: Harper & Brothers, 1960).

9. Gabriel Vahanian, *No Other God* (New York: George Braziller, 1966), p. 32.

10. Joseph Fletcher, *Situation Ethics: The New Morality* (Philadelphia: Westminster Press, 1966), p. 59.

11. Ibid., p. 68. The point is obscured, however, by his earlier assertion concerning love that it "is for the sake of people and it is not a good-in-itself," p. 61.

12. Ibid., pp. 95, 71, 26, 31.

13. Ibid., p. 67.

14. Ibid., p. 61.

15. Paul Ramsey, *Deeds and Rules in Christian Ethics* (New York: Charles Scribner's Sons, 1967), pp. 216–217.

16. Paul L. Lehmann, *Ethics in a Christian Context* (New York: Harper & Row, 1963), p. 17.

17. Ibid., pp. 131, 159, etc.

18. Lehmann acknowledges that "ethics, as Kant has eloquently and elaborately explained, is intrinsically volitional, being concerned with the willing acceptance of a claim" (ibid., pp. 75–76).

19. It may be unfortunate semantically that Lehmann elected to make this point by substituting "is" for "ought" in the situation of specific choice or action. By insisting upon the terminology "What I *am* to do" he suggests to many readers either that a person facing a decision actually has no freedom of choice or that among the available alternatives it does not matter ethically which is chosen. But each of these interpretations would, I think, be far from Lehmann's intention in insisting upon an "indicative" ethic.

20. Lehmann, *Ethics in a Christian Context,* pp. 123, 85, 159.

21. Ibid., p. 141.

22. John C. Bennett, *Christian Ethics and Social Policy* (New York: Charles Scribner's Sons, 1946), pp. 76–77. The term "middle axioms" originated with the ecumenical movement at the time of the 1937 Oxford Conference on Life and Work, although it was not there defined with much precision. See W. A. Visser 't Hooft and J. H. Oldham, *The Church and Its Function in Society* (Chicago: Willett, Clark & Co., 1937), p. 210.

23. Bennett, *Christian Ethics and Social Policy,* pp. 120–121.

24. See Paul Ramsey, *Basic Christian Ethics* (New York: Charles Scribner's Sons, 1950), p. 340. Before his death in 1988, Ramsey acknowledged that his position had changed significantly at this point since that book was written.

25. Ramsey, *Deeds and Rules in Christian Ethics,* p. 123. In this essay, Ramsey endeavors to appropriate the insights of Professor John Rawls to the task of Christian social ethics.

26. Ibid., p. 125.

27. Ibid., pp. 127, 128, 129.

28. See also John Rawls, "Two Concepts of Rules," in *Ethics,* vol. 76, no. 3 (April 1966), pp. 192–207.

29. Ramsey, *Deeds and Rules in Christian Ethics,* pp. 135, 137.

30. Ibid., p. 128.

31. To be sure, Ramsey's just-war principle of discrimination, developed in his book *War and the Christian Conscience: How Shall Modern War Be Conducted Justly?* (Durham, N.C.: Duke University Press, 1961), does specify that certain acts in war may be considered immoral regardless of beneficent consequences. The torture or murder of innocent hostages in order to influence the will of an enemy would be such an act, even if entered into from the most loving of motives. But it is doubtful whether Ramsey can make this stick as a general rule apart from an

assessment either of consequences (such as, in the long run and on the whole more lovelessness will be set loose among people when such deeds are done regardless of hoped-for gains in the short run) or of the relationship between the act and its motivation.

32. See Edgar S. Brightman, *Moral Laws* (Nashville: Abingdon Press, 1933); L. Harold DeWolf, *Responsible Freedom: Guidelines to Christian Action* (New York: Harper & Row, 1971); and Walter G. Muelder, *Moral Law in Christian Social Ethics* (Richmond, Va.: John Knox Press, 1966).

33. Muelder, *Moral Laws,* pp. 152–156.

34. John Howard Yoder, *The Politics of Jesus* (Grand Rapids: Wm. B. Eerdmans Publishing Co. 1972), p. 110.

35. Ibid., p. 192.

36. John Ferguson, *The Politics of Love: The New Testament and Non-Violent Revolution* (Cambridge, England: James Clarke & Co., 1974), pp. 114, 115.

37. Stanley Hauerwas, *A Community of Character: Toward a Constructive Christian Social Ethic* (Notre Dame, Ind.: University of Notre Dame Press, 1981), pp. 39–40.

38. James W. McClendon, Jr., *Ethics: Systematic Theology* (Nashville: Abingdon Press, 1986).

Chapter 4: Initial Presumption and the Burden of Proof

1. Thus Joseph Fletcher comments that "when John Bennett pleads, in the spirit of Luther's *pecca fortiter* [sin boldly], that 'there are situations in which the best we can do is evil,' we have to oppose what he says—much as we admire its spirit. . . . *The situationist holds that whatever is the most loving thing in the situation is the right and good thing.* It is not excusably evil, it is positively good" (*Situation Ethics: The New Morality,* pp. 64–65; Philadelphia: Westminster Press, 1966). In making this kind of statement Fletcher must neglect the important distinction between "evil" and "sin." See our discussion of the problem of necessary evil in chapter 6.

2. The term "presumption" employed here is not to be taken to mean the kind of overreaching behavior we label "presumptuousness." Nor should the term be taken as a synonym for "assumption" or "presupposition," although the meanings of all these words are close. The correct sense of the word is suggested by the legal analogy—which the chapter will use as illustration—as in "John Doe is *presumed* to be innocent until proven guilty" or "in American law there is a *presumption* of innocence."

3. This possibility was strikingly illustrated in 1971–72 in the famous case of the Harrisburg Seven, who were charged on flimsy evidence of conspiracies against the U.S. Government. After the government finished several weeks of unconvincing testimony, the defense simply rested without presenting any evidence at all. The judge agreed that the prosecution had failed to make its case. A similar ploy was attempted by the defense in another famous case more than a decade later, in 1985–86. In this case, the Sanctuary case, *United States v. Aguilar et al.,* the defendants (who were accused of violating U.S. immigration laws by harboring illegal aliens from Central America) also rested their case without presenting their own witnesses. But this time a jury found all but one of the defendants guilty as

charged. Most lawyers consider the tactic a risky one, but it does illustrate the meaning of legal presumption.

4. President John F. Kennedy accepted the advice of the Central Intelligence Agency and the Joint Chiefs of Staff to authorize a previously planned invasion of Cuba at the Bay of Pigs in 1961, despite his own considerable misgivings. In doing so he placed the burden of proof against his own judgment and that of others on his staff (such as Arthur M. Schlesinger, Jr.) who were not military or intelligence specialists. After the resulting debacle, he is reported to have developed a considerable mistrust of the judgment of such specialists and to have relied upon them subsequently only for narrow opinions within the confines of their specialized expertise. A year later, during the Cuban missile crisis, he more cautiously refused the advice of military leaders to bomb the offending missile bases and instead worked out a more general political solution on the basis of the advice of generalists. For the details of these fascinating executive decisions see Arthur M. Schlesinger, Jr., *A Thousand Days: John F. Kennedy in the White House* (Boston: Houghton Mifflin Co., 1965), p. 296; Robert F. Kennedy, *Thirteen Days: A Memoir of the Cuban Missile Crisis* (New York: W. W. Norton & Co., 1969), p. 36; and Kenneth P. O'Donnell and David F. Powers, *"Johnny, We Hardly Knew Ye": Memories of John Fitzgerald Kennedy* (Boston: Little, Brown & Co., 1972), pp. 312ff. and 361ff.

5. See Milton Friedman, *Capitalism and Freedom* (Chicago: University of Chicago Press, 1962); Milton and Rose Friedman, *Free to Choose* (New York: Harcourt Brace Jovanovich, 1979); and Michael Harrington, *Socialism* (New York: Bantam Books, 1973). I shall discuss the use of economic and political ideologies as presumptions in chapter 8.

6. See Philip Wogaman, "The Vietnam War and Paul Ramsey's Conscience," in *Dialog*, vol. 6, no. 4 (Autumn 1967), pp. 292–298.

7. Pius XI, *Quadragesimo Anno*, in *Seven Great Encyclicals* (Glen Rock, N.J.: Paulist Press, 1963 [1931]), para. 79, p. 147.

8. John XXIII, *Pacem in Terris*, in ibid., paras. 140–141, pp. 318–319.

9. Students of twentieth-century British moral philosophy will observe some parallels between the use of presumption in this volume and W. D. Ross's use of the term *"prima facie* duties," at least in his recognition that even obviously binding moral responsibilities may have to be set aside for the sake of moral duties of greater weight. See W. D. Ross, *The Right and the Good* (Oxford: Clarendon Press, 1930), especially pp. 18–47.

10. The following conditions are usually cited, in one form or another, as criteria for justified war: (1) the cause must be just, (2) war must be duly declared by a legitimate political authority, (3) the war truly must be a last resort, (4) the means of waging war must be fair and just, (5) there must be a reasonable expectation of victory, (6) it must be reasonably predictable that the evil of the war itself will be less than the anticipated and present evil if the war is not undertaken, (7) throughout hostilities, the combatants must maintain a right intention, and (8) the war must be viewed only as means to a better peace.

11. Paul Tillich, *Love, Power, and Justice* (New York: Oxford University Press, 1954), p. 49.

12. What might Jeremy Bentham, with his celebrated moral "calculus," have done if he could have had modern computers into which all the elements could be programmed! But even a mind as intricate as Bentham's cannot anticipate in detail

the depth and detail of the moral life and the circumstances it must confront in the actual world. We must never forget that moral judgment is quite as much art as it is science!

Chapter 5: Positive Moral Presumptions of Christian Faith

1. For a more extended discussion of the problem of evil, see my *Faith and Fragmentation: Christianity for a New Age* (Philadelphia: Fortress Press, 1985), esp. pp. 125–139.

2. This point is now well accepted in the literature of medical ethics, having been emphasized as early as 1970 in Paul Ramsey's influential *The Patient as Person* (New Haven: Yale University Press, 1970).

3. Frederick Elder, *Crisis in Eden* (Nashville: Abingdon Press, 1970), pp. 83ff.

4. United Methodist Council of Bishops, *In Defense of Creation: The Nuclear Crisis and a Just Peace* (Nashville: United Methodist Board of Discipleship, 1986), p. 92. The bishops were promptly attacked for their arrogance in believing that God's total work of creation could be threatened by humankind. However, the bishops had not asserted that *all* of God's creation could be destroyed in a nuclear war on this one planet. But what would be destroyed in such a war is God's creation, reflecting God's good purposes.

5. Bertrand Russell, *Why I Am Not a Christian, and Other Essays,* ed. Paul Edwards (New York: Simon & Schuster, 1957). This is from the essay "A Free Man's Worship," originally published in 1903, p. 115.

6. Apart from deterrence, the most persuasive ethical case for capital punishment may well be that based upon retribution. Some philosophers, including Walter Berns, argue that without a punishment that fits the crime it is impossible to take our full humanity as moral agents seriously. Only by holding people fully responsible for their antisocial behavior do we show real respect for them. See Walter Berns, *For Capital Punishment: Crime and the Morality of the Death Penalty* (New York: Basic Books, 1979). Even if it were possible to construct punishments exactly fitting crimes, it seems to me that Berns's discussion presupposes the wrong basis for affirming the ultimate worth of individual human life. That worth is not derived from our assumption of moral responsibility (important as that is) but from our being valued by the center and source of all being, God. This is exactly the issue addressed by Paul in his pivotal distinction between salvation by grace and salvation by "works of the law." I have addressed issues of criminal justice more fully in my book *Christian Perspectives on Politics* (Philadelphia: Fortress Press, 1988), ch. 14.

7. One biographer, however, quotes President Truman as saying, "I wanted to save a half million boys on our side and as many on the other side. I never lost any sleep over my decision" (Alfred Steinberg, *The Man from Missouri: The Life and Times of Harry S. Truman,* p. 259; New York: G. P. Putnam's Sons, 1962).

8. Americans who think of their own country as an ideal exemplar of respect for freedom usually are thinking of the dominant mainstream of respectable opinion, with which they associate themselves. Freedom has certainly been accorded the expression of mainstream views. But such Americans often forget that important test cases before the U.S. Supreme Court have usually involved the views and practices of less popular sectarian groups, such as Jehovah's Witnesses and the Communist Party.

9. L. Harold DeWolf, *Responsible Freedom: Guidelines to Christian Action* (New York: Harper & Row, 1971), pp. 102–110.

10. Paul L. Lehmann, *Ethics in a Christian Context* (New York: Harper & Row, 1963), pp. 57ff.

11. Joseph Haroutunian, *God with Us: A Theology of Transpersonal Life* (Philadelphia: Westminster Press, 1965), p. 17.

12. The term "race" is, itself, ambiguous and arbitrary. It may be defined as a social category based on socially perceived physical differences. The net consensus after much scientific study of "race" is that the term says much more about sociology than about biology. Any single physical characteristic (such as skin coloration, hair, nose, stature) taken to mark the members of what are socially referred to as "races" can be replicated within other "racial" groups, and members of "races" can be found who do not have this or that specified physical characteristic. Intellectual, moral, and emotional traits alleged to be characteristic of certain "racial" groups are, if real to any extent, social and cultural in origin. From a moral standpoint, therefore, it is a very risky proposition to treat race ontologically.

13. Remember that not all separatism is, strictly speaking, racial. There exists among black Americans a whole fabric of symbols and meanings expressing the common experience of oppression. People who have experienced oppression together have something in common as a basis for relationship that can hardly be present in their relationships with those who have not had this experience. Intense common experience is an authentic basis for friendship that is not exclusionary in principle. It becomes exclusionary when other kinds of deep human relationship not founded in the particular common experience are resisted. In racial relations it is very important for persons of groups with a history of repressing others to be brought into a deep human understanding of what that repression has meant to its victims.

14. This is a point that Martin Luther King, Jr., appears to have understood very well. Far from retreating from relationships, his movement encouraged black people to assert new forms of moral leadership *in* the old relationships, thus transforming them.

15. See William T. Blackstone, "On the Meaning and Justification of Equality Principle," in William T. Blackstone, ed., *The Concept of Equality* (Minneapolis: Burgess Publishing Co., 1969), pp. 115ff.

16. G. W. F. Hegel, *The Phenomenology of Mind,* tr. J. B. Baillie, 2nd rev. ed. (New York: Macmillan Co., 1931), pp. 229–240. Suggested by Andrew J. Reck, "The Metaphysics of Equality," in Blackstone, ed., *The Concept of Equality,* p. 138.

17. Ralf Dahrendorf, "On the Origin of Society Inequality," in Blackstone, ed., *The Concept of Equality,* pp. 106, 108.

18. The alienative effects of wealth and power are obvious enough and have been the object of literature since humanity became literate. The similar effects of social prestige are not so obvious. Nevertheless, the deference from others that is implied by prestige may be even more dangerous. Entering into every relationship between persons of high prestige and those who defer to them there is the implication that the opinions, tastes, and so on of the former are alone worthy of consideration. Authentic interpersonal communication is thus greatly impeded. The pattern of racial inequality in American life made genuine relationship between whites and blacks almost impossible for this reason. The higher prestige of the whites and the

requirement that black people show deference through ritualized patterns of speech and behavior effectively destroyed mutuality at any deep level. Consequently, both white and black Americans were diminished as persons. An important part of the "loneliness" of which prominent people sometimes ambivalently complain is exactly this. How can one help being lonely if there is no one from whom one can expect genuine, honest response as a fellow human being? Still, prestige is a fascinating goal. It gives one the illusory promise that "up there" (in status terms) one will find the fuller response from others that is involved in the quest for human fulfillment.

19. John Rawls, *A Theory of Justice* (Cambridge, Mass.: Harvard University Press, 1972), pp. 14–15.

20. J. Philip Wogaman, *Guaranteed Annual Income: The Moral Issues* (Nashville: Abingdon Press, 1968), pp. 71–74.

21. Charles S. Milligan, "How to Decide," *Christian Century,* vol. 95, no. 1 (Jan. 4–11, 1978), p. 22.

22. James W. McClendon, Jr., *Ethics: Systematic Theology* (Nashville: Abingdon Press, 1986), p. 52.

Chapter 6: Negative Moral Presumptions

1. John Dillenberger, *God Hidden and Revealed: The Interpretation of Luther's Deus Absconditus and Its Significance for Religious Thought* (Philadelphia: Muhlenberg Press, 1953), p. xvi.

2. Harry F. Ward, *In Place of Profit: Social Incentives in the Soviet Union* (New York: Charles Scribner's Sons, 1933).

3. Reinhold Niebuhr at one point went so far as to argue that Marxist communism poses greater danger even than Nazism, since the latter lacked the smokescreen of universal utopian idealism that has masked the former's unscrupulous policies: "The important point is that the ruthless power operates behind a screen of pretended ideal ends, a situation which is both more dangerous and more evil than pure cynical defiance of moral ends" (*Christian Realism and Political Problems,* pp. 37–38; New York: Charles Scribner's Sons, 1953). I am unwilling to go this far because Marxism does avoid the barbarities of racism, because it does have some openness to new truth via its conception of science (although its social science remains highly dogmatic), and because its attitude toward ultimate human freedom does have some ambiguous possibilities. Greater openness in several Marxist countries in recent years appears to vindicate the more charitable view.

4. Quoted by Mark Sherwin, *The Extremists* (New York: St. Martin's Press, 1963), p. 110.

5. Fred Schwarz, *You Can Trust the Communists (to Be Communists)* (Englewood Cliffs, N.J.: Prentice-Hall, 1960), p. 2: "You can trust the Communists. They are extremely trustworthy. You can trust a cancer cell to obey the laws of its lawless growth. You can trust an armed bank robber to take the money and try to escape. Similarly, you can trust the Communists to act in accordance with the laws of their being."

6. Gail Kennedy, ed., *Democracy and the Gospel of Wealth* (Boston: D. C. Heath & Co., 1949), p. xii.

7. World Council of Churches, *Man's Disorder and God's Design: The Amsterdam Assembly Series* (New York: Harper & Brothers, 1948), n.p.

8. Walter Rauschenbusch, *Christianity and the Social Crisis* (New York: Macmillan Co., 1907), pp. 361–362.

9. Saul D. Alinsky, *Reveille for Radicals* (Chicago: University of Chicago Press, 1945).

10. *The Stoic Philosophy of Seneca,* tr. Moses Hadas (Magnolia, Mass.: Peter Smith, 1965), p. 236.

11. Ibid.

12. "A good man would be under compulsion to wage no wars at all, if there were not such things as just wars. A just war, moreover, is justified only by the injustice of an aggressor; and that injustice ought to be a source of grief to any good man, because it is human injustice" (Augustine, *City of God* XIX. 7; see also ch. 12).

13. Leo Tolstoy, *My Religion* (New York: Thomas Y. Crowell Co., 1885).

14. See especially Leo Tolstoy, *The Kingdom of God Is Within You,* tr. Leo Wiener (New York: Farrar, Straus & Cudahy, 1961 [1905]).

15. Jacques Ellul, *Violence: Reflections from a Christian Perspective,* tr. Cecelia Gaul Kings (New York: Seabury Press, 1969), pp. 93ff.

16. More than a tendency: in another book, Ellul flatly states that "no present-day authority can claim to be instituted by God, for all authority is set in the framework of a totalitarian state. This is why I decide for anarchy" (*The Ethics of Freedom,* p. 396; Grand Rapids: Wm. B. Eerdmans Publishing Co., 1976).

17. See especially John Howard Yoder, *The Politics of Jesus* (Grand Rapids: Wm. B. Eerdmans Publishing Co., 1972); *Karl Barth and the Problem of War* (Nashville: Abingdon Press, 1970); and *When War Is Unjust* (Minneapolis: Augsburg Publishing House, 1984).

18. Yoder, *The Politics of Jesus,* p. 241.

19. Ibid., p. 236.

20. Ibid., p. 239.

21. Ibid., p. 112.

22. Ibid., p. 245.

23. Yoder, *Karl Barth and the Problem of War,* pp. 73–74.

24. Ellul, *Violence,* p. 167.

25. Leo Tolstoy, "Notes for Officers," in *Tolstoy's Writings on Civil Disobedience and Non-Violence* (New York: Bergman Publishers, 1967), p. 36.

26. James W. McClendon, Jr., has correctly stated my view that "Christians must sometimes do evil because worse consequences would at those times come of doing good." And I suspect he has correctly interpreted Yoder when he writes that "Yoder simply denies that *Christians* have been charged with making the world come out right. . . . It is God not we who must bear final responsibility for the strategy of dealing with the world by way of the cross rather than by the ways of violence and its power" (*Ethics: Systematic Theology,* p. 74; Nashville: Abingdon Press, 1986). Obviously, none of us has full responsibility for "making the world come out right," and I would be the last to argue for that. But have either Yoder or McClendon reflected sufficiently on the fact that God's actions in human history are and always have been through *people?* For further comments on the position of writers like Yoder and McClendon, see my *Christian Perspectives on Politics* (Philadelphia: Fortress Press, 1988), esp. chs. 3 and 8.

27. Karl Barth, *Church Dogmatics,* ed. G. W. Bromiley and T. F. Torrance, III/4 (Edinburgh: T. & T. Clark, 1961), p. 455.

Chapter 7: Polar Moral Presumptions

1. L. Harold DeWolf, *Responsible Freedom: Guidelines to Christian Action* (New York: Harper & Row, 1971), p. 176.

2. Edward LeRoy Long, Jr., *A Survey of Christian Ethics,* (New York: Oxford University Press, 1967), esp. sect. IV. See also his *A Survey of Recent Christian Ethics* (New York and Oxford: Oxford University Press, 1982).

3. Aristotle, *Nichomachean Ethics,* tr. W. D. Ross, II. 9.

4. George J. Stigler, "The Proper Goals of Economic Policy," in *Journal of Business,* July 1958, p. 714. Such views have been echoed more recently by such writers as Milton Friedman and George Gilder and have enjoyed substantial ideological support during the Reagan era in the United States.

5. Benito Mussolini, *The Political and Social Doctrine of Fascism,* tr. Jane Soames (London: Hogarth Press, 1933), reprinted in John Somerville and Ronald E. Santoni, eds., *Social and Political Philosophy: Readings from Plato to Gandhi* (Garden City, N.Y.: Doubleday & Co., Anchor Books, 1963), p. 426.

6. Karl Barth, *Christ and Adam,* tr. T. A. Small (New York: Harper & Brothers, 1956), p. 91.

7. Milton Friedman, *Capitalism and Freedom* (Chicago: University of Chicago Press, 1972).

8. H. Richard Niebuhr, *The Responsible Self: An Essay in Christian Moral Philosophy* (New York: Harper & Row, 1963), pp. 61, 68.

9. In another context, I have argued that there is one form of freedom that should be considered absolute—that is, not simply presumptive: our freedom from any requirement to profess beliefs which we do not hold or to engage in forms of worship which we do not accept. What such a denial of freedom comes down to is the obliteration of the freedom side of the polarity altogether. We cannot say quite the same thing in respect to freedom of expression of ideas, although I continue to believe that that freedom should be treated as a "near absolute." See J. Philip Wogaman, *Protestant Faith and Religious Liberty* (Nashville: Abingdon Press, 1967), pp. 182–190.

10. Henry David Thoreau, "On the Duty of Civil Disobedience," in Somerville and Santoni, eds., *Social and Political Philosophy,* p. 282.

11. Robert Nozick, *Anarchy, State, and Utopia* (New York: Basic Books, 1974).

12. Pope John XXIII suggested the need for invoking a higher level of collectivity in his encyclical *Pacem in Terris:* "It can be said, therefore, that at this historical moment the present system of organization and the way its principle of authority operates on a world basis no longer correspond to the objective requirements of the universal common good" (para. 135). Similarly, the U.S. Catholic Bishops, in their 1986 "Pastoral Letter on Catholic Social Teaching and the U.S. Economy," observe that "the common good may sometimes demand that the right to own be limited by public involvement in the planning or ownership of certain sectors of the economy. Support of private ownership does not mean that anyone has the right to unlimited accumulation of wealth" (para. 115).

13. Note, for example, Milton Kotler's comment in a work on neighborhood government: "In short, our knowledge has been misguided in the direction of globalism. World power, not local liberty, captivated our imaginations for so long that it has distracted us from practical thought and civic emotions. For who really

cares about the globe! That issue was settled when we discovered it was round" (*Neighborhood Government: The Local Foundations of Political Life,* p. xii; Indianapolis: Bobbs-Merrill Co., 1969).

14. See Peter L. Berger and Richard John Neuhaus, *To Empower People: The Role of Mediating Structures in Public Policy* (Washington, D.C.: American Enterprise Institute, 1977), and Michael Novak, ed., *Democracy and Mediating Structures: A Theological Inquiry* (Washington, D.C.: American Enterprise Institute for Public Policy Research, 1980). My own essay on "The Church as Mediating Institution: Theological and Philosophical Perspective," in the latter volume (pp. 69–81), emphasized the importance of mediating structures providing linkages between the individual and centers of real social power.

15. Walter Rauschenbusch, *Christianity and the Social Crisis* (New York: Macmillan Co., 1907), p. 90.

16. Walter Rauschenbusch, *Christianizing the Social Order* (New York: Macmillan Co., 1912), pp. 128ff.

17. William James quoted by John K. Roth, *Freedom and the Moral Life: The Ethics of William James* (Philadelphia: Westminster Press, 1969), p. 70.

18. Diane M. Yeager, " 'Can't You See that I'm Dancing': The Counterpoint of the Serious and the Ludic in the Life Well-Lived," in Larry L. Rasmussen, ed., *The Annual of the Society of Christian Ethics—1984,* p. 213.

Chapter 8: Presumptions of Human Authority

1. One of the best summaries of the insights of reference group theory remains Robert K. Merton, *Social Theory and Social Structure,* rev. & enl. ed. (Chicago: Free Press of Glencoe, 1957), pp. 225–386.

2. Charles Hampden-Turner, *From Poverty to Dignity: A Strategy for Poor Americans* (Garden City, N.Y.: Doubleday & Co., 1974), pp. 23–27.

3. I have been particularly struck by the pioneering small-group experiments of Solomon E. Asch, who demonstrated empirically the near impossibility of individuals to express public disagreement with a group even when the group was demonstrably wrong. But Asch also noted that people were much more likely to dissent if they perceived that even one other person also disagreed with the group's conclusions. See Solomon E. Asch, "Effects of Group Pressure Upon the Modification and Distortion of Judgments," in Eleanor E. Maccoby, Theodore M. Newcomb, and Eugene L. Hartley, eds., *Readings in Social Psychology,* 3rd ed. (New York: Henry Holt & Co., 1958), pp. 174–183.

4. Observing the generation gap of the 1960s, the anthropologist Margaret Mead shrewdly observed that "there are no elders who know what those who have been reared within the last twenty years know about the world into which they were born" (*Culture and Commitment: A Study of the Generation Gap,* p. 78; Garden City, N.Y.: Doubleday & Co., 1970). The pace of change and, with it, the diminishing of traditional authorities have not appeared to abate in the two decades since she recorded those words.

5. What Max Weber refers to as "charismatic authority" should possibly be excluded, although it should be remembered that this form of authority includes elements of rationality along with the nonrational persuasiveness of the leader. Charismatic authority can be either Christian or the furthest thing from it, but our

response to it is so largely intuitive it is difficult to anticipate its emergence intelligently. Without totally excluding this form of human authority and without discounting either its inevitability or its desirability in human society, our own discussion of forms of human moral authority will be confined to those that can be defined and anticipated rationally.

6. I am somewhat uncomfortable with the proposal of Bruce Birch and Larry Rasmussen that the canon as a whole should be utilized as the framework of control in Christian ethics. "Even when it presents us with difficult tensions and contradictions," they write, "attention to the canon requires that the totality of the biblical witness be weighed in reaching moral judgments. To pick out some portions as relevant and to reject others is to create one's own canon. Ethical statements based on such a limited canon are more often than not misleading" (Bruce C. Birch and Larry L. Rasmussen, *Bible and Ethics in the Christian Life,* p. 183; Minneapolis: Augsburg Publishing House, 1976). While I agree that Christians should be familiar with the whole canon and be open to whatever any part of it may contribute, it seems to me a mistake to invite the view that all its parts are of equal value. The point is that we do approach the Bible with a hermeneutical control that, in effect, does create a canon within a canon. For instance, on the basis of my own understanding of the revelation of God in Jesus Christ, there is a basis of selectivity in my reading of all the scripture—and even a basis for my rejection of some of what I read. Needless to say, I agree with much that Birch and Rasmussen have to say concerning the applicability of the Bible to Christian ethics.

7. Paul L. Lehmann, *Ethics in a Christian Context* (New York: Harper & Row, 1963), esp. pp. 45–101.

8. I do not wish to overstate this point. Sub-Christian valuations reflecting racism, sexism, nationalism, and selfish class interests have certainly intruded into the vast corpus of denominational and ecumenical pronouncements at many points. Nevertheless, the challenge to transcend such valuations is also evident. A business leader of my acquaintance, after voting against the interests of his own corporation at an international ecumenical gathering, was heard to say, "Well, I didn't come here as a representative of the ——— Company!"

9. Quoted by Hans Küng, *Infallible? An Inquiry,* tr. Edward Quinn (Garden City, N.Y.: Doubleday & Co., 1971), p. 98.

10. Ibid., pp. 98–99.

11. *Lumen Gentium,* sect. 25.

12. Pope John XXIII is alleged to have remarked, "I'm not infallible; I'm infallible only when I speak *ex cathedra.* But I'll never speak *ex cathedra."* Quoted by Küng, *Infallible? An Inquiry,* p. 87.

13. Edward Schillebeeckx, "The Problem of the Infallibility of the Church's Office: A Theological Reflection," in Edward Schillebeeckx and Bas van Iersel, eds., *Truth and Certainty,* tr. David Smith (New York: Herder & Herder, 1973), p. 93.

14. Küng, *Infallible? An Inquiry,* pp. 181–185.

15. Charles E. Curran, *Contemporary Problems in Moral Theology* (Notre Dame, Ind.: Fides Publishers, 1970), p. 264.

16. I am aware of the irony of citing Küng, Schillebeeckx, and Curran on the teaching authority of the Roman Catholic Church. After the publication of *A*

Christian Method of Moral Judgment, in which these scholars were also discussed, each of the three was repudiated by the Vatican as a legitimate spokesperson for Catholic theology. In one sense that unhappy development clouds the extent to which the Vatican may be open to definitions of the magisterium that would be acceptable in the ecumenical community. But it is also possible that these three thinkers, by articulating ecumenically discussible conceptions of the magisterium, may also have anticipated official future thinking in their own church. For documentation and commentary on the Curran case and its implications, see Charles E. Curran, *Faithful Dissent* (Kansas City, Mo.: Sheed & Ward, 1986), and Charles E. Curran and Richard A. McCormick, S.J., eds., *Readings in Moral Theology No. 6: Dissent in the Church* (New York: Paulist Press, 1988).

17. Alexander Miller, *The Renewal of Man* (Garden City, N.Y.: Doubleday & Co., 1955), quoted in Harmon L. Smith and Louis W. Hodges, *The Christian and His Decisions: An Introduction to Christian Ethics* (Nashville: Abingdon Press, 1969), p. 154.

18. I do not mean to suggest that all Christians in any previous generation supported such outrages, but only that enough did to give great traditional weight to them.

19. Paul Ramsey, *Who Speaks for the Church?* (Nashville: Abingdon Press, 1967), pp. 135–136. Ramsey's specific objection was to the stance taken by the World Council of Churches' Conference on Church and Society in 1966 in opposition to the Vietnam War—a point at which the conference's view has arguably stood up better than Ramsey's to the test of time.

20. David Halberstam, *The Best and the Brightest* (New York: Random House, 1972).

21. See J. P. Bunker, "Surgical Manpower: A Comparison of Operations and Surgeons in the United States and in England and Wales," *New England Journal of Medicine,* vol. 282 (1970), pp. 135–144, and E. A. Vayda, "A Comparison of Surgical Rates in Canada and England and Wales," *New England Journal of Medicine,* vol. 289 (1973), pp. 1224–1229.

22. Ramsey, *Who Speaks for the Church?,* p. 138.

23. Daniel D. McCracken, "Ethical Problems of the Expert Witness in National Decision Making Involving the Assessment of Technology," unpublished B.D. thesis (New York: Union Theological Seminary, 1970), pp. 42–50.

24. Quoted by Sebastian de Grazia, *The Political Community: A Study of Anomie* (Chicago: University of Chicago Press, 1948), p. 189.

25. Michael Novak, *The Experience of Nothingness* (New York: Harper & Row, 1970), p. 6. In his more recent books, such as *The Spirit of Democratic Capitalism* (New York: Simon & Schuster, 1982), Novak sharply segregates the sphere of government from spheres of economics and culture, effectively placing the burden of proof against government in most areas of contemporary life.

26. Letter to Bishop Mandell Creighton, April 5, 1887.

27. Cf. Edward H. Madden, *Civil Disobedience and Moral Law in Nineteenth-Century American Philosophy* (Seattle: University of Washington Press, 1968), esp. ch. 6. I have discussed this problem more extensively in J. Philip Wogaman, *Christian Perspectives on Politics* (Philadelphia: Fortress Press, 1988), esp. pp. 205–206.

Chapter 9: Ideological Presumptions

1. Quoted by Harry M. Johnson, "Ideology and the Social System," *Encyclopedia of the Social Sciences* (New York: Macmillan Co., 1968), p. 76.

2. The terms "ideology" and "utopia" are distinguished by Karl Mannheim on the basis of their supportive or shattering effects on the status quo. See *Ideology and Utopia: An Introduction to the Sociology of Knowledge* (New York: Harcourt, Brace and World, 1936). In a sense, the two terms, even as employed by Mannheim, point toward the same ethical reality: social ideals that transcend any particular situation. In this chapter, therefore, the term "ideology" includes what is usually meant by the term "utopia." The tendency of ideological consciousness is to treat particular forms of social organization as ideal, whether these be past, present, or potential.

3. These themes are represented by James Cone, *God of the Oppressed* (New York: Seabury Press, 1975); Cornel West, *Prophesy Deliverance! An Afro-American Revolutionary Christianity* (Philadelphia: Westminster Press, 1982); Rosemary Radford Ruether, *To Change the World: Christology and Cultural Criticism* (New York: Crossroad Publishing Co., 1981); Gustavo Gutiérrez, *A Theology of Liberation* (Maryknoll, N.Y.: Orbis Books, 1973); and José Miguez Bonino, *Toward a Christian Political Ethics* (Philadelphia: Fortress Press, 1983).

4. Jan Milič Lochman, *Church in a Marxist Society: A Czechoslovak View* (New York: Harper & Row, 1970), is one of the better illustrations of this literature.

5. Christopher Dawson, *The Historical Reality of Christian Culture: A Way to the Renewal of Human Life* (New York: Harper & Brothers, 1960), p. 36. See also T. S. Eliot, *Christianity and Culture* (New York: Harcourt Brace, 1960 [1940]) and *The Idea of a Christian Society* (London: Faber & Faber, 1939), for similarly romantic conceptions of Christian civilization.

6. Walter Rauschenbusch, *Christianizing the Social Order* (New York: Macmillan Co., 1912), p. 127.

7. Elsewhere I have made similar points at greater length in criticizing the sectarian tendencies of Stanley Hauerwas and James W. McClendon, Jr. See J. Philip Wogaman, *Christian Perspectives on Politics* (Philadelphia: Fortress Press, 1988), ch. 8.

8. I have seen no evidence that would support the view that most of the identifiable homosexual population possesses such physiological characteristics. John Money does cite impressive evidence of the existence of such characteristics, however, in his "Sin, Sickness, or Status? Homosexual Gender Identity and Psychoneuroendocrinology," in *American Psychologist,* vol. 42, no. 4 (April 1987), pp. 384–399. See also Alan P. Bell, Martin S. Weinberg, and Sue Kiefer Hammersmith, *Sexual Preference: Its Development in Men and Women* (Bloomington: Indiana University Press, 1981), esp. ch. 19.

9. It is important to note that the state is not, by definition, simply coercive. R. M. MacIver's analysis of the state in *The Web of Government* (New York: Macmillan Co., 1947) emphasizes throughout that civil society is an infinitely complex social phenomenon through which most activity is voluntary. In characterizing the state as society acting as a whole, I am partly influenced by Talcott Parson's view that political power is "capacity to control the relational system as a system." See Talcott Parsons, *The Social System* (Chicago: Free Press, 1951), p. 126. Note also MacIver's comment that political power "alone is the organ of the whole commu-

nity" (*The Web of Government,* p. 94). I have gone into this in greater depth in Wogaman, *Christian Perspectives on Politics,* esp. ch. 2.

10. I agree with Neumann that political power primarily represents the power of influence. See Franz Neumann, *The Democratic and the Authoritarian State,* ed. Herbert Marcuse (Chicago: Free Press of Glencoe, 1957). Anything that affects or influences the will of human beings is potentially political.

11. Most twentieth-century fascism seems to have populist rootage, although it is often a populism perverted by popular prejudices, inflamed by demagoguery, and manipulated by business interests. That is the characteristic formula of Italian fascism, German Nazism, Spanish Falangism, and Argentinian Peronismo, and it has also been characteristic of the less successful fascist-type movements in the Western democracies. The phenomenon of "working class totalitarianism" has been explored with insight by Seymour Martin Lipset, *Political Man: The Social Bases of Politics* (Garden City, N.Y.: Doubleday & Co., 1960).

12. Benito Mussolini, in John Somerville and Ronald E. Santoni, eds., *Social and Political Philosophy* (Garden City, N.Y.: Doubleday & Co., Doubleday Anchor Book), p. 437.

13. This is less true of Tolstoyan anarchism, for Tolstoy insisted on using nonviolent means to achieve the dismantling of the state. It may be noted in passing that anarchism can appear in both left-wing and right-wing form, so far as its economic predispositions are concerned. The right-wing form is well represented by the Libertarians and such thinkers as Robert Nozick, who insist upon absolute laissez-faire economic policies. See Nozick, *Anarchy, State, and Utopia* (New York: Basic Books, 1974).

14. Jacques Maritain, *Man and the State* (Chicago: University of Chicago Press, 1951), pp. 38, 44.

15. Quoted by George H. Sabine, *A History of Political Theory,* 3rd ed. (New York: Holt, Rinehart & Winston, 1961), p. 396.

16. Amsterdam Assembly, *The Church and the Disorder of Society* (New York: Harper & Brothers, 1948), p. 200.

17. Some proponents of laissez-faire capitalism believe that the free market inherently creates enough competition so that government regulations are not even needed for that role. See, e.g., George Gilder, *Wealth and Poverty* (New York: Basic Books, 1981), pp. 37–38.

18. Max Weber's well-known *Protestant Ethic and the Spirit of Capitalism* remains one of the most discerning analyses of the relationship between Protestant (particularly Calvinist) Christianity and the peculiar forms of capitalism which developed in Western Europe and North America, although aspects of that study have been questioned by other writers. On the question of deserving, I have been struck by how recurrently writers committed to laissez-faire principles support the notion that wealth follows merit and poverty reflects the failings of the poor. Gilder, for instance, remarks that what poor people need most of all in order to succeed is "the spur of their poverty" (*Wealth and Poverty,* p. 118).

19. That remains true despite the persistent efforts of such governments as that of President Reagan in the United States and Prime Minister Margaret Thatcher in the United Kingdom to return to as pure a form of laissez-faire capitalism as possible. The failure to dismantle major social welfare institutions despite this deep ideological commitment, sustained in both countries for a decade or so, suggests that

the ideology is in tension with real human needs and inclinations at important points.

20. Such points were lifted up by the Oxford Conference of Life and Work (1937) and the First Assembly of the World Council of Churches (1948), which had to assess capitalism in the context of the Great Depression and profound ideological conflicts, particularly at that time, in the Western world.

21. Joseph A. Schumpeter, *Capitalism, Socialism, and Democracy,* 3rd ed. (New York: Harper & Brothers, 1950), p. 415.

22. J. Philip Wogaman, *The Great Economic Debate: An Ethical Analysis* (Philadelphia: Westminster Press, 1977). My more recent *Economics and Ethics: A Christian Inquiry* (Philadelphia: Fortress Press, 1986) assumes the presently existing welfare-capitalist (or mixed economy) system in most Western countries in order to suggest key economic priorities for such countries and in order to criticize the laissez-faire excesses of the Reagan and Thatcher era in the United States and the United Kingdom.

Chapter 10: Being, Deciding, and Doing

1. Laszek Kolakowski, "The Conspiracy of Ivory Tower Intellectuals," in Arthur P. Mendel, ed., *Essential Works of Marxism* (New York: Bantam Books, 1961), p. 348.

2. Thurman W. Arnold, *The Folklore of Capitalism* (New Haven: Yale University Press, 1937), pp. 13–14. The criticism may not be wholly warranted. Certainly it does not characterize the socialist leader's own motives. Moreover, a part of the folklore of American liberal political history is that many of Thomas's proposals found their way, in time, into the party platforms of the major parties and thence into respectability and enactment. Nevertheless, it cannot be maintained seriously that Thomas was an effective political strategist, and the main thrust of Arnold's criticism seems to me to be fully justified several decades after it was made.

Index